MASS EFFECT™
REDEMPTION

ILLUSTRATION BY
DARYL MANDRYK

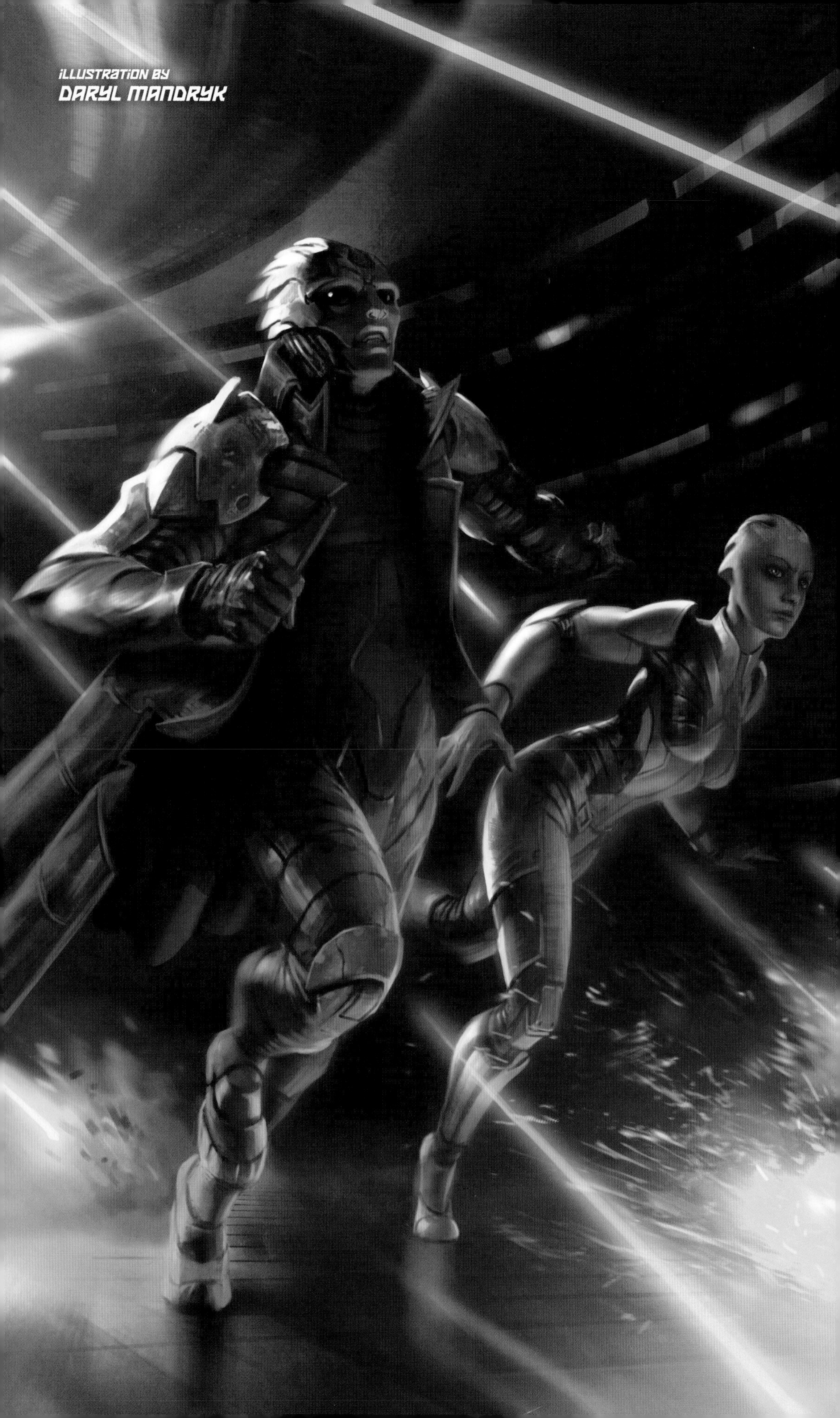

MASS EFFECT™
REDEMPTION

STORY
MAC WALTERS

SCRIPT
JOHN JACKSON MILLER

ART
OMAR FRANCIA

COLORS
MICHAEL ATIYEH

LETTERING
MICHAEL HEISLER

DARK HORSE BOOKS®

PUBLISHER
MIKE RICHARDSON

ASSISTANT EDITOR
BRENDAN WRIGHT

EDITOR
DAVE MARSHALL

DESIGNERS
STEPHEN REICHERT AND TINA ALESSI

MASS EFFECT: REDEMPTION

This volume collects issues #1 through #4 of the Dark Horse comic-book series *Mass Effect: Redemption*.

Special thanks to BioWare, including:
DEREK WATTS, Art Director; CASEY HUDSON, Executive Producer;
AARYN FLYNN, Studio GM, BioWare Edmonton;
RAY MUZYKA and GREG ZESCHUK, BioWare Co-Founders

Published by Dark Horse Books,
A division of Dark Horse Comics, Inc.
10956 SE Main Street | Milwaukie, OR 97222

darkhorse.com
masseffect.com

LIBRARY OF CONGRESS CATALOGING-IN-PUBLICATION DATA

Walters, Mac.
Mass effect : redemption / story, Mac Walters ; script, John Jackson Miller ; art, Omar Francia.
p. cm.
ISBN 978-1-59582-481-3
1. Graphic novels. I. Miller, John Jackson. II. Francia, Omar. III. Title.
PN6727.W277M37 2010
741.5'943--dc22
2009051705

First standard edition: June 2010
ISBN: 978-1-59582-481-3

Custom edition: June 2010
ISBN: 978-1-59582-601-5

1 3 5 7 9 10 8 6 4 2
Printed at Midas Printing International, Ltd., Huizhou, China

MIKE RICHARDSON President and Publisher   NEIL HANKERSON Executive Vice President   TOM WEDDLE Chief Financial Officer   RANDY STRADLEY Vice President of Publishing   MICHAEL MARTENS Vice President of Business Development   ANITA NELSON Vice President of Marketing, Sales, and Licensing   DAVID SCROGGY Vice President of Product Development   DALE LAFOUNTAIN Vice President of Information Technology   DARLENE VOGEL Director of Purchasing   KEN LIZZI General Counsel   DAVEY ESTRADA Editorial Director   SCOTT ALLIE Senior Managing Editor   CHRIS WARNER Senior Books Editor   DIANA SCHUTZ Executive Editor   CARY GRAZZINI Director of Design and Production   LIA RIBACCHI Art Director   CARA NIECE Director of Scheduling

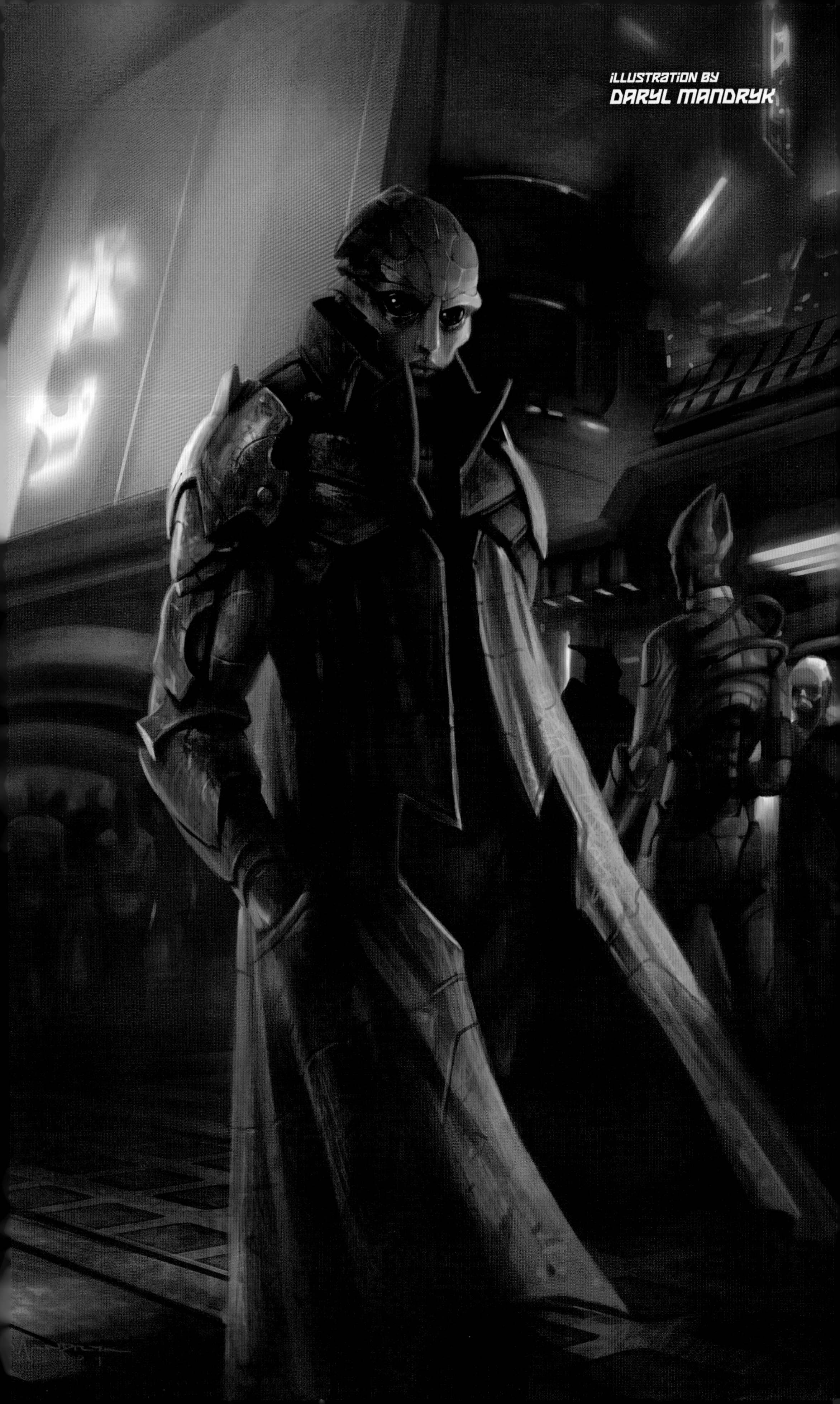
ILLUSTRATION BY
DARYL MANDRYK

The stars teem with life . . . and death.

In the generation since discovering the **mass relay** near Pluto, humanity has used the ancient device to make its presence felt in the cosmos. Welcomed into the **Citadel Council**, the people of Earth have proven adroit and adaptive—to the consternation of some longer-established species.

But tragedy struck one of Earth's greatest heroes just weeks after rescuing the galactic capital, the **Citadel**, from a devastating strike. **Commander Shepard**, one of the few elite agents known as **Spectres**, was lost in a mysterious attack on the **Normandy**.

Now, Shepard's friends—including the intrepid asari, **Dr. Liara T'Soni**—want answers. But Shepard's enemies are searching for something, too. Something worth killing for . . .

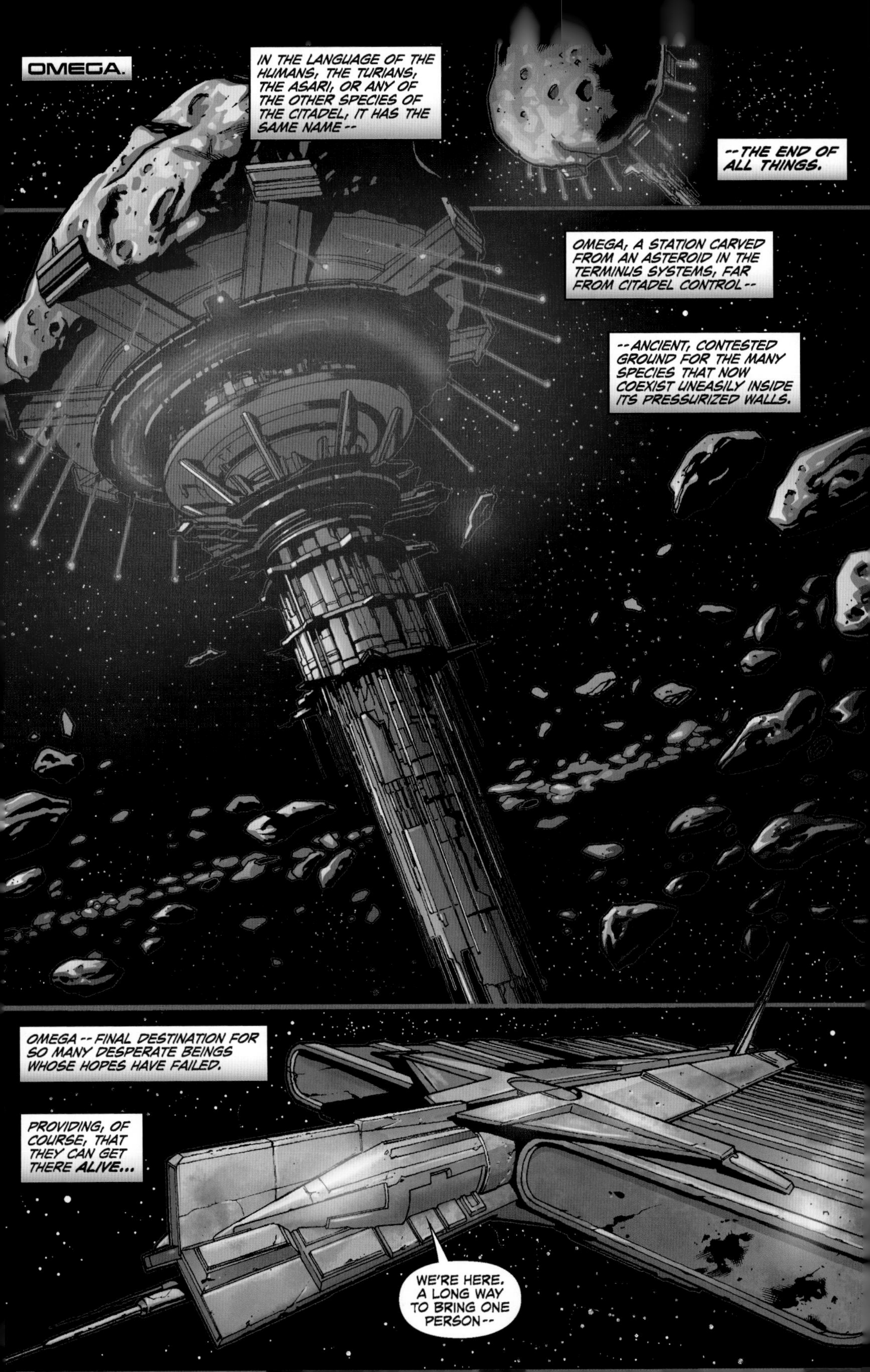
OMEGA.
IN THE LANGUAGE OF THE HUMANS, THE TURIANS, THE ASARI, OR ANY OF THE OTHER SPECIES OF THE CITADEL, IT HAS THE SAME NAME--
--THE END OF ALL THINGS.
OMEGA, A STATION CARVED FROM AN ASTEROID IN THE TERMINUS SYSTEMS, FAR FROM CITADEL CONTROL--
--ANCIENT, CONTESTED GROUND FOR THE MANY SPECIES THAT NOW COEXIST UNEASILY INSIDE ITS PRESSURIZED WALLS.
OMEGA--FINAL DESTINATION FOR SO MANY DESPERATE BEINGS WHOSE HOPES HAVE FAILED.
PROVIDING, OF COURSE, THAT THEY CAN GET THERE ALIVE...
WE'RE HERE. A LONG WAY TO BRING ONE PERSON--

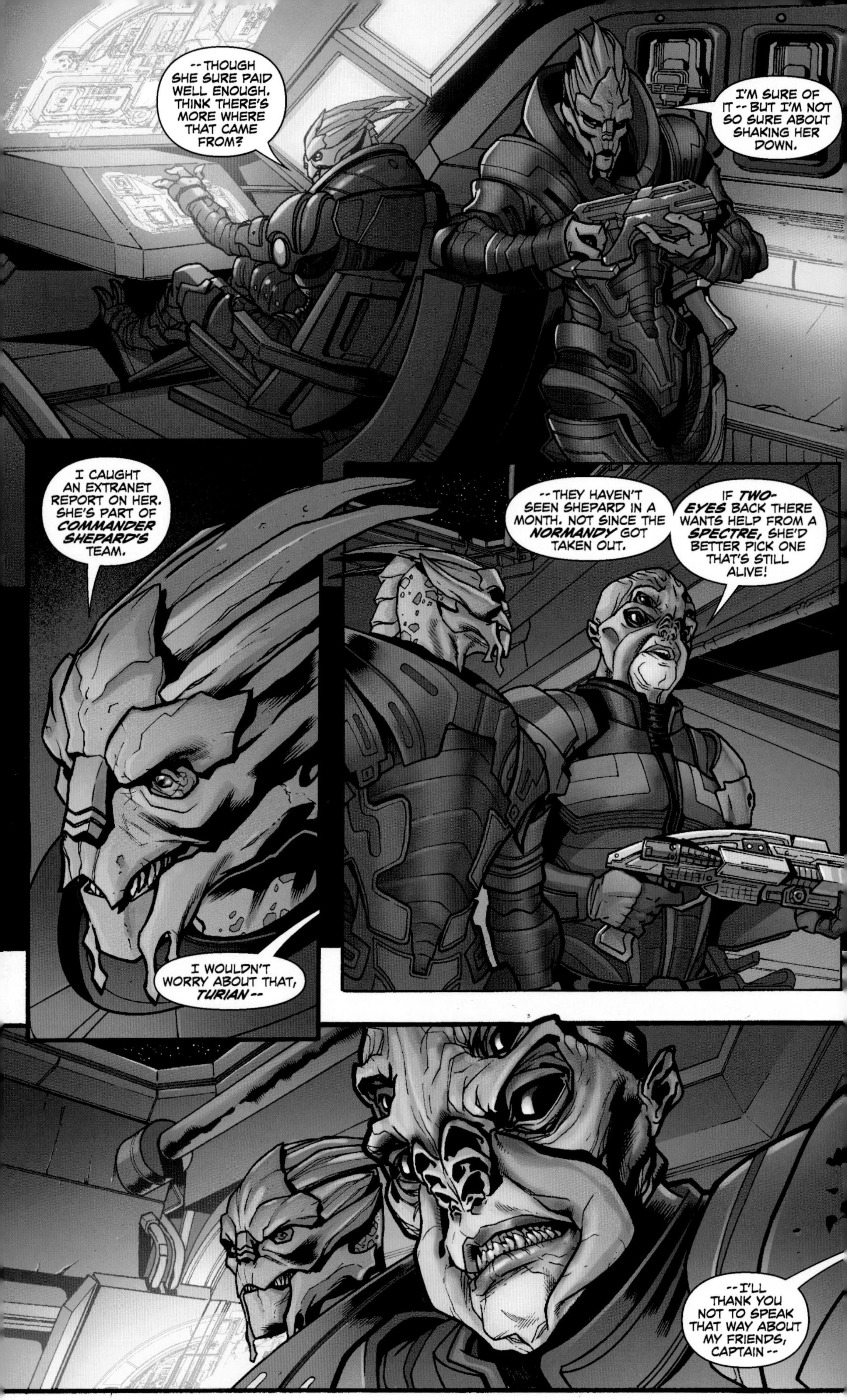

--THOUGH SHE SURE PAID WELL ENOUGH. THINK THERE'S MORE WHERE THAT CAME FROM?
I'M SURE OF IT--BUT I'M NOT SO SURE ABOUT SHAKING HER DOWN.
I CAUGHT AN EXTRANET REPORT ON HER. SHE'S PART OF *COMMANDER SHEPARD'S* TEAM.
--THEY HAVEN'T SEEN SHEPARD IN A MONTH. NOT SINCE THE *NORMANDY* GOT TAKEN OUT.
IF *TWO-EYES* BACK THERE WANTS HELP FROM A *SPECTRE,* SHE'D BETTER PICK ONE THAT'S STILL ALIVE!
I WOULDN'T WORRY ABOUT THAT, *TURIAN*--
--I'LL THANK YOU NOT TO SPEAK THAT WAY ABOUT MY FRIENDS, CAPTAIN--

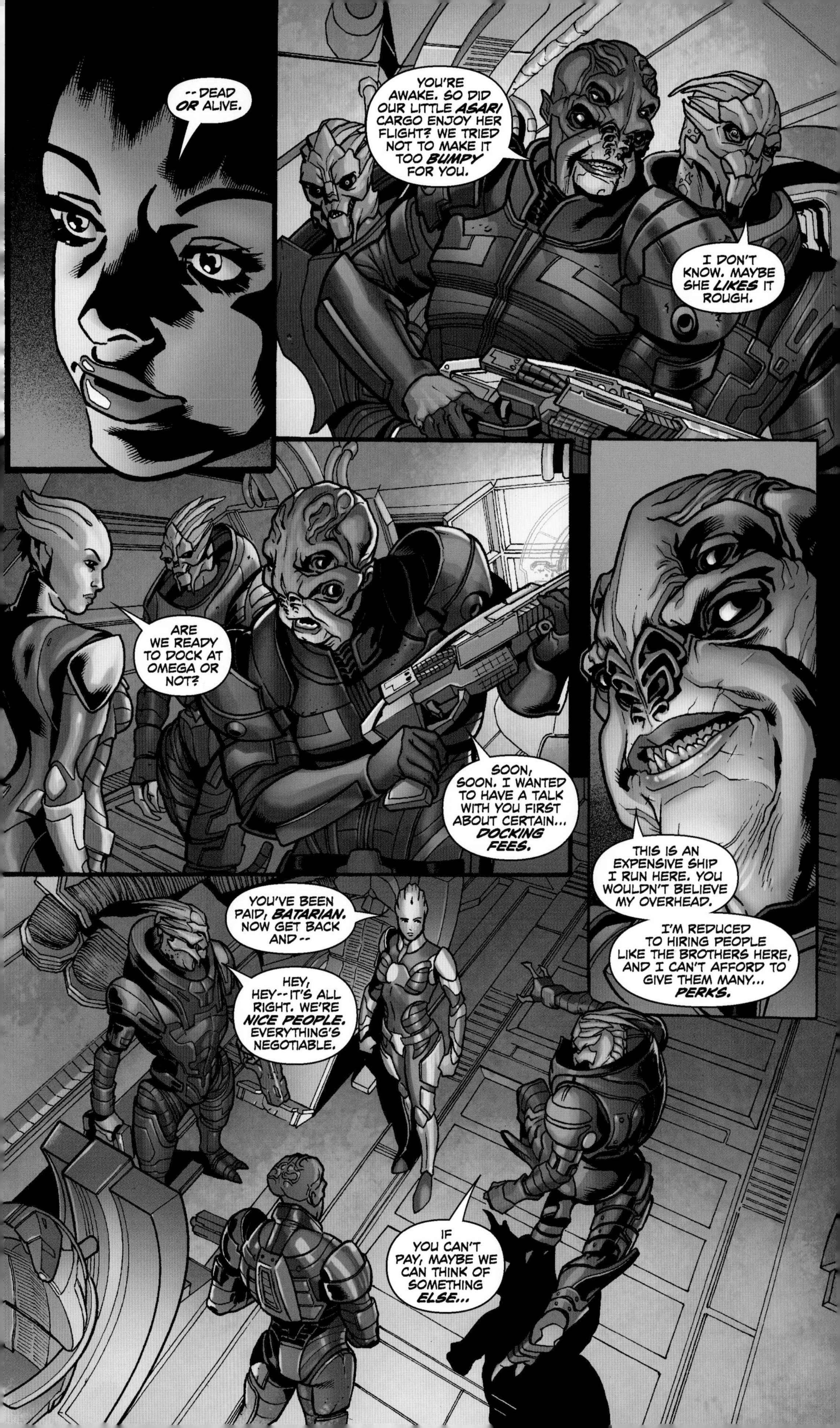

--DEAD OR ALIVE.
YOU'RE AWAKE. SO DID OUR LITTLE ASARI CARGO ENJOY HER FLIGHT? WE TRIED NOT TO MAKE IT TOO BUMPY FOR YOU.
I DON'T KNOW. MAYBE SHE LIKES IT ROUGH.
ARE WE READY TO DOCK AT OMEGA OR NOT?
SOON, SOON. I WANTED TO HAVE A TALK WITH YOU FIRST ABOUT CERTAIN... DOCKING FEES.
THIS IS AN EXPENSIVE SHIP I RUN HERE. YOU WOULDN'T BELIEVE MY OVERHEAD.
I'M REDUCED TO HIRING PEOPLE LIKE THE BROTHERS HERE, AND I CAN'T AFFORD TO GIVE THEM MANY... PERKS.
YOU'VE BEEN PAID, BATARIAN. NOW GET BACK AND--
HEY, HEY--IT'S ALL RIGHT. WE'RE NICE PEOPLE. EVERYTHING'S NEGOTIABLE.
IF YOU CAN'T PAY, MAYBE WE CAN THINK OF SOMETHING ELSE...

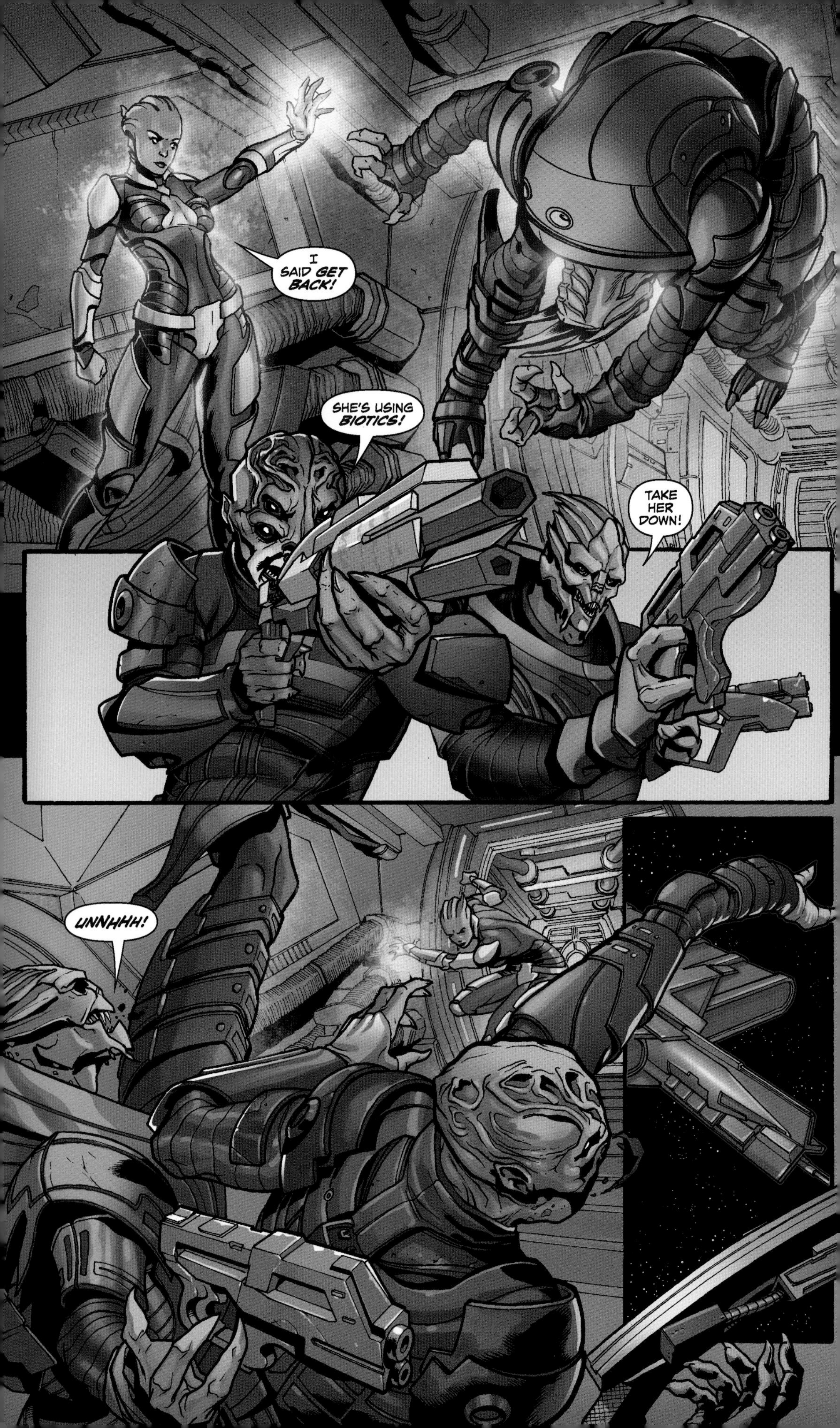
I SAID GET BACK!
SHE'S USING BIOTICS!
TAKE HER DOWN!
UNNHHH!

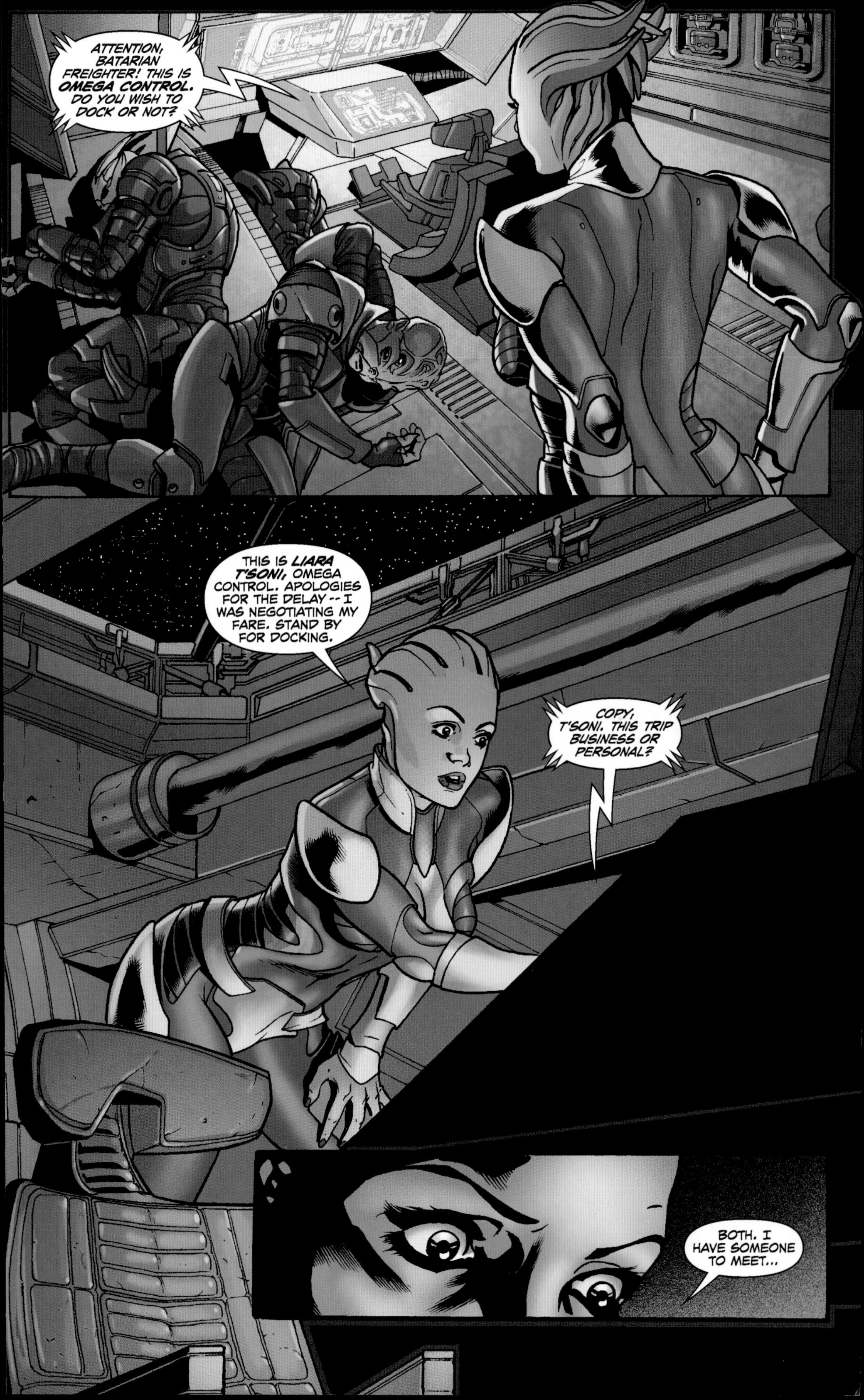
ATTENTION, BATARIAN FREIGHTER! THIS IS OMEGA CONTROL. DO YOU WISH TO DOCK OR NOT?
THIS IS LIARA T'SONI, OMEGA CONTROL. APOLOGIES FOR THE DELAY -- I WAS NEGOTIATING MY FARE. STAND BY FOR DOCKING.
COPY, T'SONI. THIS TRIP BUSINESS OR PERSONAL?
BOTH. I HAVE SOMEONE TO MEET...

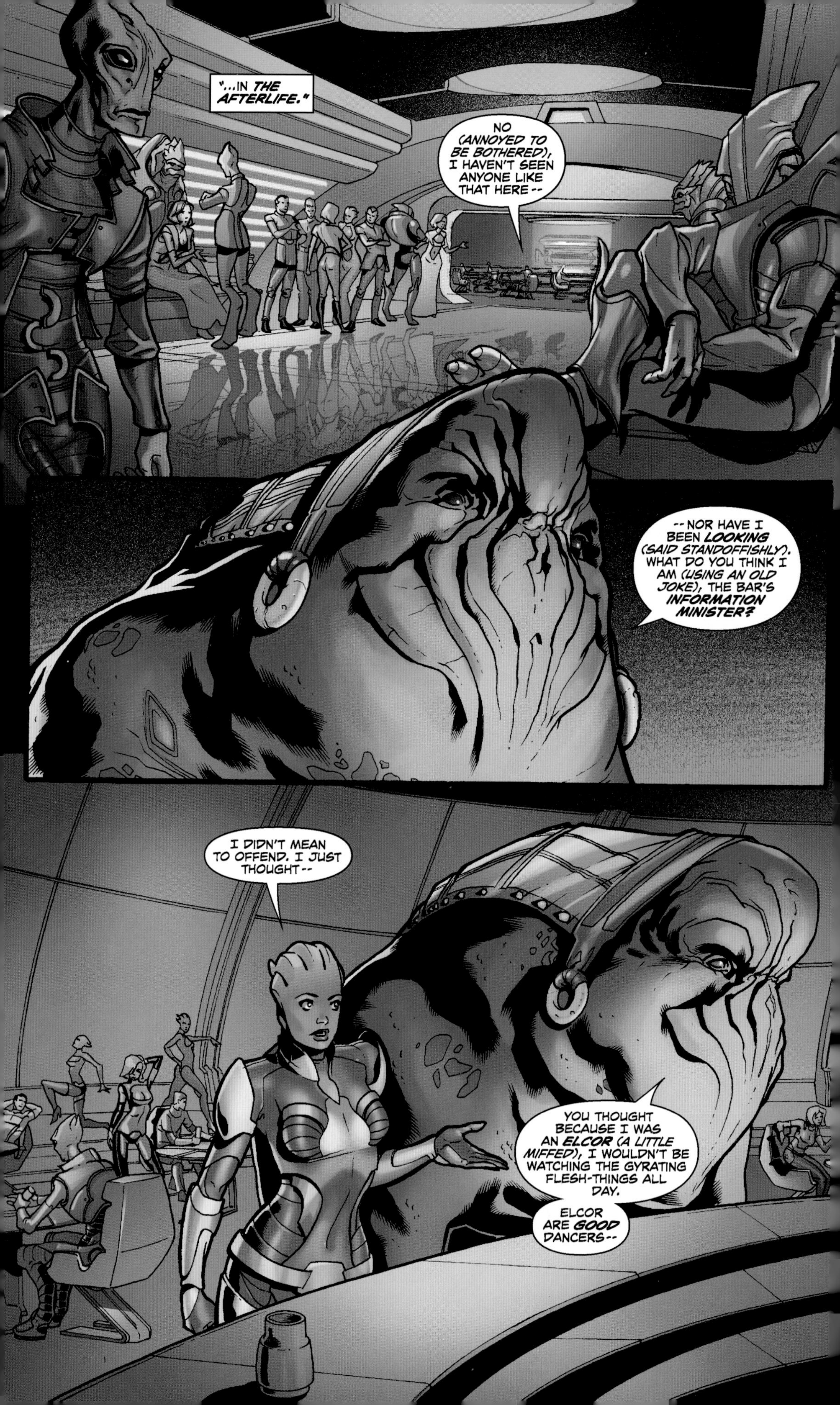
"...IN *THE AFTERLIFE.*"
NO (*ANNOYED TO BE BOTHERED*), I HAVEN'T SEEN ANYONE LIKE THAT HERE--
--NOR HAVE I BEEN ***LOOKING*** (*SAID STANDOFFISHLY*). WHAT DO YOU THINK I AM (*USING AN OLD JOKE*), THE BAR'S ***INFORMATION MINISTER?***
I DIDN'T MEAN TO OFFEND. I JUST THOUGHT--
YOU THOUGHT BECAUSE I WAS AN ***ELCOR*** (*A LITTLE MIFFED*), I WOULDN'T BE WATCHING THE GYRATING FLESH-THINGS ALL DAY.
ELCOR ARE ***GOOD*** DANCERS--

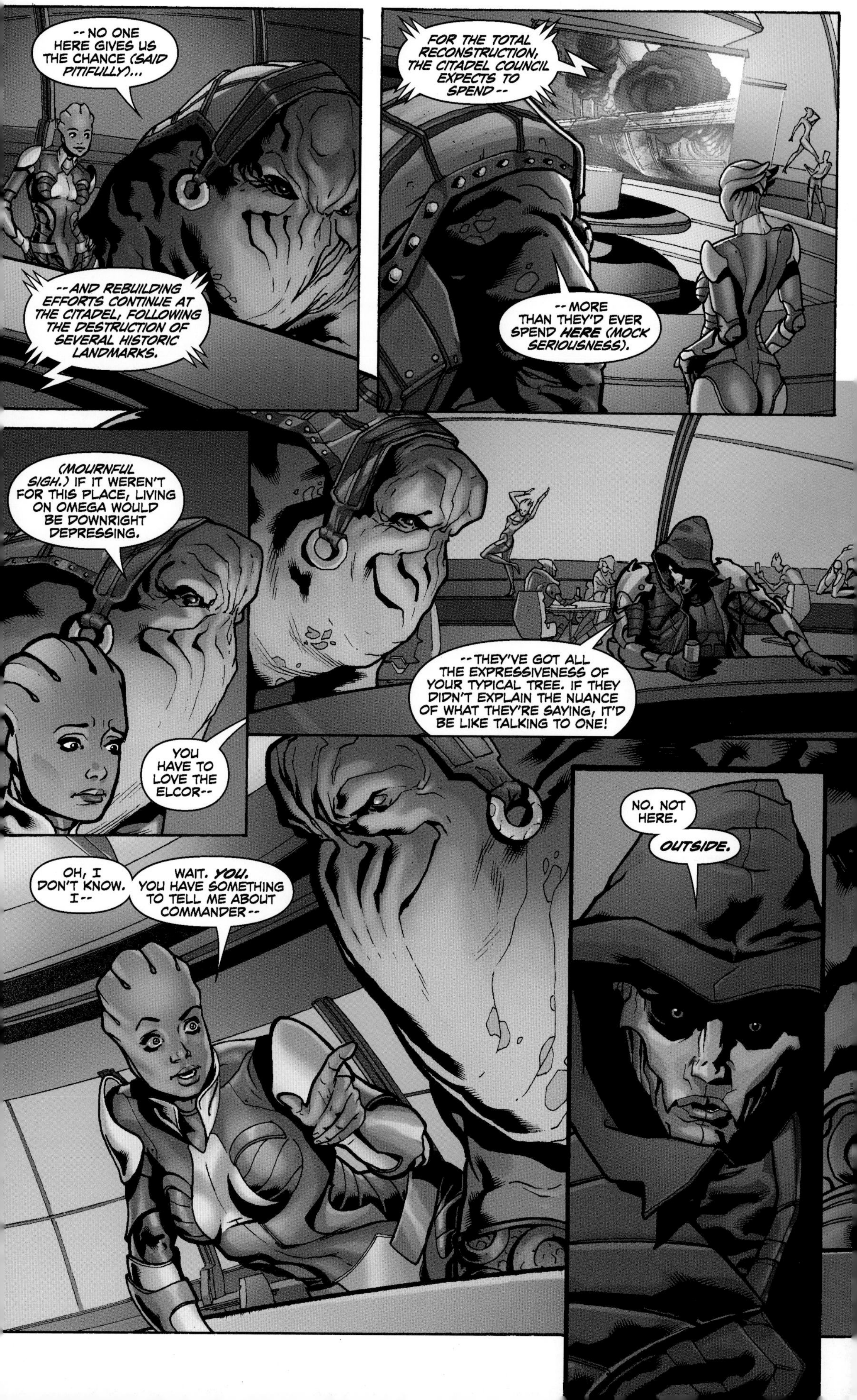
--NO ONE HERE GIVES US THE CHANCE (SAID PITIFULLY)...
--AND REBUILDING EFFORTS CONTINUE AT THE CITADEL, FOLLOWING THE DESTRUCTION OF SEVERAL HISTORIC LANDMARKS.
FOR THE TOTAL RECONSTRUCTION, THE CITADEL COUNCIL EXPECTS TO SPEND--
--MORE THAN THEY'D EVER SPEND *HERE* (MOCK SERIOUSNESS).
(MOURNFUL SIGH.) IF IT WEREN'T FOR THIS PLACE, LIVING ON OMEGA WOULD BE DOWNRIGHT DEPRESSING.
YOU HAVE TO LOVE THE ELCOR--
--THEY'VE GOT ALL THE EXPRESSIVENESS OF YOUR TYPICAL TREE. IF THEY DIDN'T EXPLAIN THE NUANCE OF WHAT THEY'RE SAYING, IT'D BE LIKE TALKING TO ONE!
OH, I DON'T KNOW. I--
WAIT. ***YOU.*** YOU HAVE SOMETHING TO TELL ME ABOUT COMMANDER--
NO. NOT HERE.
OUTSIDE.

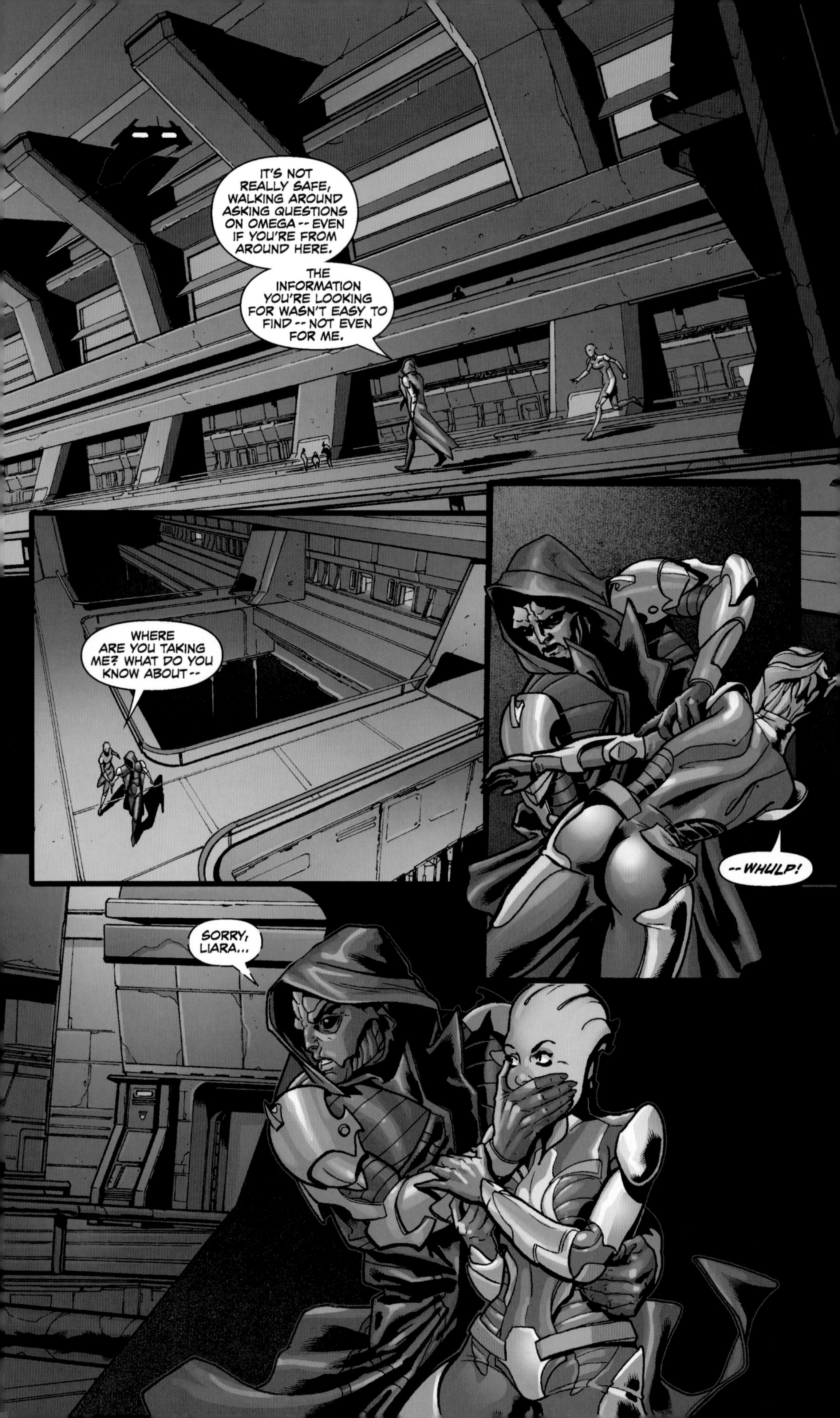
IT'S NOT REALLY SAFE, WALKING AROUND ASKING QUESTIONS ON OMEGA -- EVEN IF YOU'RE FROM AROUND HERE.
THE INFORMATION YOU'RE LOOKING FOR WASN'T EASY TO FIND -- NOT EVEN FOR ME.
WHERE ARE YOU TAKING ME? WHAT DO YOU KNOW ABOUT --
--WHULP!
SORRY, LIARA...

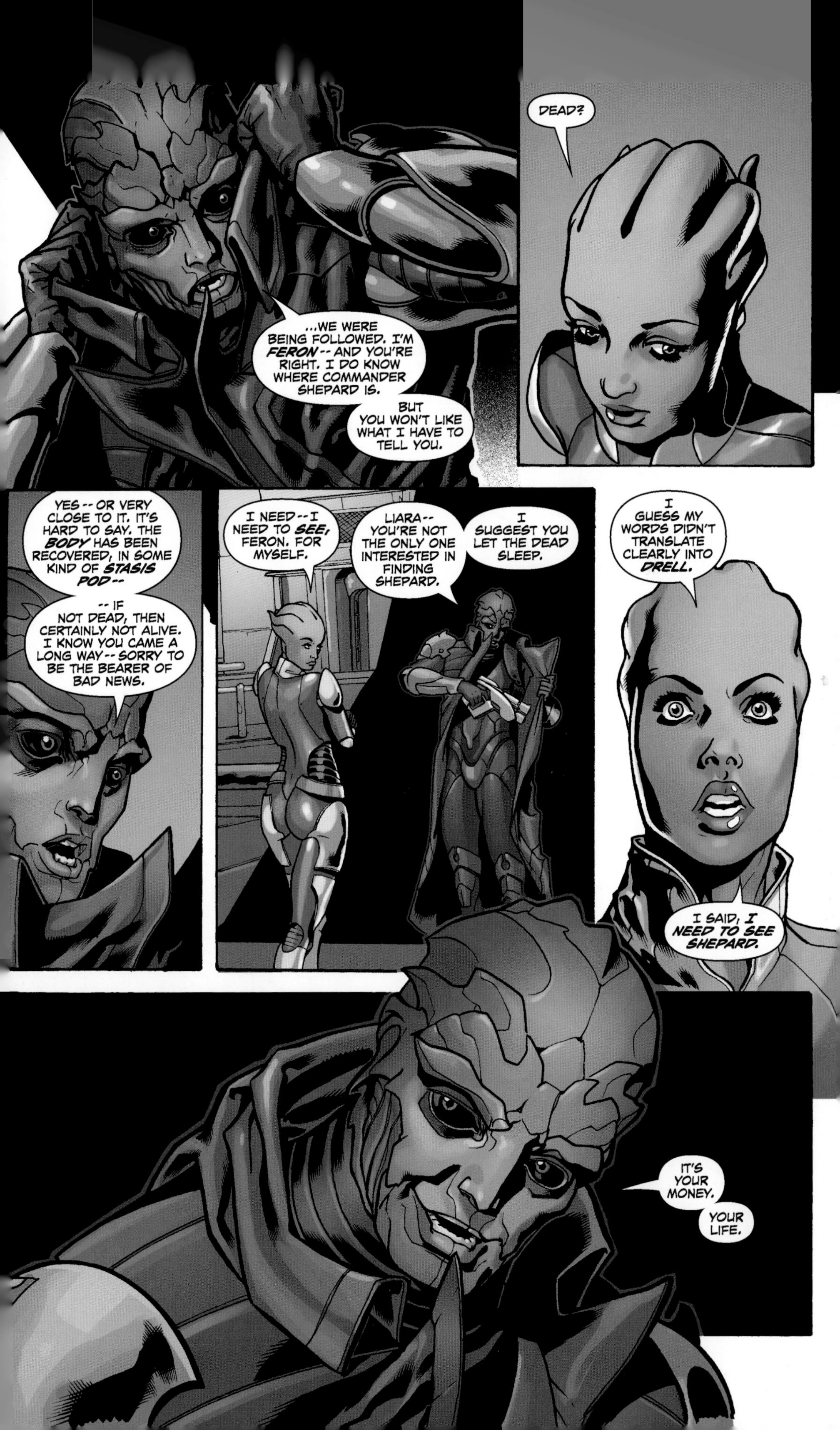
...WE WERE BEING FOLLOWED. I'M FERON -- AND YOU'RE RIGHT. I DO KNOW WHERE COMMANDER SHEPARD IS.
BUT YOU WON'T LIKE WHAT I HAVE TO TELL YOU.
DEAD?
YES -- OR VERY CLOSE TO IT. IT'S HARD TO SAY. THE BODY HAS BEEN RECOVERED, IN SOME KIND OF STASIS POD --
-- IF NOT DEAD, THEN CERTAINLY NOT ALIVE. I KNOW YOU CAME A LONG WAY -- SORRY TO BE THE BEARER OF BAD NEWS.
I NEED -- I NEED TO SEE, FERON. FOR MYSELF.
LIARA -- YOU'RE NOT THE ONLY ONE INTERESTED IN FINDING SHEPARD.
I SUGGEST YOU LET THE DEAD SLEEP.
I GUESS MY WORDS DIDN'T TRANSLATE CLEARLY INTO DRELL.
I SAID, I NEED TO SEE SHEPARD.
IT'S YOUR MONEY.
YOUR LIFE.

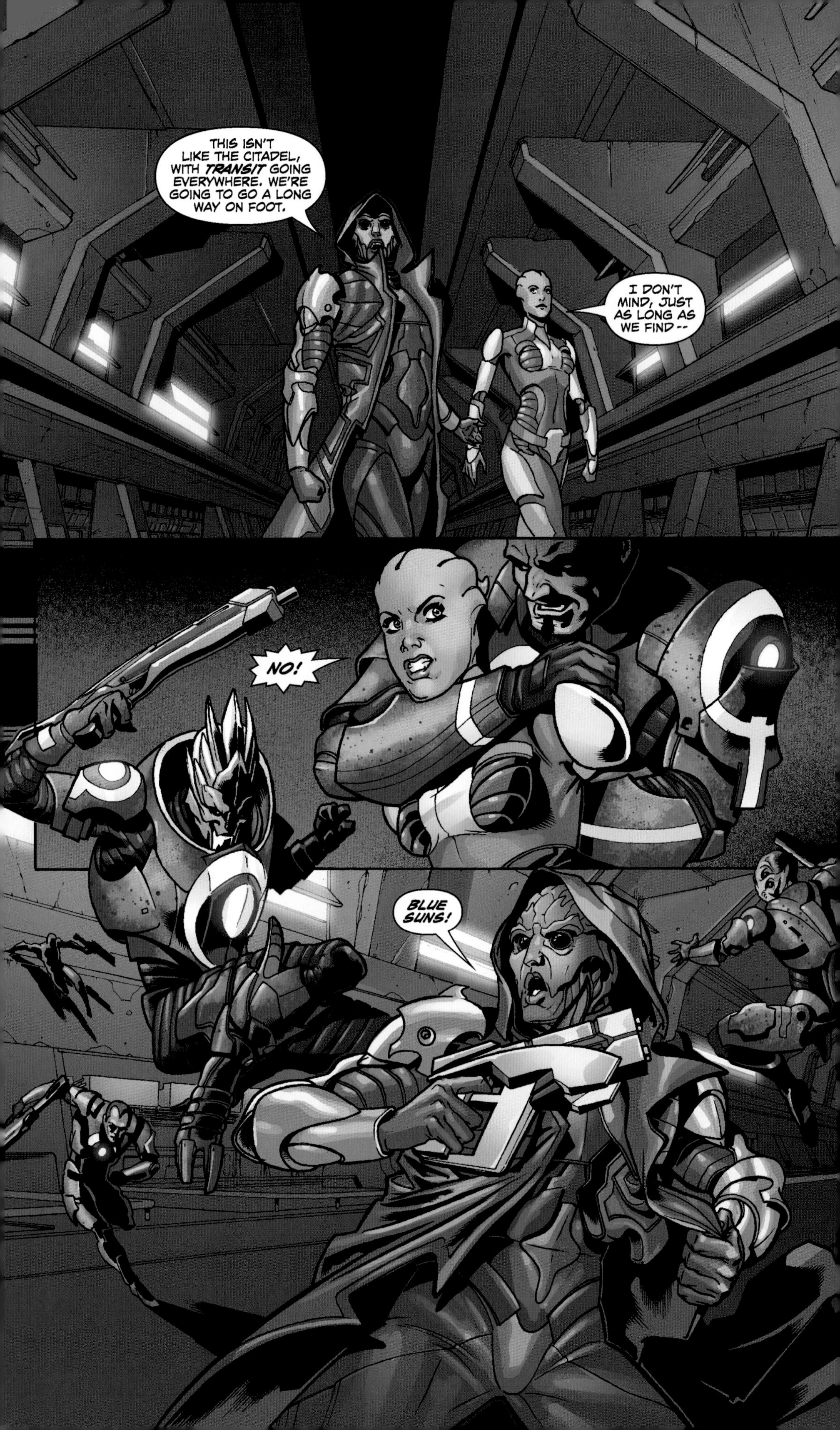
THIS ISN'T LIKE THE CITADEL, WITH *TRANSIT* GOING EVERYWHERE. WE'RE GOING TO GO A LONG WAY ON FOOT.
I DON'T MIND, JUST AS LONG AS WE FIND --
NO!
BLUE SUNS!

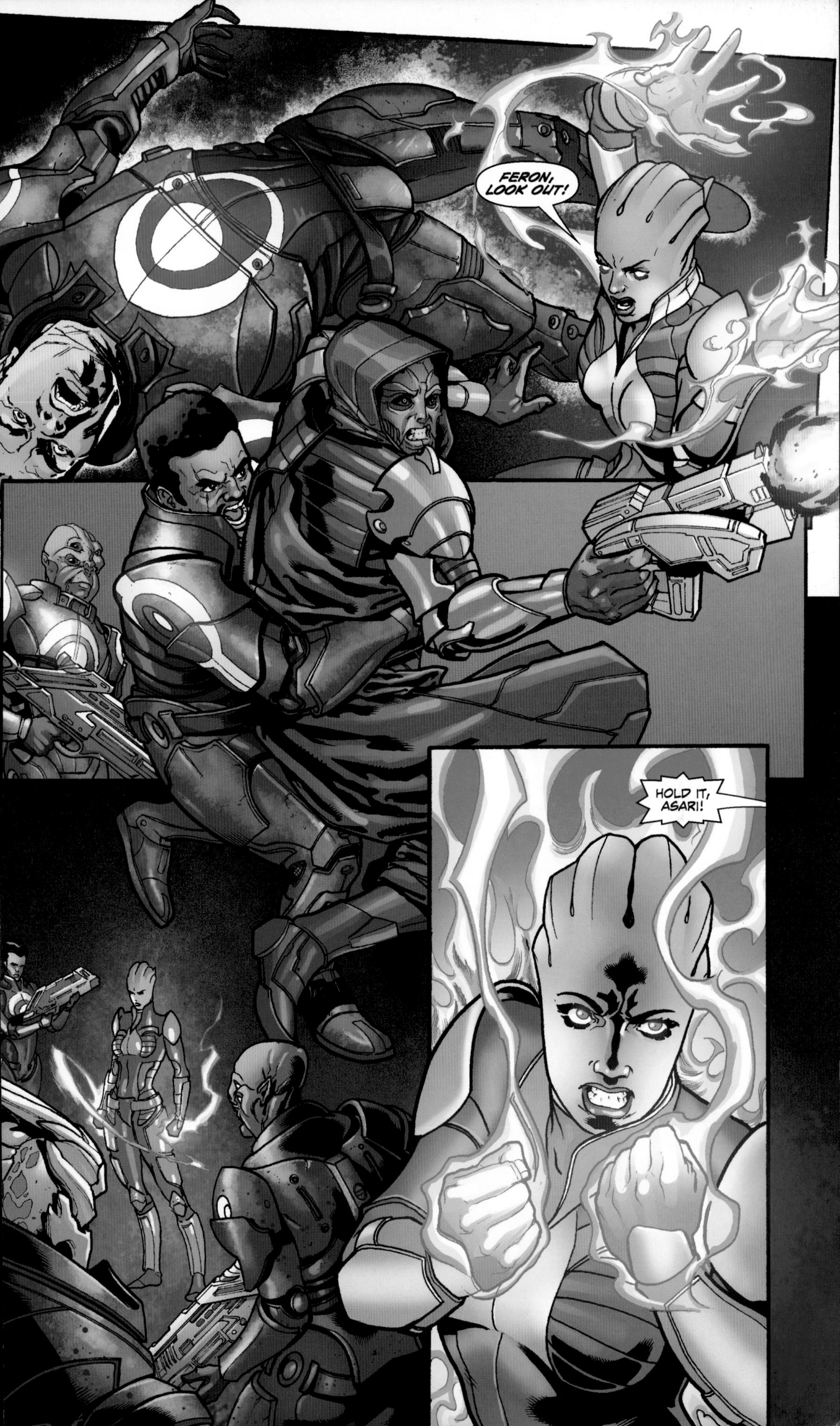
FERON, LOOK OUT!
HOLD IT, ASARI!

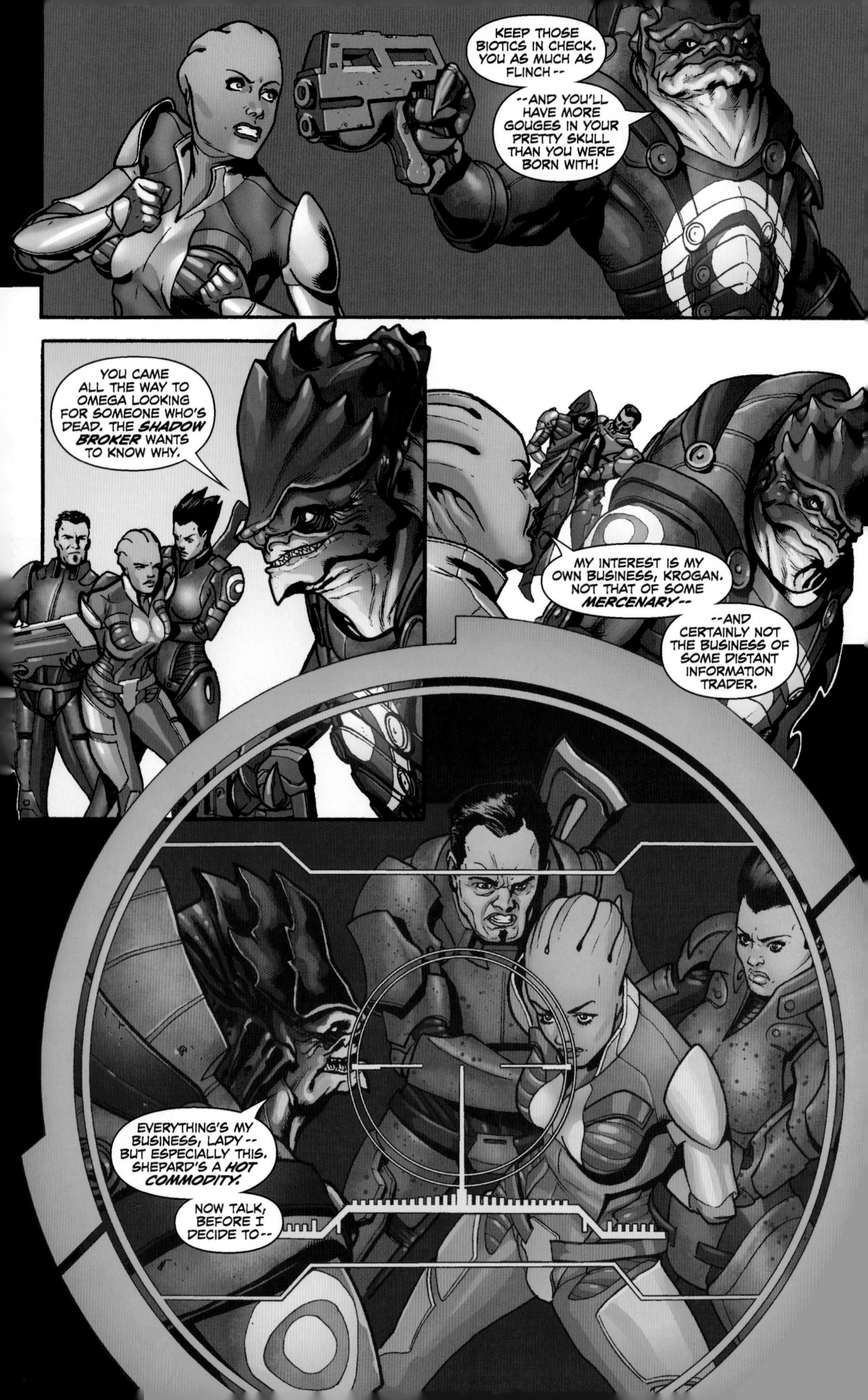
KEEP THOSE BIOTICS IN CHECK. YOU AS MUCH AS FLINCH --
--AND YOU'LL HAVE MORE GOUGES IN YOUR PRETTY SKULL THAN YOU WERE BORN WITH!
YOU CAME ALL THE WAY TO OMEGA LOOKING FOR SOMEONE WHO'S DEAD. THE *SHADOW BROKER* WANTS TO KNOW WHY.
MY INTEREST IS MY OWN BUSINESS, KROGAN. NOT THAT OF SOME *MERCENARY*--
--AND CERTAINLY NOT THE BUSINESS OF SOME DISTANT INFORMATION TRADER.
EVERYTHING'S MY BUSINESS, LADY -- BUT ESPECIALLY THIS. SHEPARD'S A *HOT COMMODITY.*
NOW TALK, BEFORE I DECIDE TO--

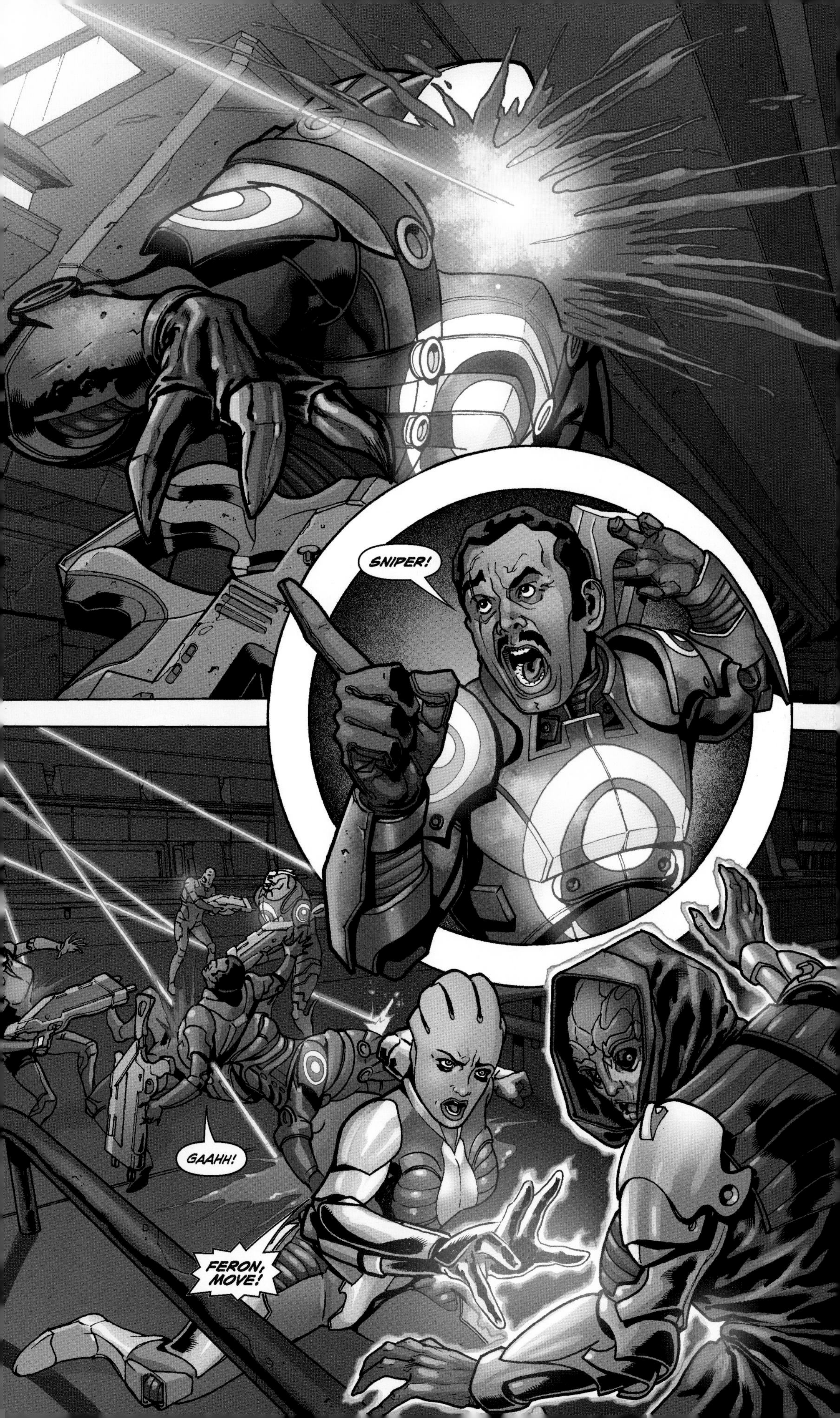
SNIPER!
GAAHH!
FERON, MOVE!

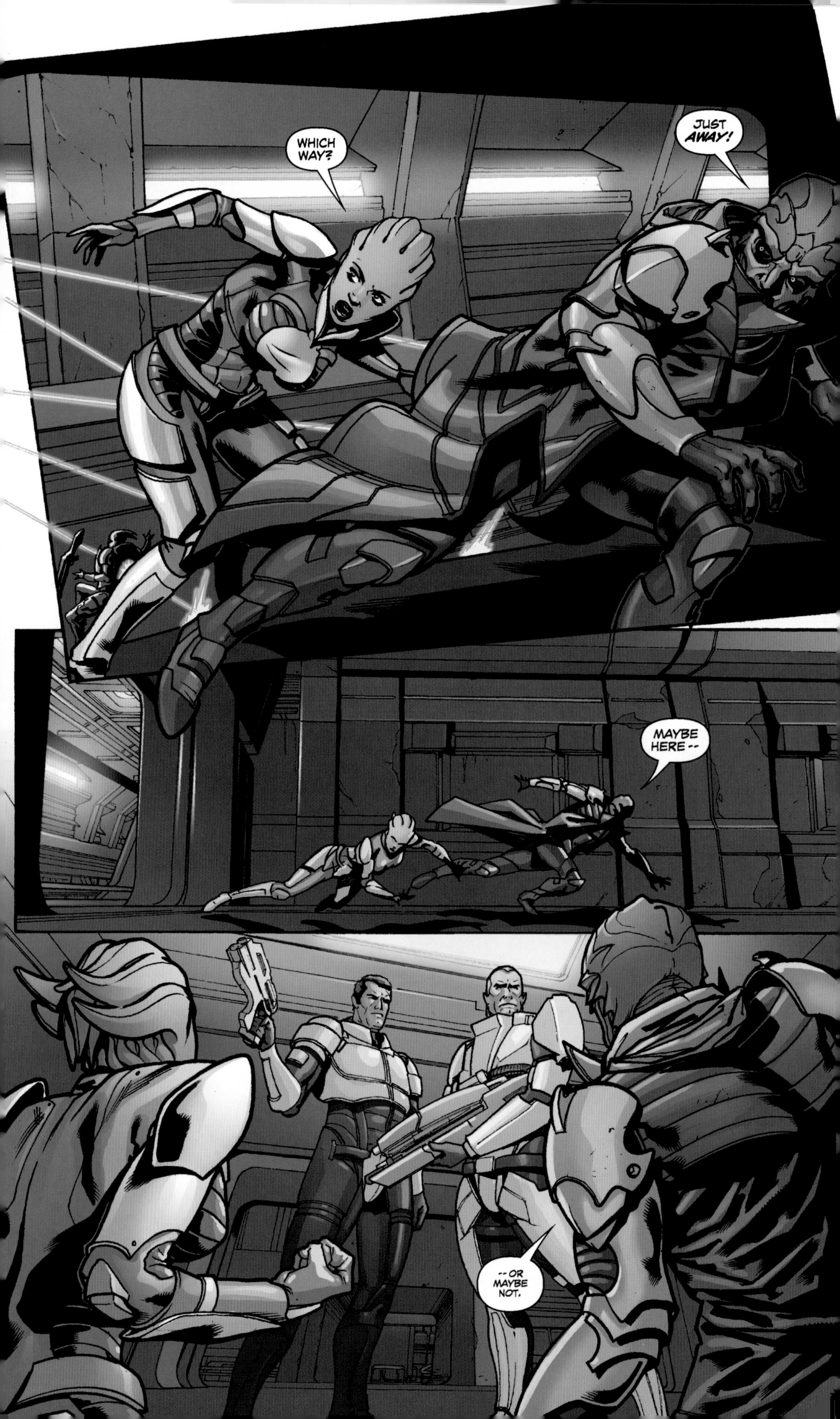
WHICH WAY?
JUST AWAY!
MAYBE HERE --
-- OR MAYBE NOT.

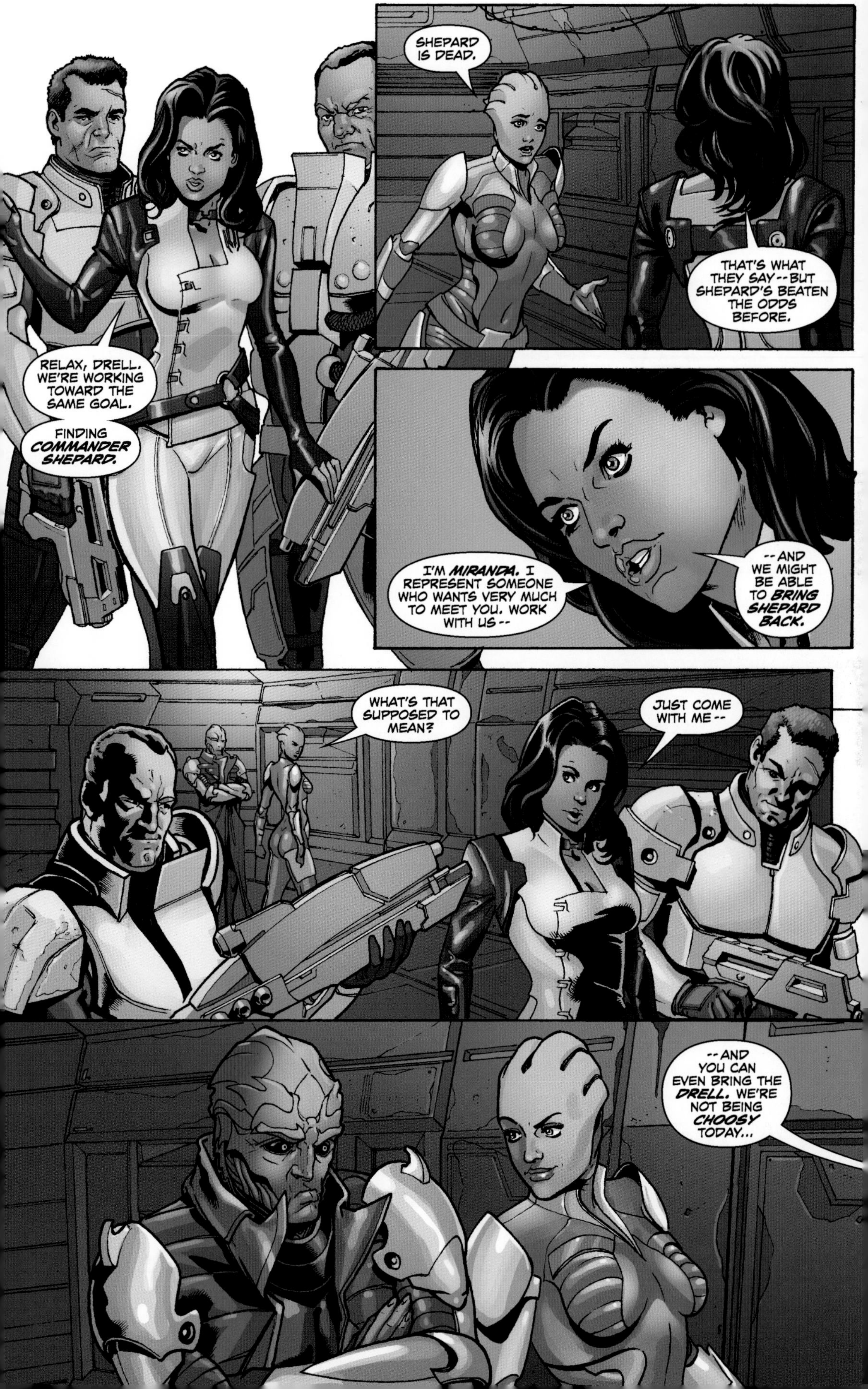
RELAX, DRELL. WE'RE WORKING TOWARD THE SAME GOAL.
FINDING *COMMANDER SHEPARD.*
SHEPARD IS DEAD.
THAT'S WHAT THEY SAY--BUT SHEPARD'S BEATEN THE ODDS BEFORE.
I'M *MIRANDA.* I REPRESENT SOMEONE WHO WANTS VERY MUCH TO MEET YOU. WORK WITH US--
--AND WE MIGHT BE ABLE TO *BRING SHEPARD BACK.*
WHAT'S THAT SUPPOSED TO MEAN?
JUST COME WITH ME--
--AND YOU CAN EVEN BRING THE *DRELL.* WE'RE NOT BEING *CHOOSY* TODAY...

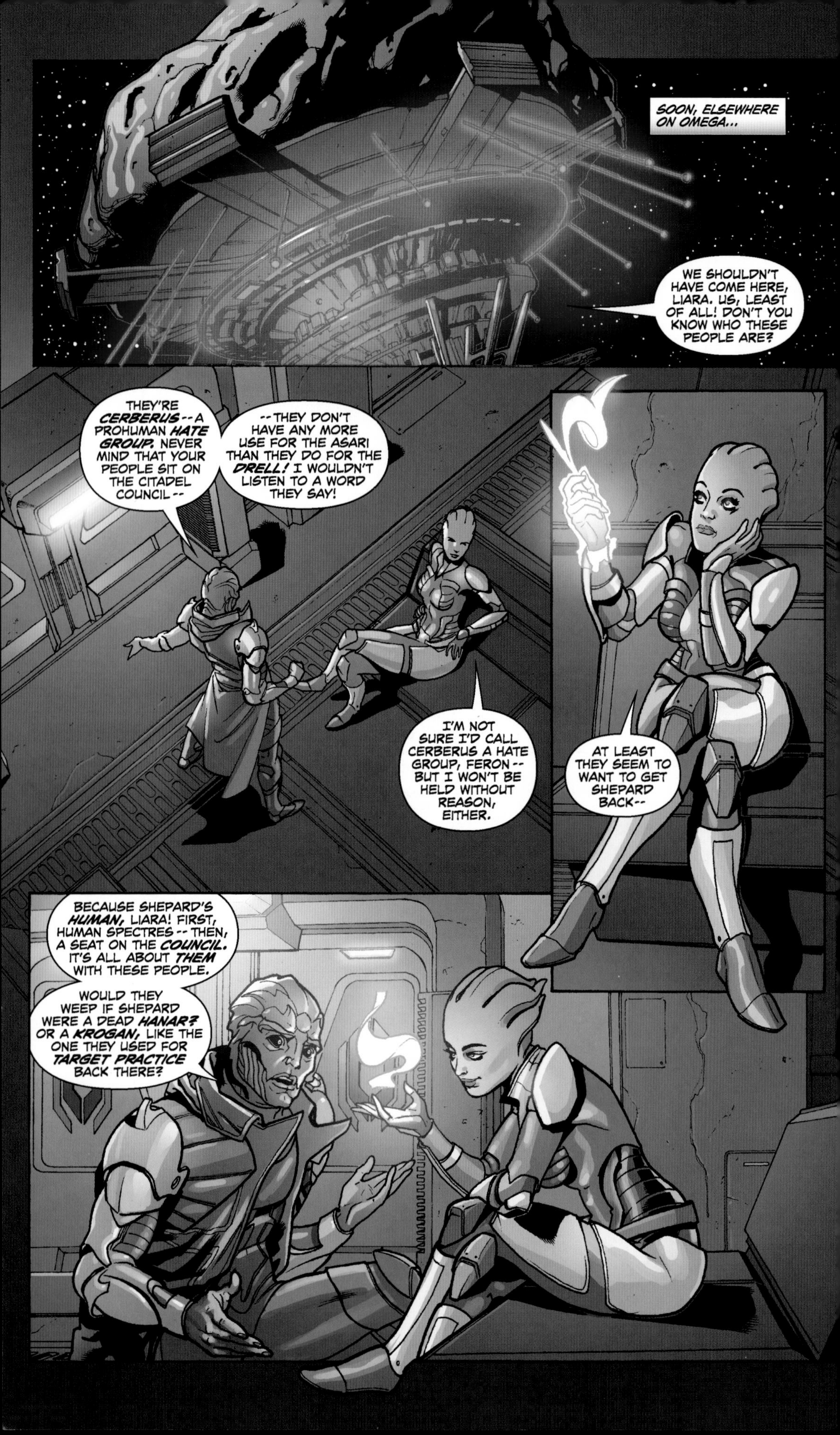
SOON, ELSEWHERE ON OMEGA...
WE SHOULDN'T HAVE COME HERE, LIARA. US, LEAST OF ALL! DON'T YOU KNOW WHO THESE PEOPLE ARE?
THEY'RE CERBERUS--A PROHUMAN HATE GROUP. NEVER MIND THAT YOUR PEOPLE SIT ON THE CITADEL COUNCIL--
--THEY DON'T HAVE ANY MORE USE FOR THE ASARI THAN THEY DO FOR THE DRELL! I WOULDN'T LISTEN TO A WORD THEY SAY!
I'M NOT SURE I'D CALL CERBERUS A HATE GROUP, FERON--BUT I WON'T BE HELD WITHOUT REASON, EITHER.
AT LEAST THEY SEEM TO WANT TO GET SHEPARD BACK--
BECAUSE SHEPARD'S HUMAN, LIARA! FIRST, HUMAN SPECTRES--THEN, A SEAT ON THE COUNCIL. IT'S ALL ABOUT THEM WITH THESE PEOPLE.
WOULD THEY WEEP IF SHEPARD WERE A DEAD HANAR? OR A KROGAN, LIKE THE ONE THEY USED FOR TARGET PRACTICE BACK THERE?

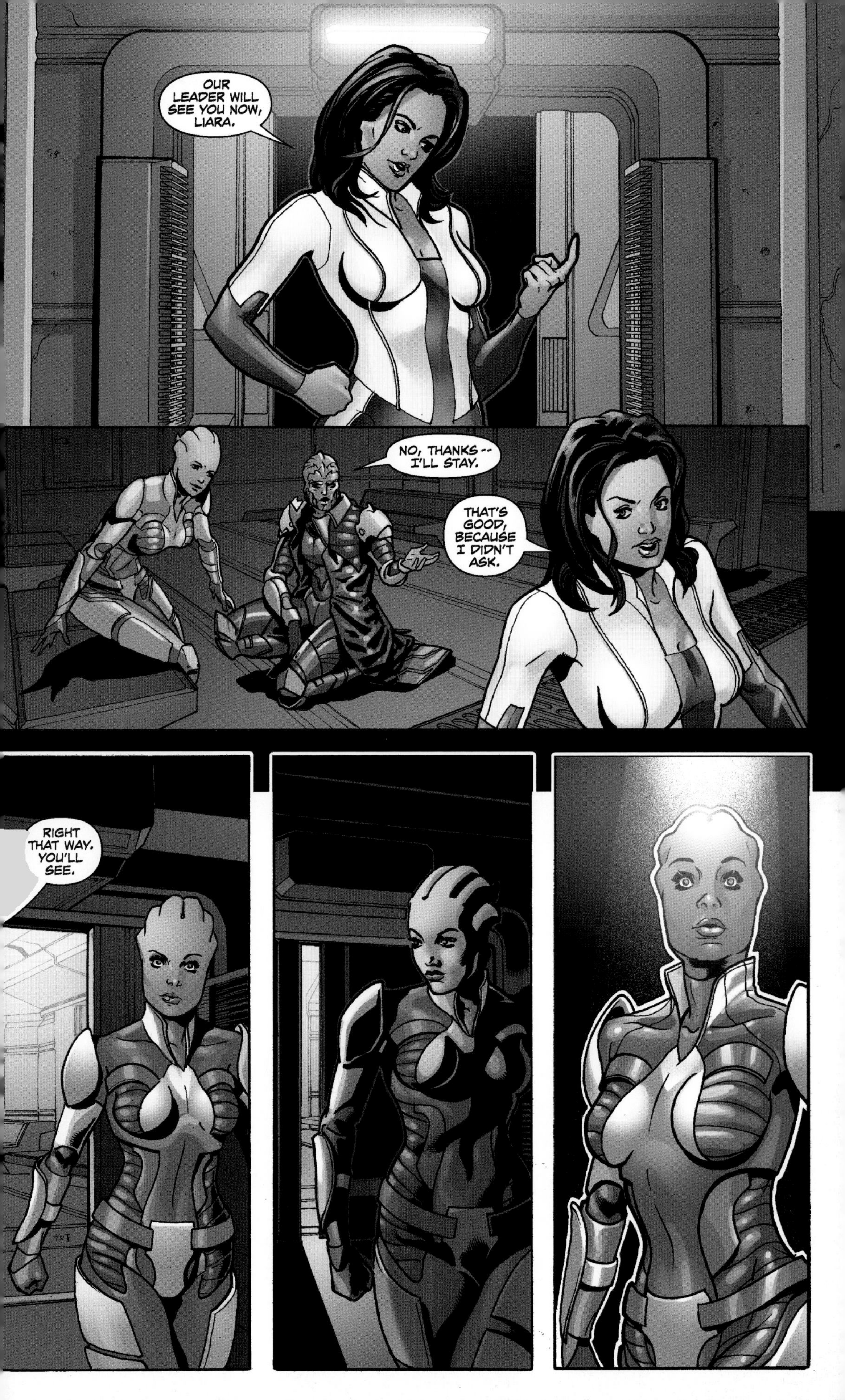
OUR LEADER WILL SEE YOU NOW, LIARA.
NO, THANKS -- I'LL STAY.
THAT'S GOOD, BECAUSE I DIDN'T ASK.
RIGHT THAT WAY. YOU'LL SEE.

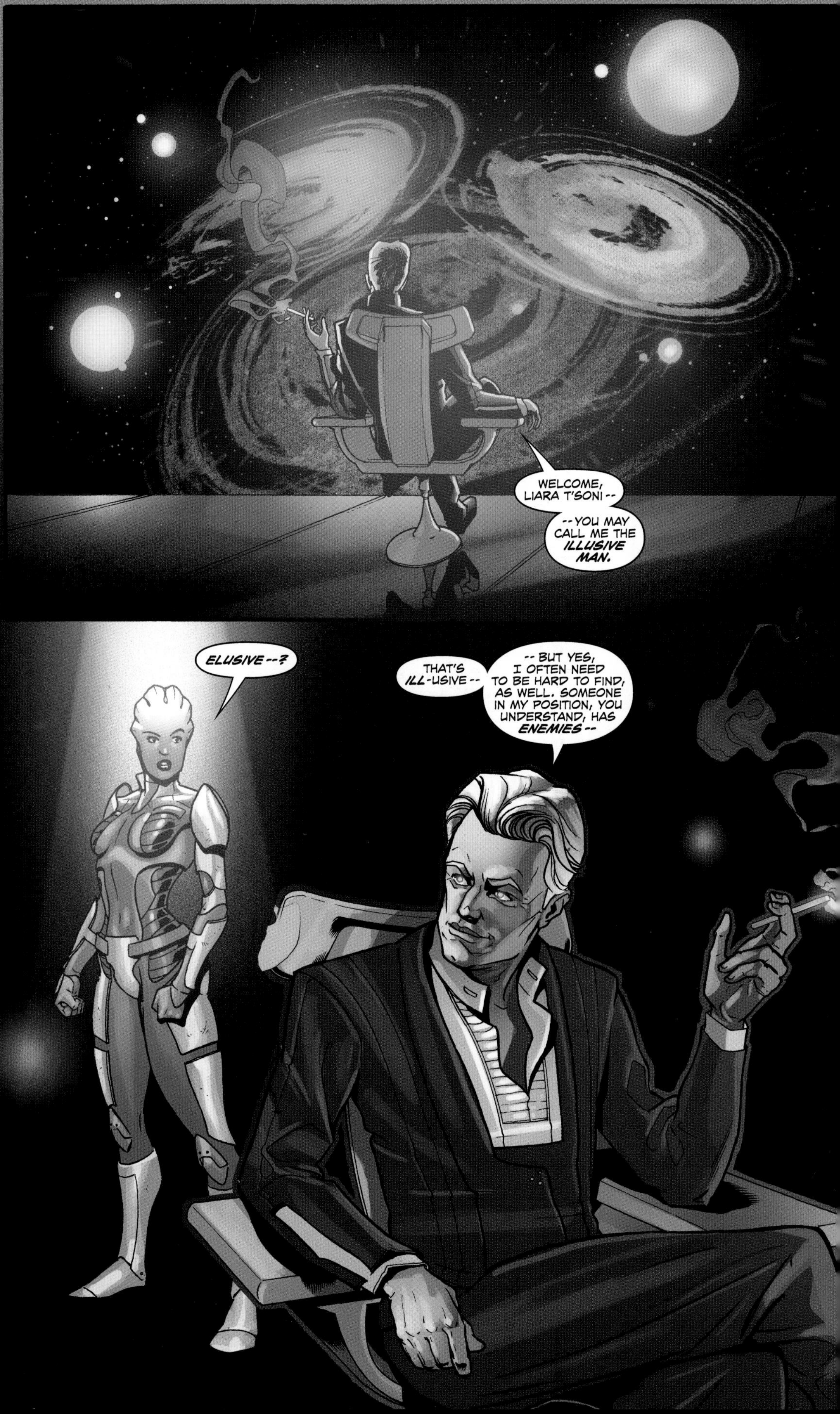
WELCOME, LIARA T'SONI --
--YOU MAY CALL ME THE *ILLUSIVE MAN.*
ELUSIVE --?
THAT'S *ILL*-USIVE --
-- BUT YES, I OFTEN NEED TO BE HARD TO FIND, AS WELL. SOMEONE IN MY POSITION, YOU UNDERSTAND, HAS *ENEMIES --*

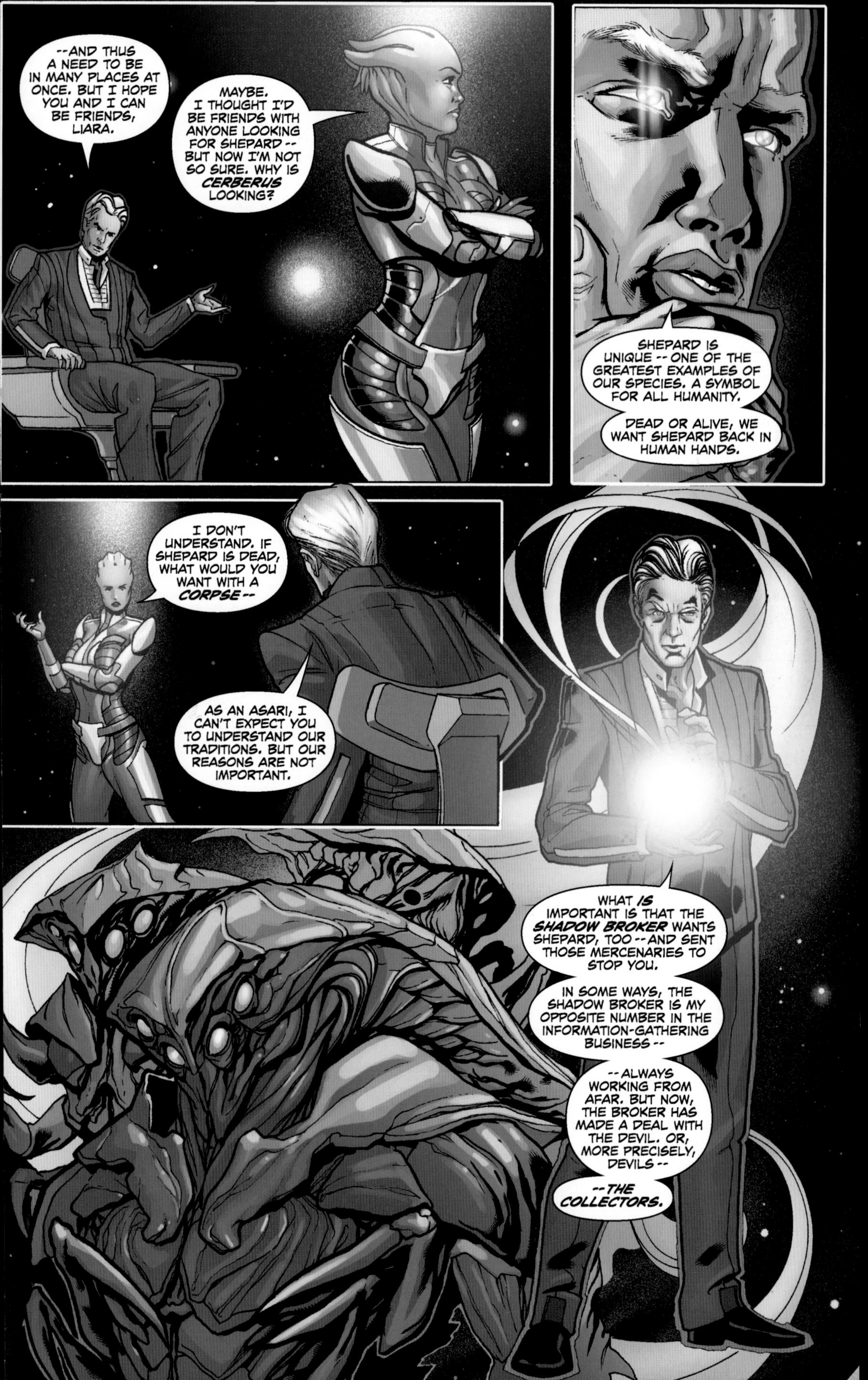
--AND THUS A NEED TO BE IN MANY PLACES AT ONCE. BUT I HOPE YOU AND I CAN BE FRIENDS, LIARA.
MAYBE. I THOUGHT I'D BE FRIENDS WITH ANYONE LOOKING FOR SHEPARD -- BUT NOW I'M NOT SO SURE. WHY IS CERBERUS LOOKING?
SHEPARD IS UNIQUE -- ONE OF THE GREATEST EXAMPLES OF OUR SPECIES. A SYMBOL FOR ALL HUMANITY.
DEAD OR ALIVE, WE WANT SHEPARD BACK IN HUMAN HANDS.
I DON'T UNDERSTAND. IF SHEPARD IS DEAD, WHAT WOULD YOU WANT WITH A CORPSE--
AS AN ASARI, I CAN'T EXPECT YOU TO UNDERSTAND OUR TRADITIONS. BUT OUR REASONS ARE NOT IMPORTANT.
WHAT IS IMPORTANT IS THAT THE SHADOW BROKER WANTS SHEPARD, TOO -- AND SENT THOSE MERCENARIES TO STOP YOU.
IN SOME WAYS, THE SHADOW BROKER IS MY OPPOSITE NUMBER IN THE INFORMATION-GATHERING BUSINESS --
-- ALWAYS WORKING FROM AFAR. BUT NOW, THE BROKER HAS MADE A DEAL WITH THE DEVIL. OR, MORE PRECISELY, DEVILS --
-- THE COLLECTORS.

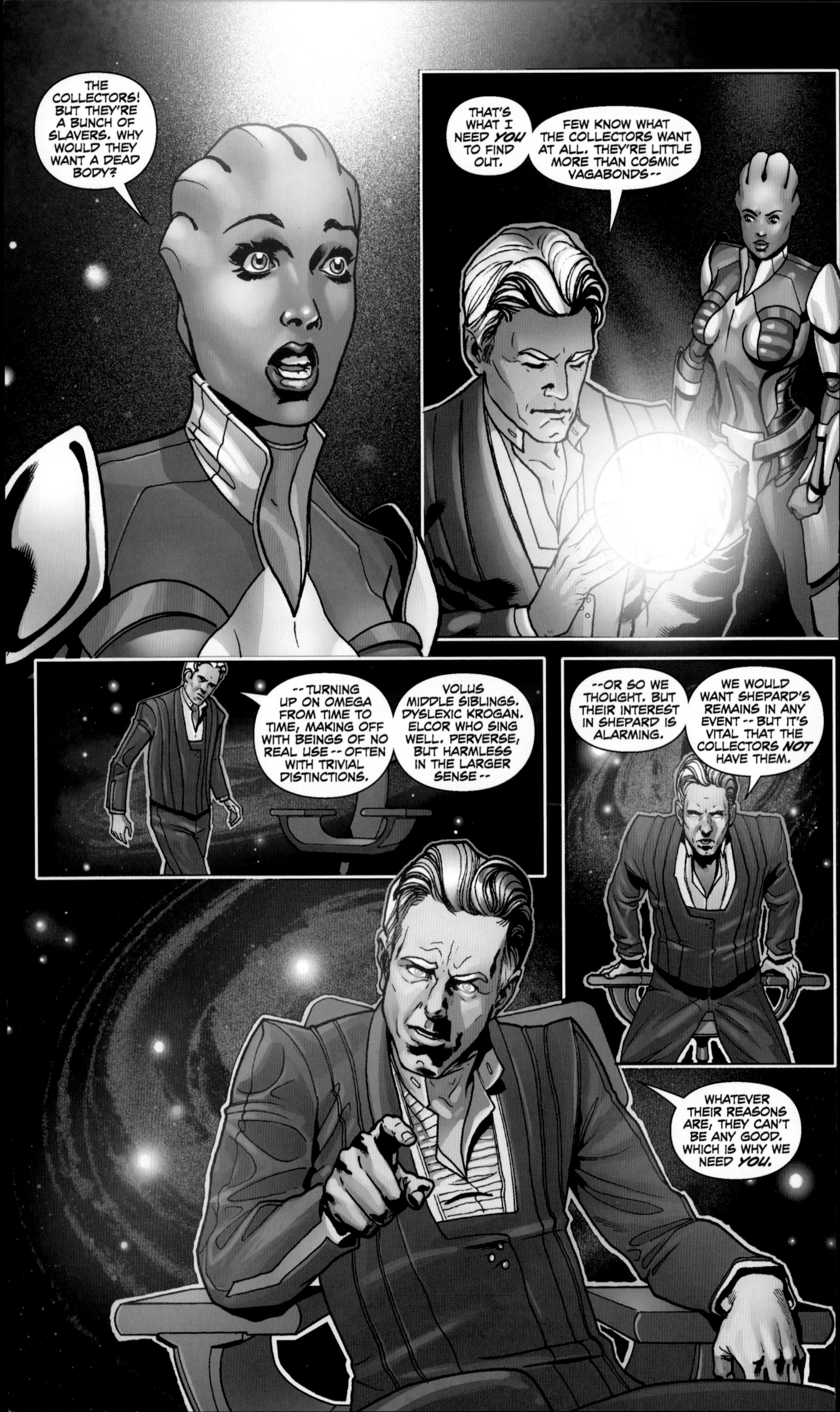
THE COLLECTORS! BUT THEY'RE A BUNCH OF SLAVERS. WHY WOULD THEY WANT A DEAD BODY?
THAT'S WHAT I NEED *YOU* TO FIND OUT.
FEW KNOW WHAT THE COLLECTORS WANT AT ALL. THEY'RE LITTLE MORE THAN COSMIC VAGABONDS--
--TURNING UP ON OMEGA FROM TIME TO TIME, MAKING OFF WITH BEINGS OF NO REAL USE--OFTEN WITH TRIVIAL DISTINCTIONS.
VOLUS MIDDLE SIBLINGS. DYSLEXIC KROGAN. ELCOR WHO SING WELL. PERVERSE, BUT HARMLESS IN THE LARGER SENSE--
--OR SO WE THOUGHT. BUT THEIR INTEREST IN SHEPARD IS ALARMING.
WE WOULD WANT SHEPARD'S REMAINS IN ANY EVENT--BUT IT'S VITAL THAT THE COLLECTORS *NOT* HAVE THEM.
WHATEVER THEIR REASONS ARE, THEY CAN'T BE ANY GOOD. WHICH IS WHY WE NEED *YOU*.

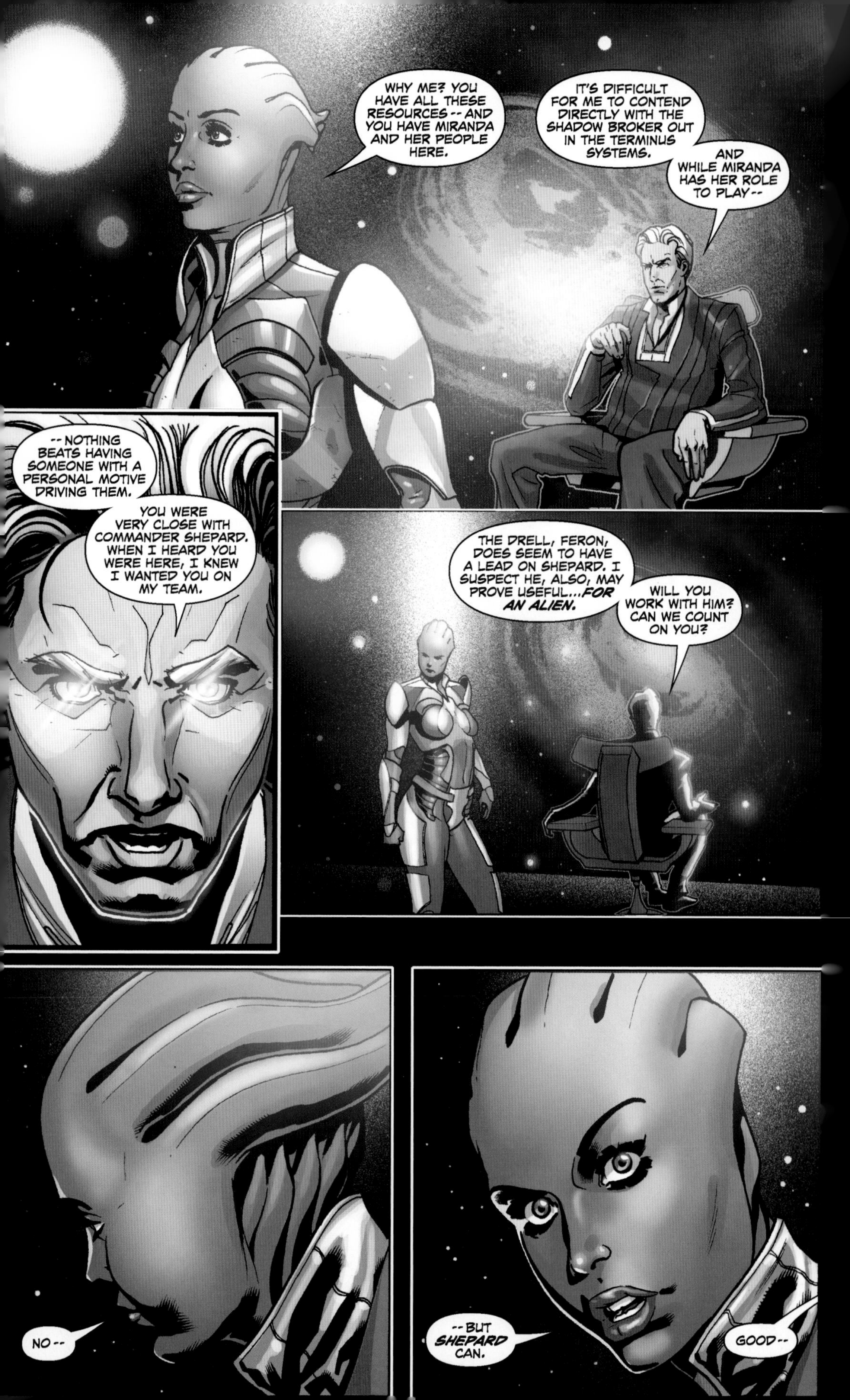
WHY ME? YOU HAVE ALL THESE RESOURCES -- AND YOU HAVE MIRANDA AND HER PEOPLE HERE.
IT'S DIFFICULT FOR ME TO CONTEND DIRECTLY WITH THE SHADOW BROKER OUT IN THE TERMINUS SYSTEMS.
AND WHILE MIRANDA HAS HER ROLE TO PLAY --
-- NOTHING BEATS HAVING SOMEONE WITH A PERSONAL MOTIVE DRIVING THEM.
YOU WERE VERY CLOSE WITH COMMANDER SHEPARD. WHEN I HEARD YOU WERE HERE, I KNEW I WANTED YOU ON MY TEAM.
THE DRELL, FERON, DOES SEEM TO HAVE A LEAD ON SHEPARD. I SUSPECT HE, ALSO, MAY PROVE USEFUL... ***FOR AN ALIEN.***
WILL YOU WORK WITH HIM? CAN WE COUNT ON YOU?
NO --
-- BUT ***SHEPARD*** CAN.
GOOD --

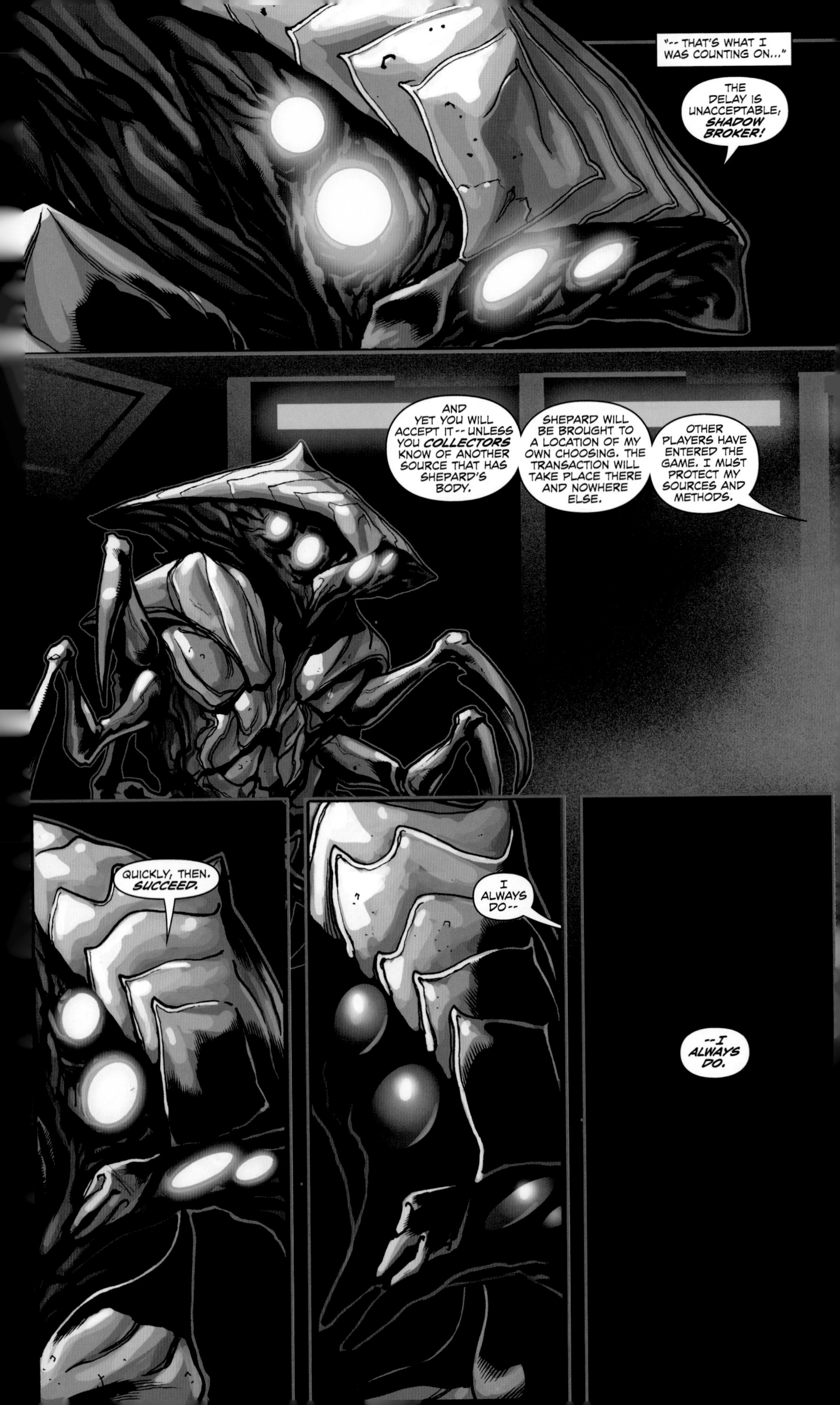
"-- THAT'S WHAT I WAS COUNTING ON..."
THE DELAY IS UNACCEPTABLE, SHADOW BROKER!
AND YET YOU WILL ACCEPT IT -- UNLESS YOU COLLECTORS KNOW OF ANOTHER SOURCE THAT HAS SHEPARD'S BODY.
SHEPARD WILL BE BROUGHT TO A LOCATION OF MY OWN CHOOSING. THE TRANSACTION WILL TAKE PLACE THERE AND NOWHERE ELSE.
OTHER PLAYERS HAVE ENTERED THE GAME. I MUST PROTECT MY SOURCES AND METHODS.
QUICKLY, THEN. SUCCEED.
I ALWAYS DO --
-- I ALWAYS DO.

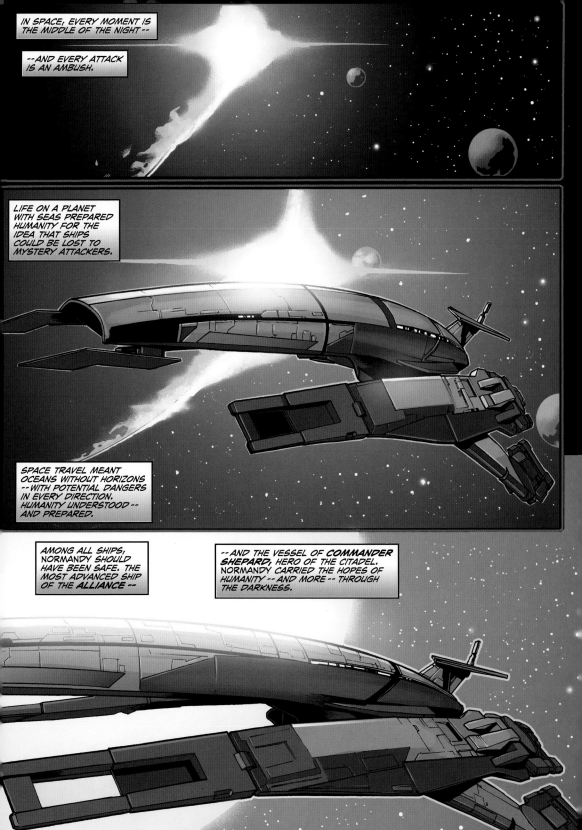

IN SPACE, EVERY MOMENT IS THE MIDDLE OF THE NIGHT--

--AND EVERY ATTACK IS AN AMBUSH.

LIFE ON A PLANET WITH SEAS PREPARED HUMANITY FOR THE IDEA THAT SHIPS COULD BE LOST TO MYSTERY ATTACKERS.

SPACE TRAVEL MEANT OCEANS WITHOUT HORIZONS -- WITH POTENTIAL DANGERS IN EVERY DIRECTION. HUMANITY UNDERSTOOD -- AND PREPARED.

AMONG ALL SHIPS, NORMANDY SHOULD HAVE BEEN SAFE. THE MOST ADVANCED SHIP OF THE **ALLIANCE** --

--AND THE VESSEL OF **COMMANDER SHEPARD**, HERO OF THE CITADEL. NORMANDY CARRIED THE HOPES OF HUMANITY -- AND MORE -- THROUGH THE DARKNESS.

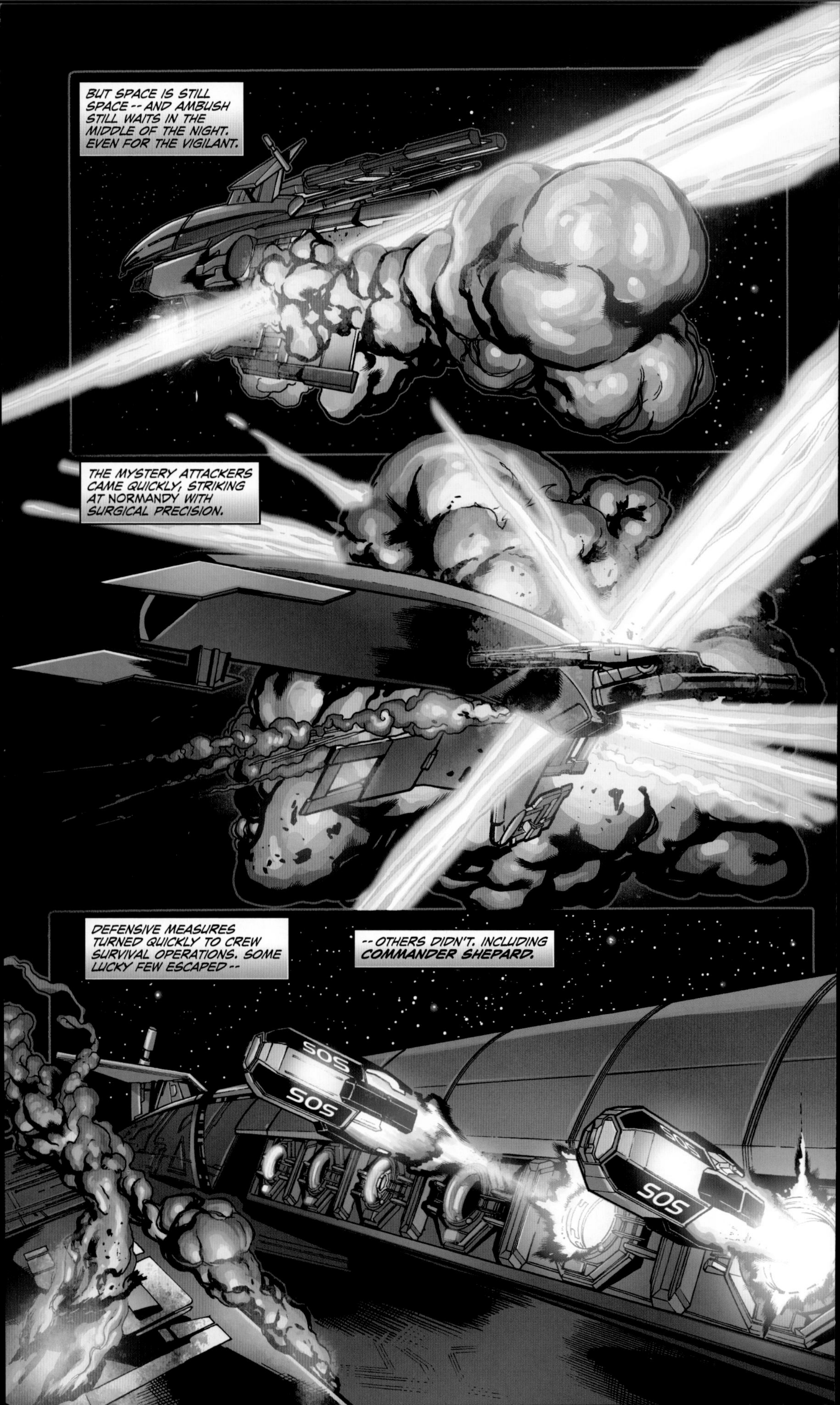
BUT SPACE IS STILL SPACE -- AND AMBUSH STILL WAITS IN THE MIDDLE OF THE NIGHT. EVEN FOR THE VIGILANT.
THE MYSTERY ATTACKERS CAME QUICKLY, STRIKING AT NORMANDY WITH SURGICAL PRECISION.
DEFENSIVE MEASURES TURNED QUICKLY TO CREW SURVIVAL OPERATIONS. SOME LUCKY FEW ESCAPED --
-- OTHERS DIDN'T. INCLUDING COMMANDER SHEPARD.
SOS
SOS
SOS
SOS

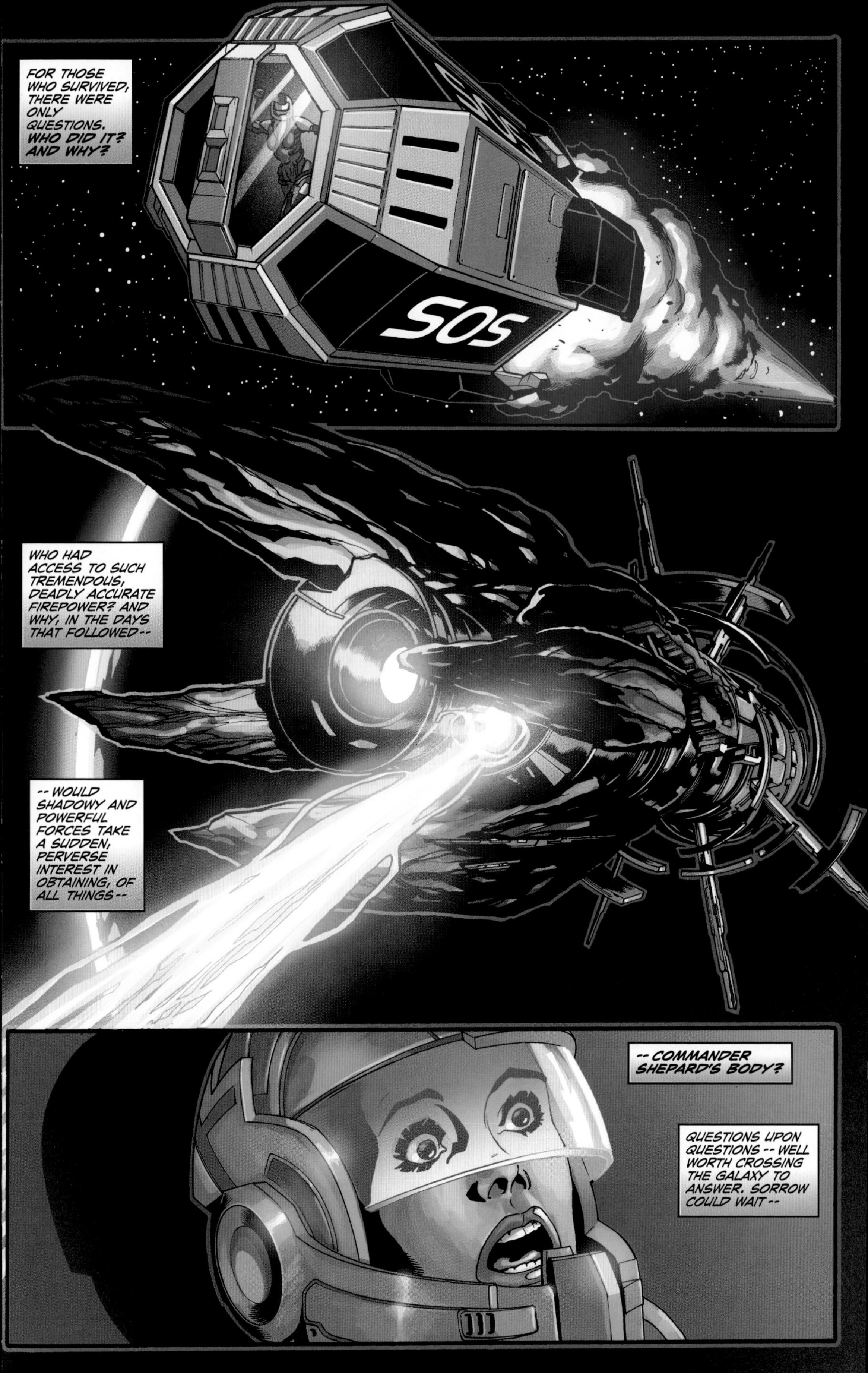
FOR THOSE WHO SURVIVED, THERE WERE ONLY QUESTIONS. WHO DID IT? AND WHY?
SOS
WHO HAD ACCESS TO SUCH TREMENDOUS, DEADLY ACCURATE FIREPOWER? AND WHY, IN THE DAYS THAT FOLLOWED--
--WOULD SHADOWY AND POWERFUL FORCES TAKE A SUDDEN, PERVERSE INTEREST IN OBTAINING, OF ALL THINGS--
--COMMANDER SHEPARD'S BODY?
QUESTIONS UPON QUESTIONS--WELL WORTH CROSSING THE GALAXY TO ANSWER. SORROW COULD WAIT--

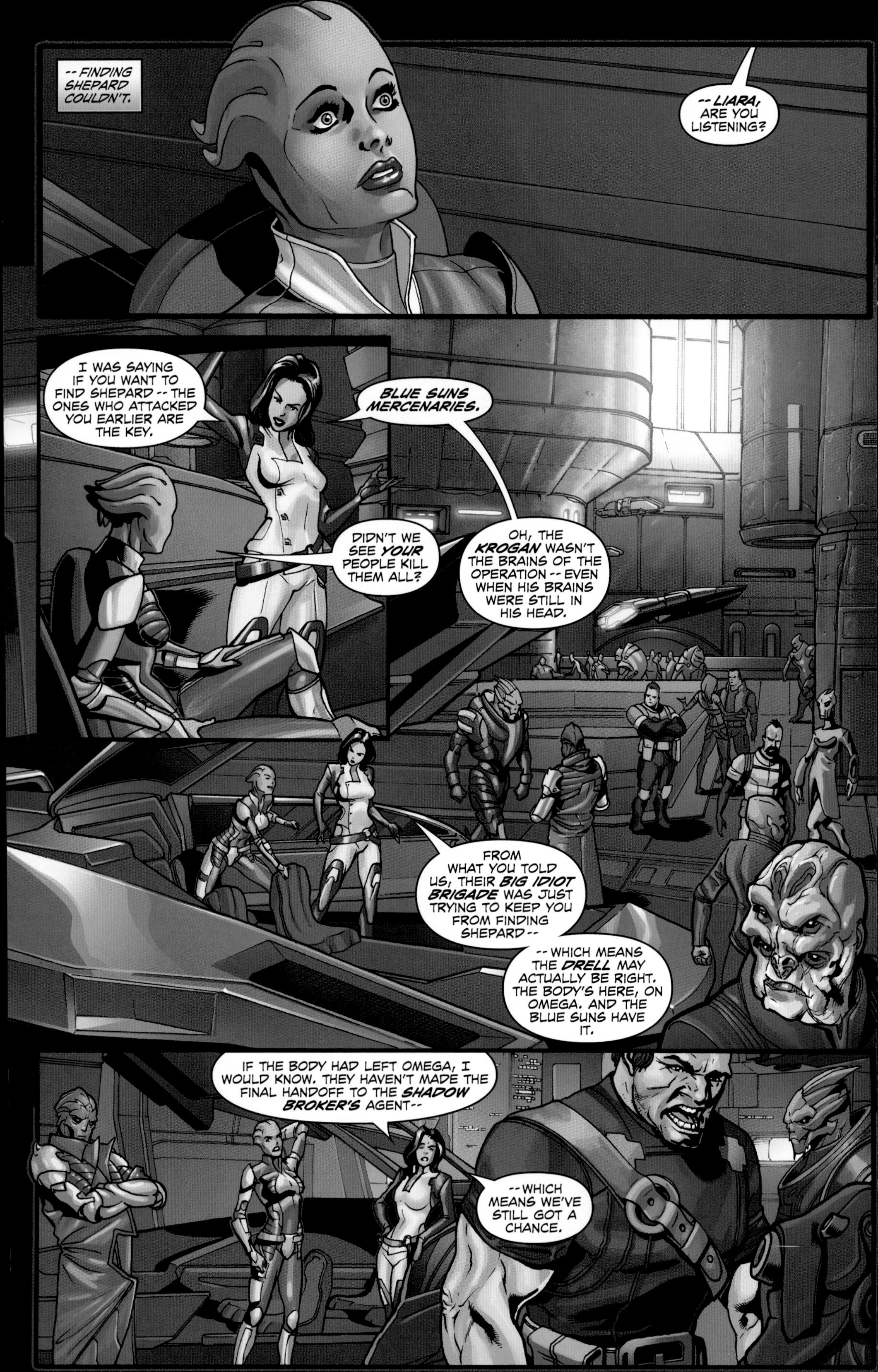
-- FINDING SHEPARD COULDN'T.
-- LIARA, ARE YOU LISTENING?
I WAS SAYING IF YOU WANT TO FIND SHEPARD -- THE ONES WHO ATTACKED YOU EARLIER ARE THE KEY.
BLUE SUNS MERCENARIES.
DIDN'T WE SEE YOUR PEOPLE KILL THEM ALL?
OH, THE KROGAN WASN'T THE BRAINS OF THE OPERATION -- EVEN WHEN HIS BRAINS WERE STILL IN HIS HEAD.
FROM WHAT YOU TOLD US, THEIR BIG IDIOT BRIGADE WAS JUST TRYING TO KEEP YOU FROM FINDING SHEPARD--
-- WHICH MEANS THE DRELL MAY ACTUALLY BE RIGHT. THE BODY'S HERE, ON OMEGA. AND THE BLUE SUNS HAVE IT.
IF THE BODY HAD LEFT OMEGA, I WOULD KNOW. THEY HAVEN'T MADE THE FINAL HANDOFF TO THE SHADOW BROKER'S AGENT--
-- WHICH MEANS WE'VE STILL GOT A CHANCE.

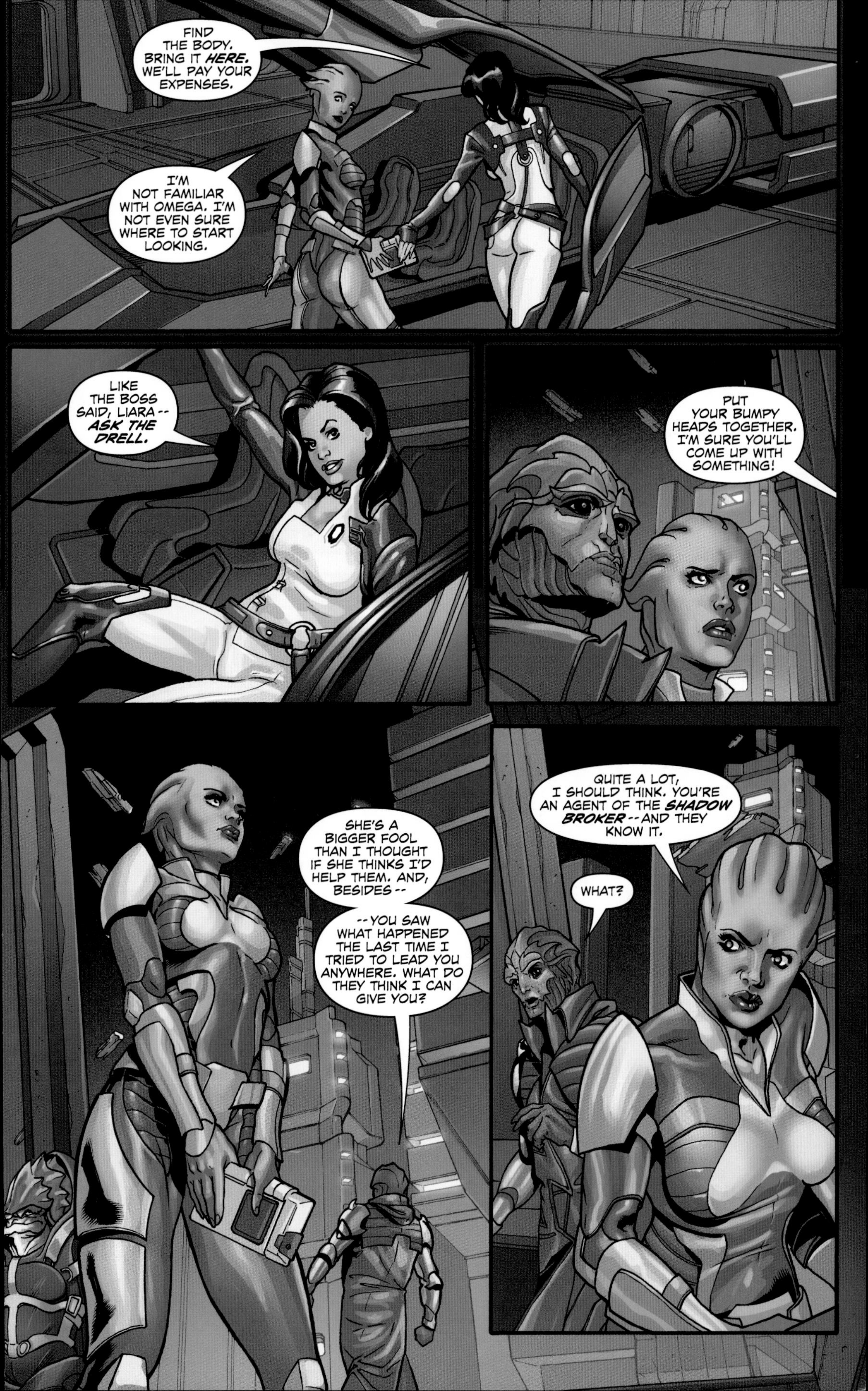

FIND THE BODY. BRING IT *HERE.* WE'LL PAY YOUR EXPENSES.
I'M NOT FAMILIAR WITH OMEGA. I'M NOT EVEN SURE WHERE TO START LOOKING.
LIKE THE BOSS SAID, LIARA -- ***ASK THE DRELL.***
PUT YOUR BUMPY HEADS TOGETHER. I'M SURE YOU'LL COME UP WITH SOMETHING!
SHE'S A BIGGER FOOL THAN I THOUGHT IF SHE THINKS I'D HELP THEM. AND, BESIDES --
-- YOU SAW WHAT HAPPENED THE LAST TIME I TRIED TO LEAD YOU ANYWHERE. WHAT DO THEY THINK I CAN GIVE YOU?
QUITE A LOT, I SHOULD THINK. YOU'RE AN AGENT OF THE ***SHADOW BROKER*** -- AND THEY KNOW IT.
WHAT?

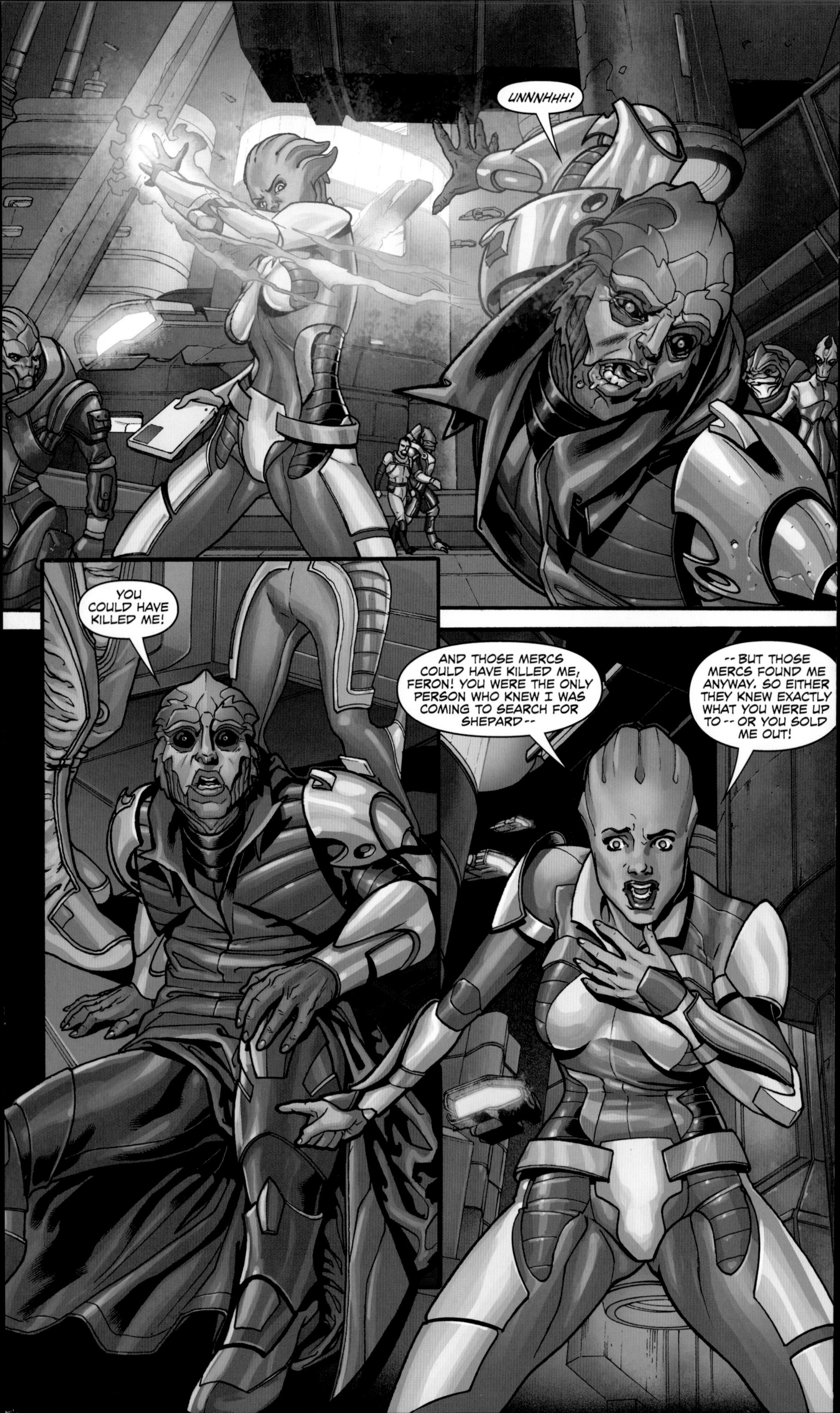
UNNNHHH!
YOU COULD HAVE KILLED ME!
AND THOSE MERCS COULD HAVE KILLED ME, FERON! YOU WERE THE ONLY PERSON WHO KNEW I WAS COMING TO SEARCH FOR SHEPARD--
--BUT THOSE MERCS FOUND ME ANYWAY. SO EITHER THEY KNEW EXACTLY WHAT YOU WERE UP TO--OR YOU SOLD ME OUT!

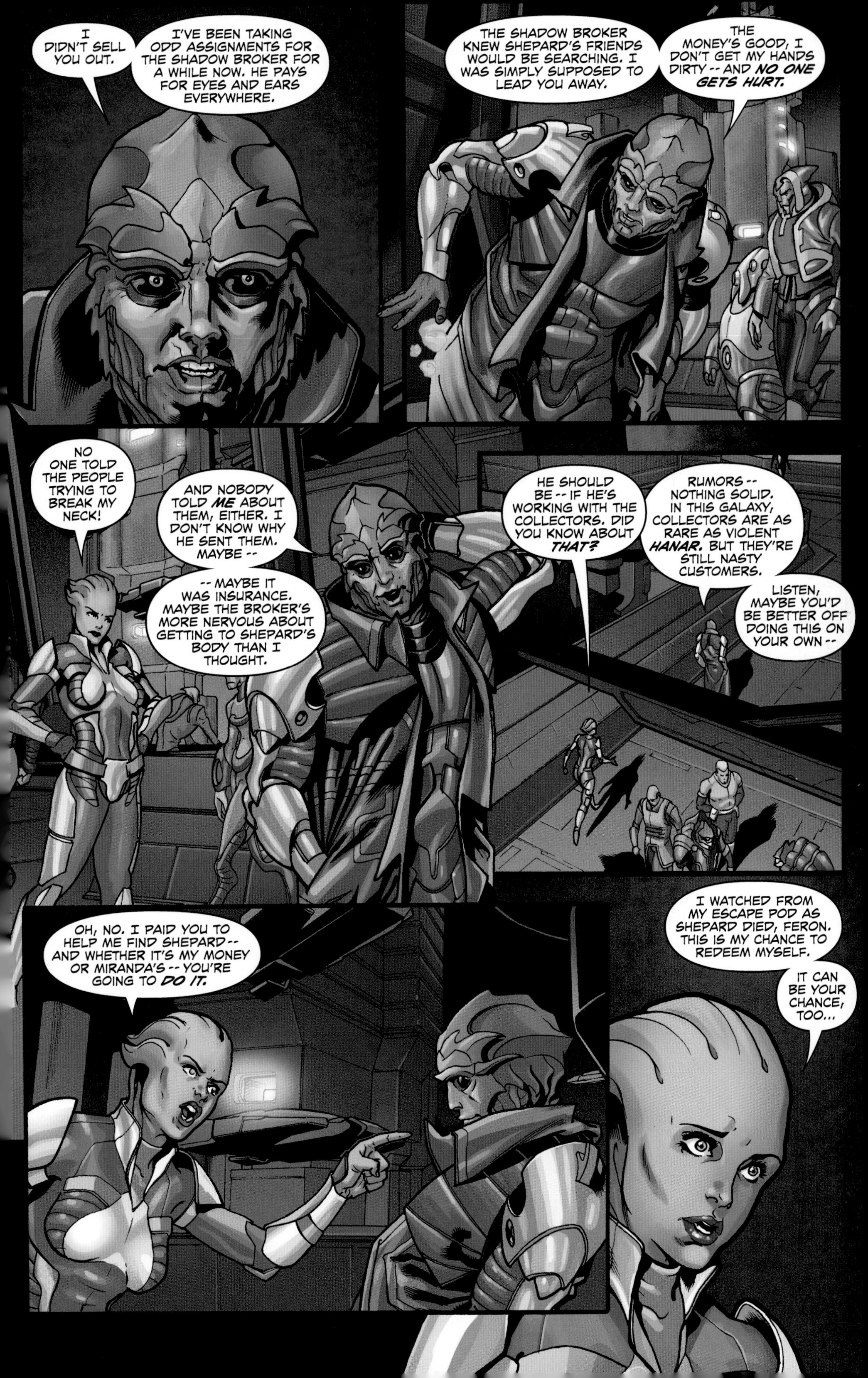
I DIDN'T SELL YOU OUT.
I'VE BEEN TAKING ODD ASSIGNMENTS FOR THE SHADOW BROKER FOR A WHILE NOW. HE PAYS FOR EYES AND EARS EVERYWHERE.
THE SHADOW BROKER KNEW SHEPARD'S FRIENDS WOULD BE SEARCHING. I WAS SIMPLY SUPPOSED TO LEAD YOU AWAY.
THE MONEY'S GOOD, I DON'T GET MY HANDS DIRTY -- AND NO ONE GETS HURT.
NO ONE TOLD THE PEOPLE TRYING TO BREAK MY NECK!
AND NOBODY TOLD ME ABOUT THEM, EITHER. I DON'T KNOW WHY HE SENT THEM. MAYBE --
-- MAYBE IT WAS INSURANCE. MAYBE THE BROKER'S MORE NERVOUS ABOUT GETTING TO SHEPARD'S BODY THAN I THOUGHT.
HE SHOULD BE -- IF HE'S WORKING WITH THE COLLECTORS. DID YOU KNOW ABOUT THAT?
RUMORS -- NOTHING SOLID. IN THIS GALAXY, COLLECTORS ARE AS RARE AS VIOLENT HANAR. BUT THEY'RE STILL NASTY CUSTOMERS.
LISTEN, MAYBE YOU'D BE BETTER OFF DOING THIS ON YOUR OWN --
OH, NO. I PAID YOU TO HELP ME FIND SHEPARD -- AND WHETHER IT'S MY MONEY OR MIRANDA'S -- YOU'RE GOING TO DO IT.
I WATCHED FROM MY ESCAPE POD AS SHEPARD DIED, FERON. THIS IS MY CHANCE TO REDEEM MYSELF.
IT CAN BE YOUR CHANCE, TOO...

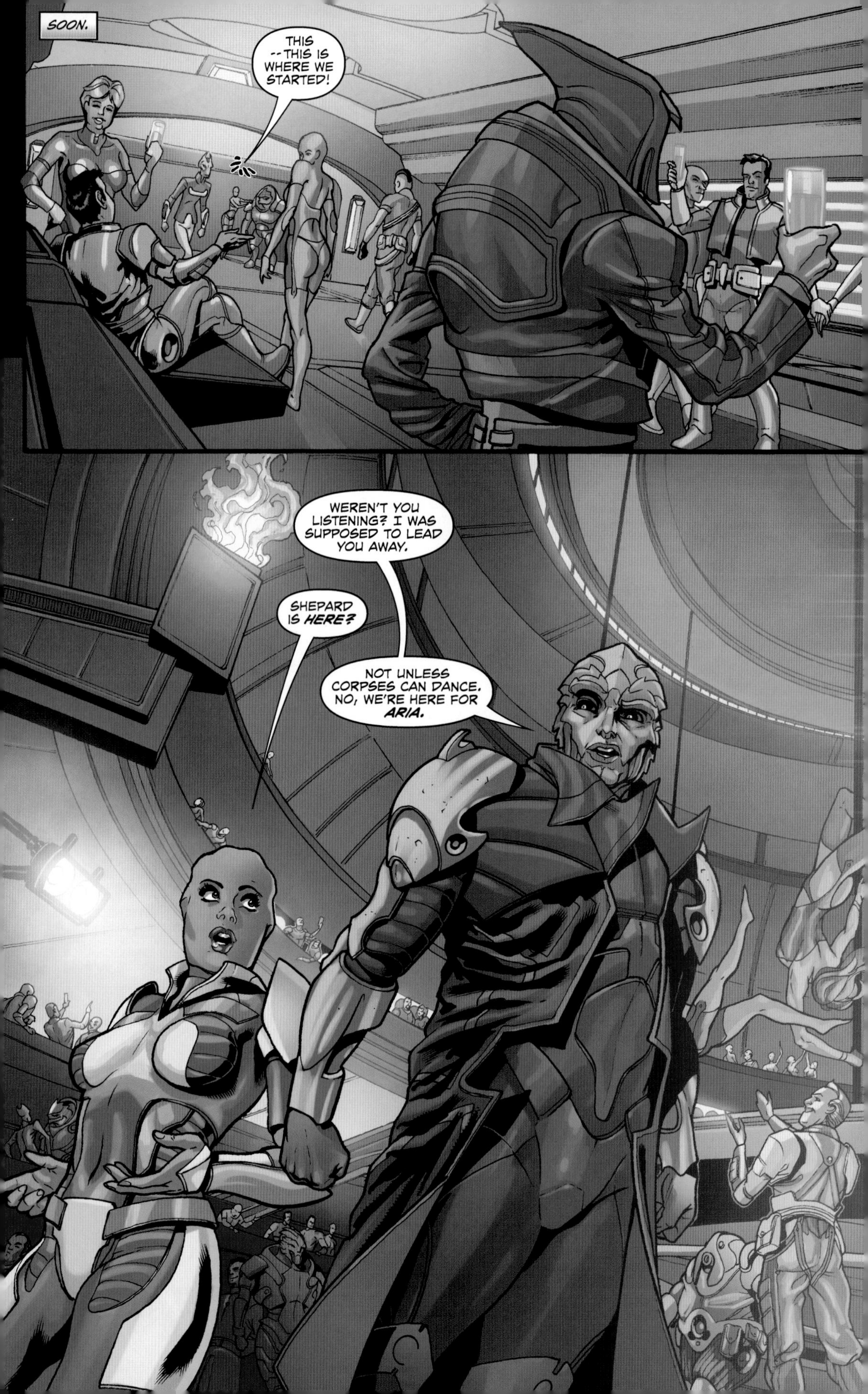
SOON.
THIS --THIS IS WHERE WE STARTED!
WEREN'T YOU LISTENING? I WAS SUPPOSED TO LEAD YOU AWAY.
SHEPARD IS *HERE?*
NOT UNLESS CORPSES CAN DANCE. NO, WE'RE HERE FOR *ARIA.*

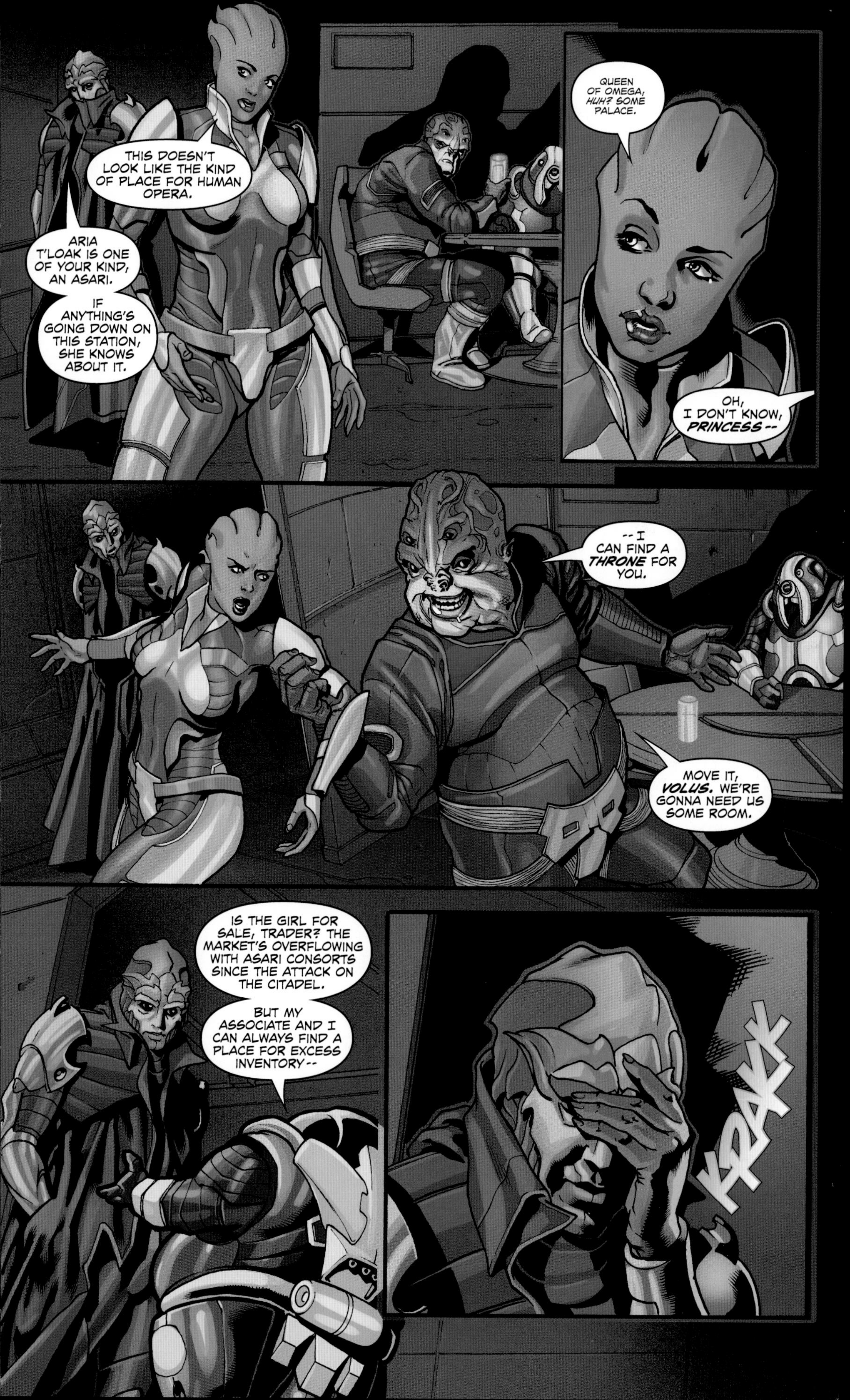
THIS DOESN'T LOOK LIKE THE KIND OF PLACE FOR HUMAN OPERA.
ARIA T'LOAK IS ONE OF YOUR KIND, AN ASARI.
IF ANYTHING'S GOING DOWN ON THIS STATION, SHE KNOWS ABOUT IT.
QUEEN OF OMEGA, *HUH?* SOME PALACE.
OH, I DON'T KNOW, ***PRINCESS*** --
-- I CAN FIND A ***THRONE*** FOR YOU.
MOVE IT, ***VOLUS.*** WE'RE GONNA NEED US SOME ROOM.
IS THE GIRL FOR SALE, TRADER? THE MARKET'S OVERFLOWING WITH ASARI CONSORTS SINCE THE ATTACK ON THE CITADEL.
BUT MY ASSOCIATE AND I CAN ALWAYS FIND A PLACE FOR EXCESS INVENTORY --
KRAKK

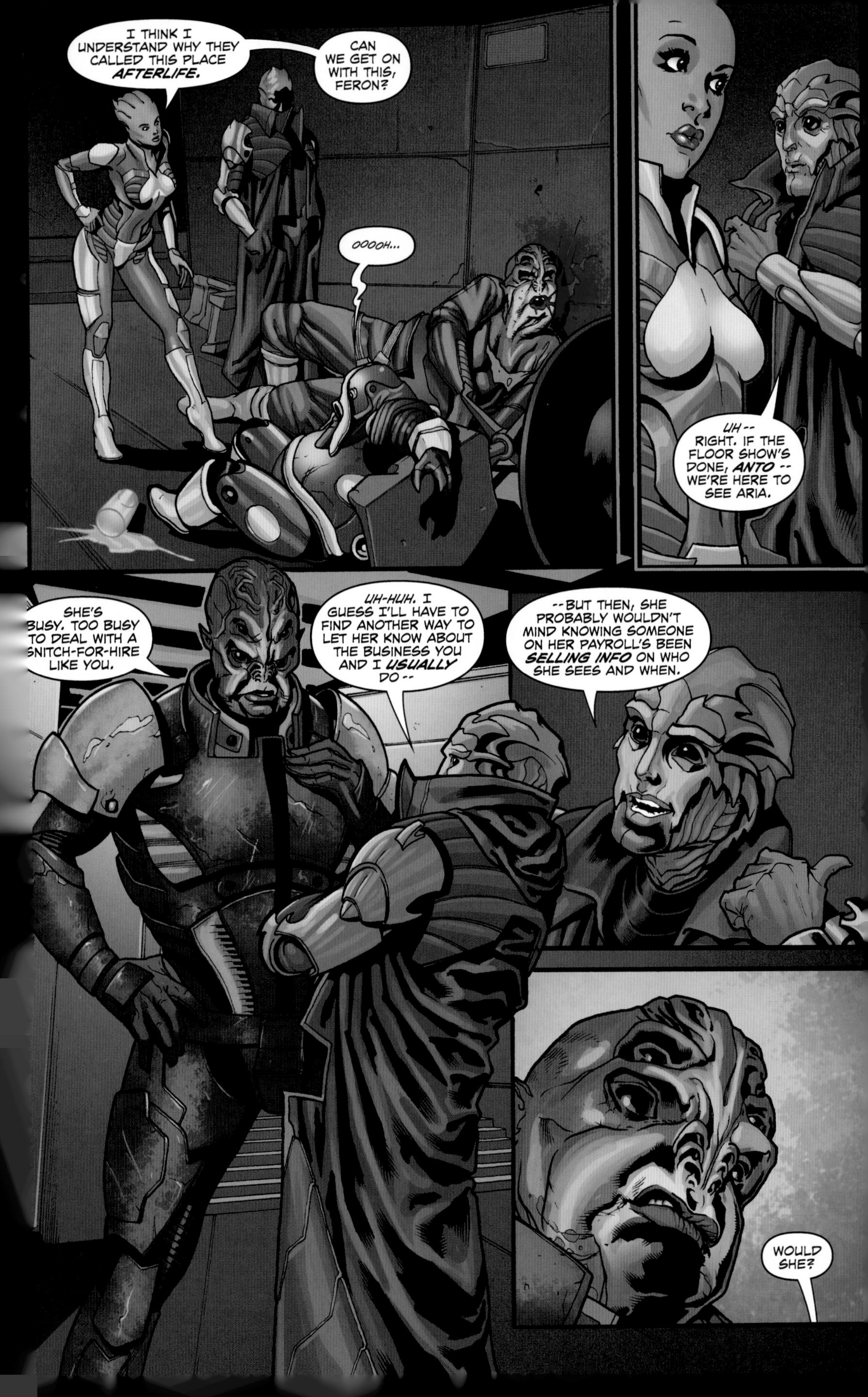
I THINK I UNDERSTAND WHY THEY CALLED THIS PLACE AFTERLIFE.
CAN WE GET ON WITH THIS, FERON?
OOOOH...
UH -- RIGHT. IF THE FLOOR SHOW'S DONE, ANTO -- WE'RE HERE TO SEE ARIA.
SHE'S BUSY. TOO BUSY TO DEAL WITH A SNITCH-FOR-HIRE LIKE YOU.
UH-HUH. I GUESS I'LL HAVE TO FIND ANOTHER WAY TO LET HER KNOW ABOUT THE BUSINESS YOU AND I USUALLY DO --
--BUT THEN, SHE PROBABLY WOULDN'T MIND KNOWING SOMEONE ON HER PAYROLL'S BEEN SELLING INFO ON WHO SHE SEES AND WHEN.
WOULD SHE?

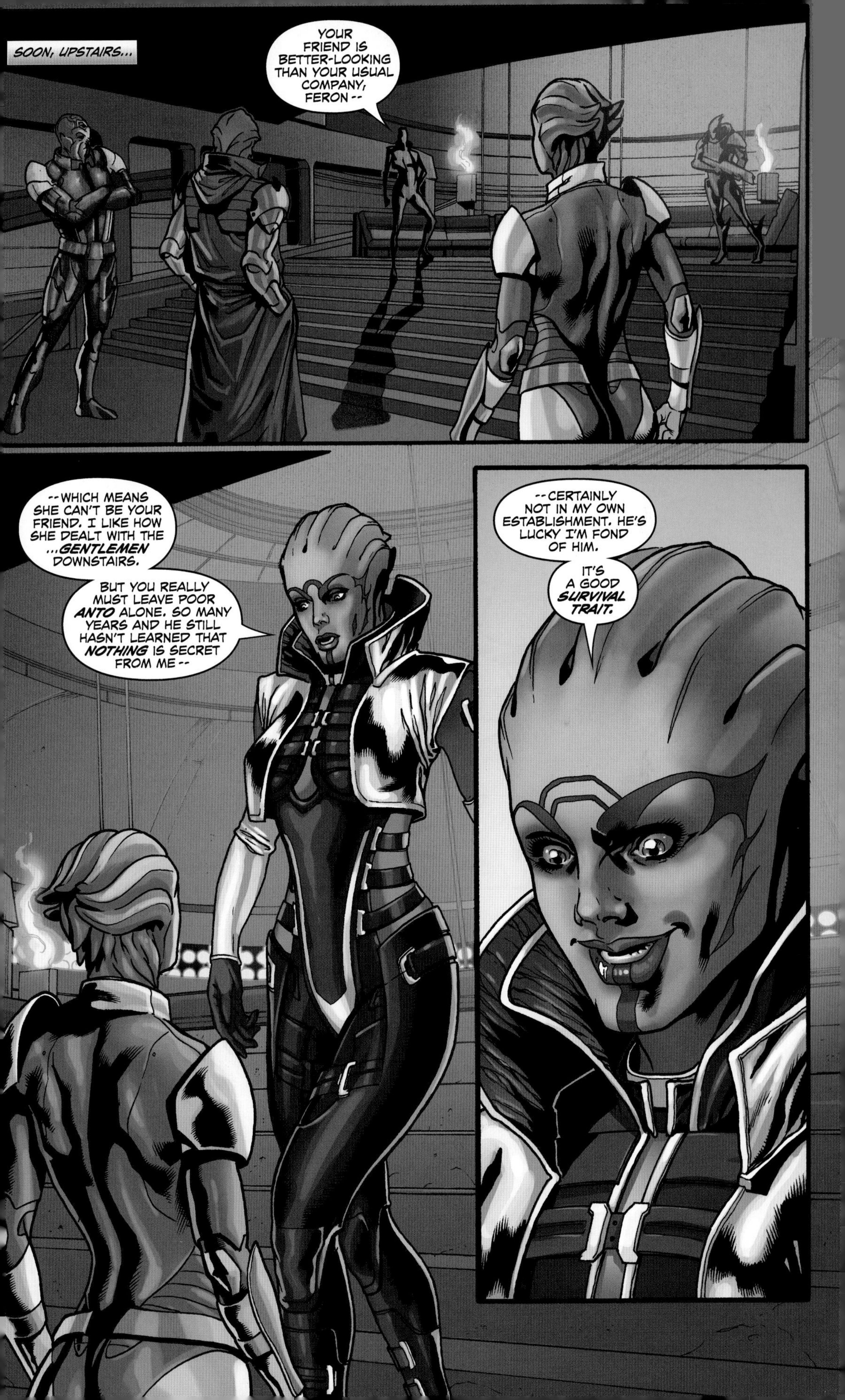
SOON, UPSTAIRS...
YOUR FRIEND IS BETTER-LOOKING THAN YOUR USUAL COMPANY, FERON --
--WHICH MEANS SHE CAN'T BE YOUR FRIEND. I LIKE HOW SHE DEALT WITH THE ...GENTLEMEN DOWNSTAIRS.
BUT YOU REALLY MUST LEAVE POOR ANTO ALONE. SO MANY YEARS AND HE STILL HASN'T LEARNED THAT NOTHING IS SECRET FROM ME --
--CERTAINLY NOT IN MY OWN ESTABLISHMENT. HE'S LUCKY I'M FOND OF HIM.
IT'S A GOOD SURVIVAL TRAIT.

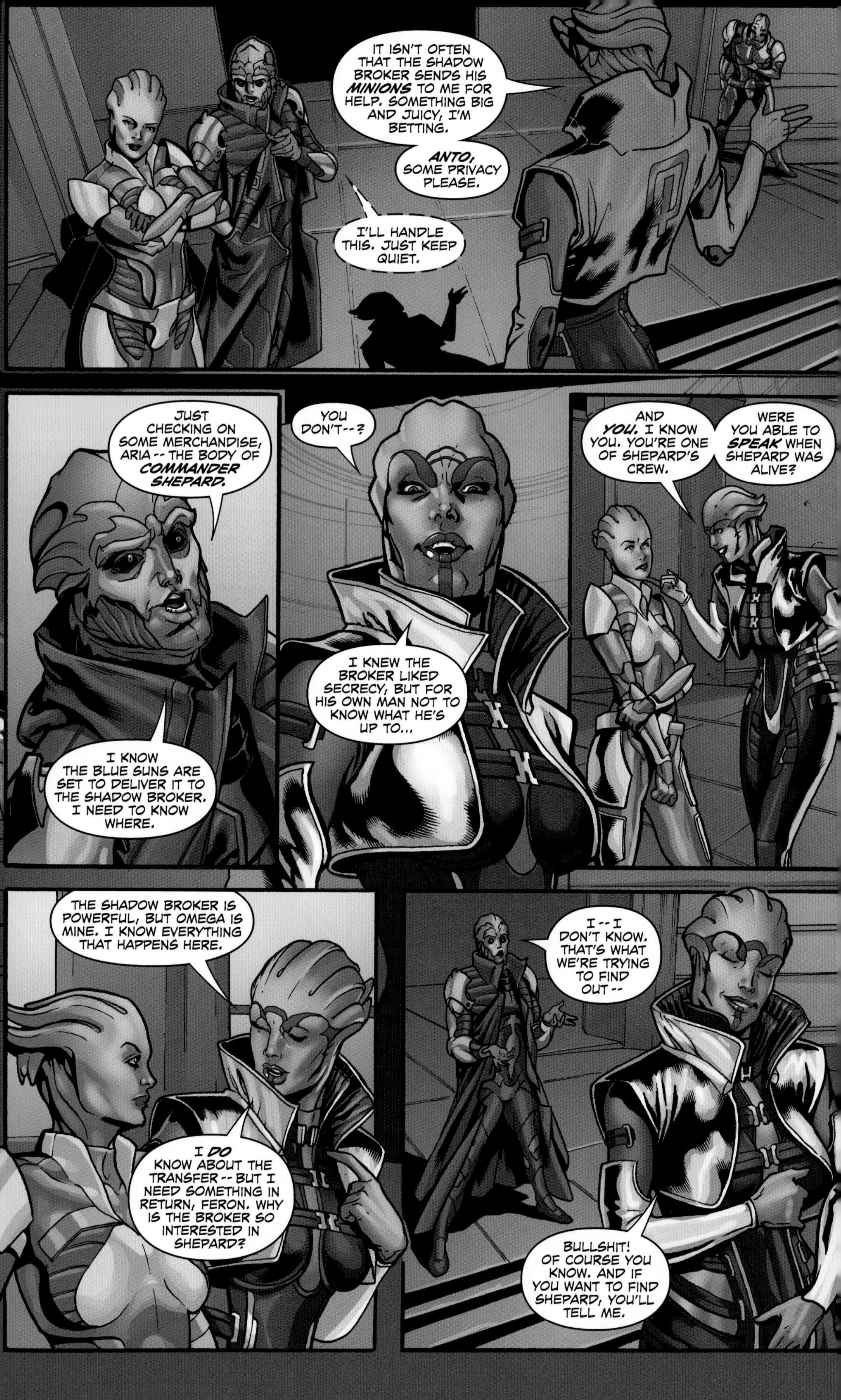
IT ISN'T OFTEN THAT THE SHADOW BROKER SENDS HIS MINIONS TO ME FOR HELP. SOMETHING BIG AND JUICY, I'M BETTING.
ANTO, SOME PRIVACY PLEASE.
I'LL HANDLE THIS. JUST KEEP QUIET.
JUST CHECKING ON SOME MERCHANDISE, ARIA -- THE BODY OF COMMANDER SHEPARD.
I KNOW THE BLUE SUNS ARE SET TO DELIVER IT TO THE SHADOW BROKER. I NEED TO KNOW WHERE.
YOU DON'T --?
I KNEW THE BROKER LIKED SECRECY, BUT FOR HIS OWN MAN NOT TO KNOW WHAT HE'S UP TO...
AND YOU. I KNOW YOU. YOU'RE ONE OF SHEPARD'S CREW.
WERE YOU ABLE TO SPEAK WHEN SHEPARD WAS ALIVE?
THE SHADOW BROKER IS POWERFUL, BUT OMEGA IS MINE. I KNOW EVERYTHING THAT HAPPENS HERE.
I DO KNOW ABOUT THE TRANSFER -- BUT I NEED SOMETHING IN RETURN, FERON. WHY IS THE BROKER SO INTERESTED IN SHEPARD?
I -- I DON'T KNOW. THAT'S WHAT WE'RE TRYING TO FIND OUT --
BULLSHIT! OF COURSE YOU KNOW. AND IF YOU WANT TO FIND SHEPARD, YOU'LL TELL ME.

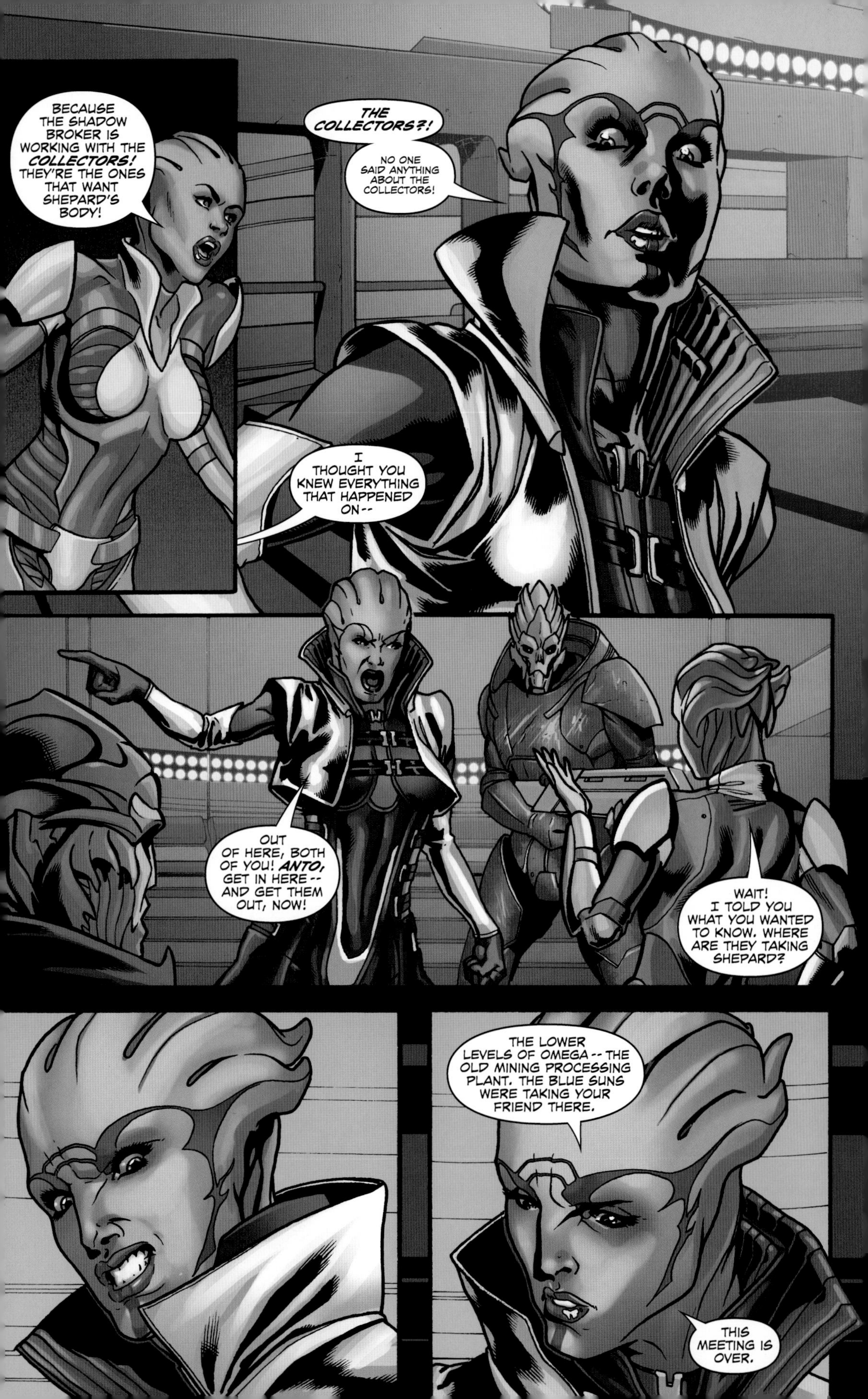
BECAUSE THE SHADOW BROKER IS WORKING WITH THE COLLECTORS! THEY'RE THE ONES THAT WANT SHEPARD'S BODY!
THE COLLECTORS?!
NO ONE SAID ANYTHING ABOUT THE COLLECTORS!
I THOUGHT YOU KNEW EVERYTHING THAT HAPPENED ON--
OUT OF HERE, BOTH OF YOU! ANTO, GET IN HERE-- AND GET THEM OUT, NOW!
WAIT! I TOLD YOU WHAT YOU WANTED TO KNOW. WHERE ARE THEY TAKING SHEPARD?
THE LOWER LEVELS OF OMEGA-- THE OLD MINING PROCESSING PLANT. THE BLUE SUNS WERE TAKING YOUR FRIEND THERE.
THIS MEETING IS OVER.

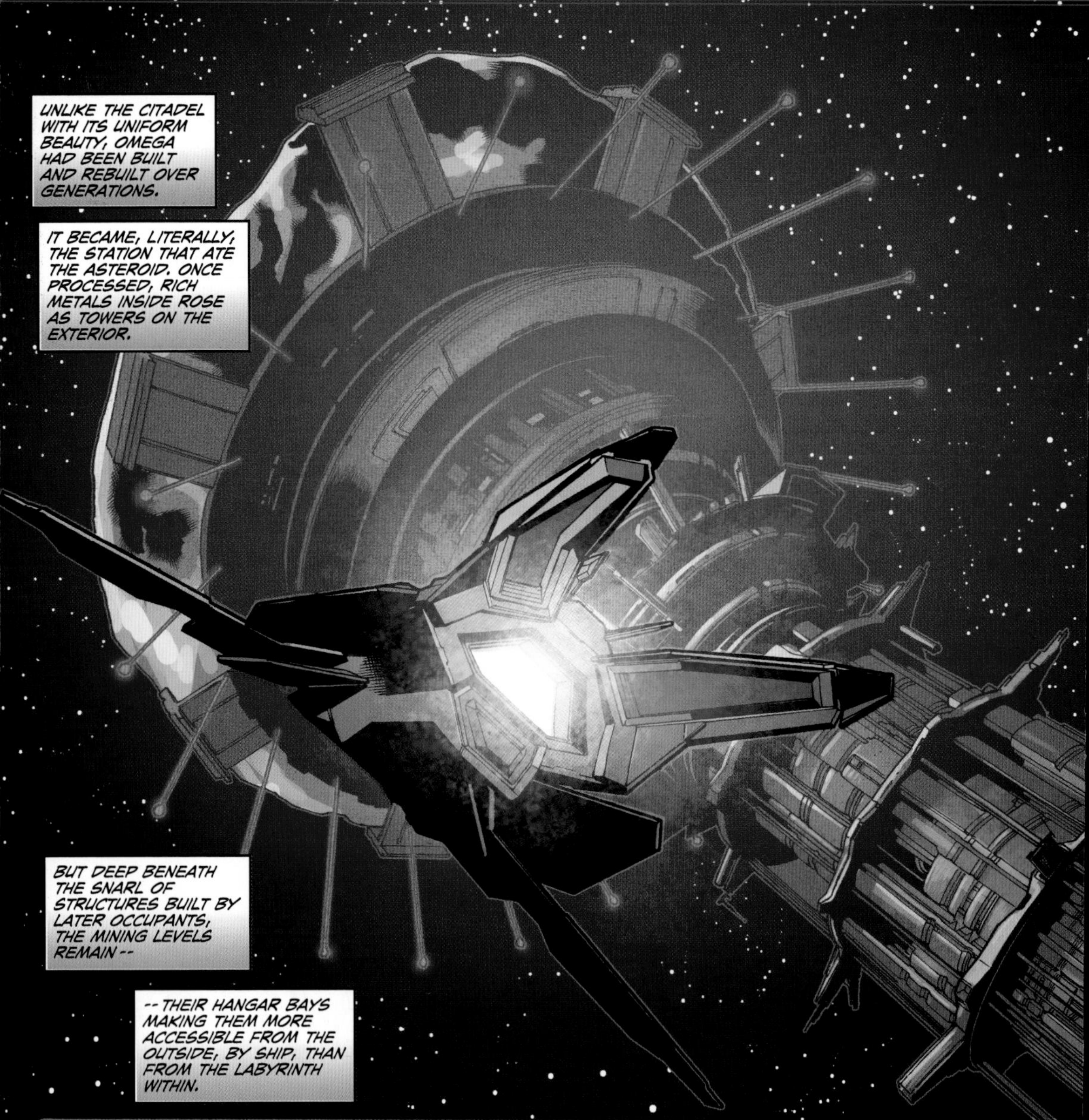
UNLIKE THE CITADEL WITH ITS UNIFORM BEAUTY, OMEGA HAD BEEN BUILT AND REBUILT OVER GENERATIONS.
IT BECAME, LITERALLY, THE STATION THAT ATE THE ASTEROID. ONCE PROCESSED, RICH METALS INSIDE ROSE AS TOWERS ON THE EXTERIOR.
BUT DEEP BENEATH THE SNARL OF STRUCTURES BUILT BY LATER OCCUPANTS, THE MINING LEVELS REMAIN --
-- THEIR HANGAR BAYS MAKING THEM MORE ACCESSIBLE FROM THE OUTSIDE, BY SHIP, THAN FROM THE LABYRINTH WITHIN.

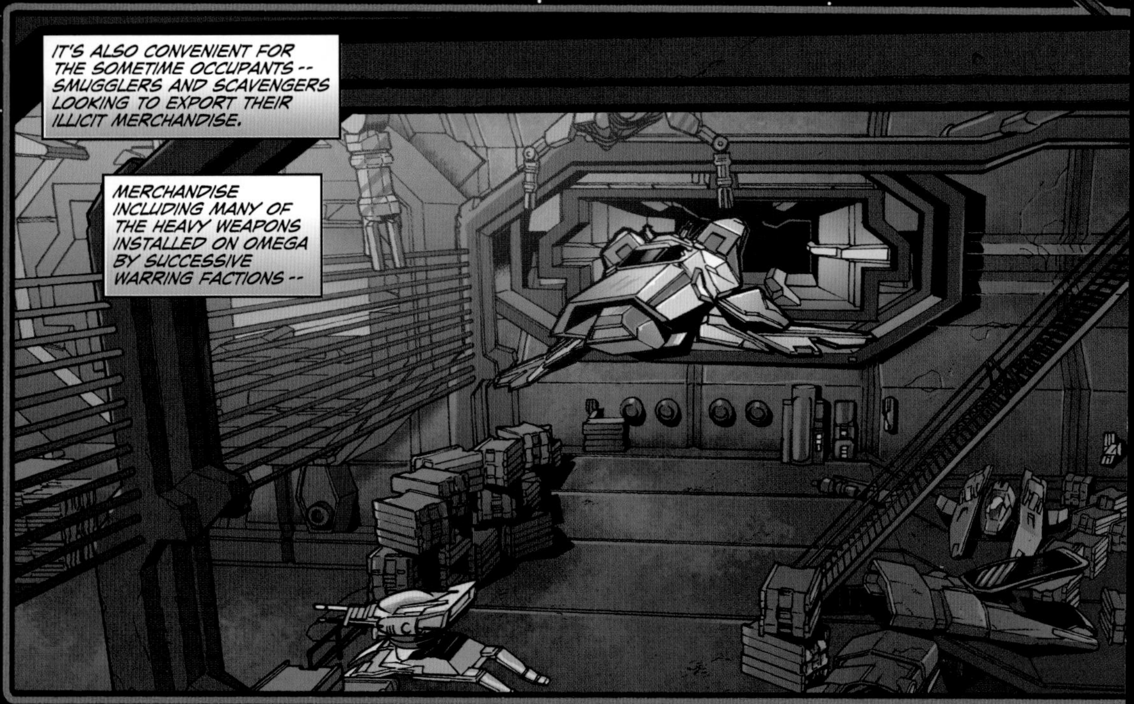
IT'S ALSO CONVENIENT FOR THE SOMETIME OCCUPANTS -- SMUGGLERS AND SCAVENGERS LOOKING TO EXPORT THEIR ILLICIT MERCHANDISE.
MERCHANDISE INCLUDING MANY OF THE HEAVY WEAPONS INSTALLED ON OMEGA BY SUCCESSIVE WARRING FACTIONS --

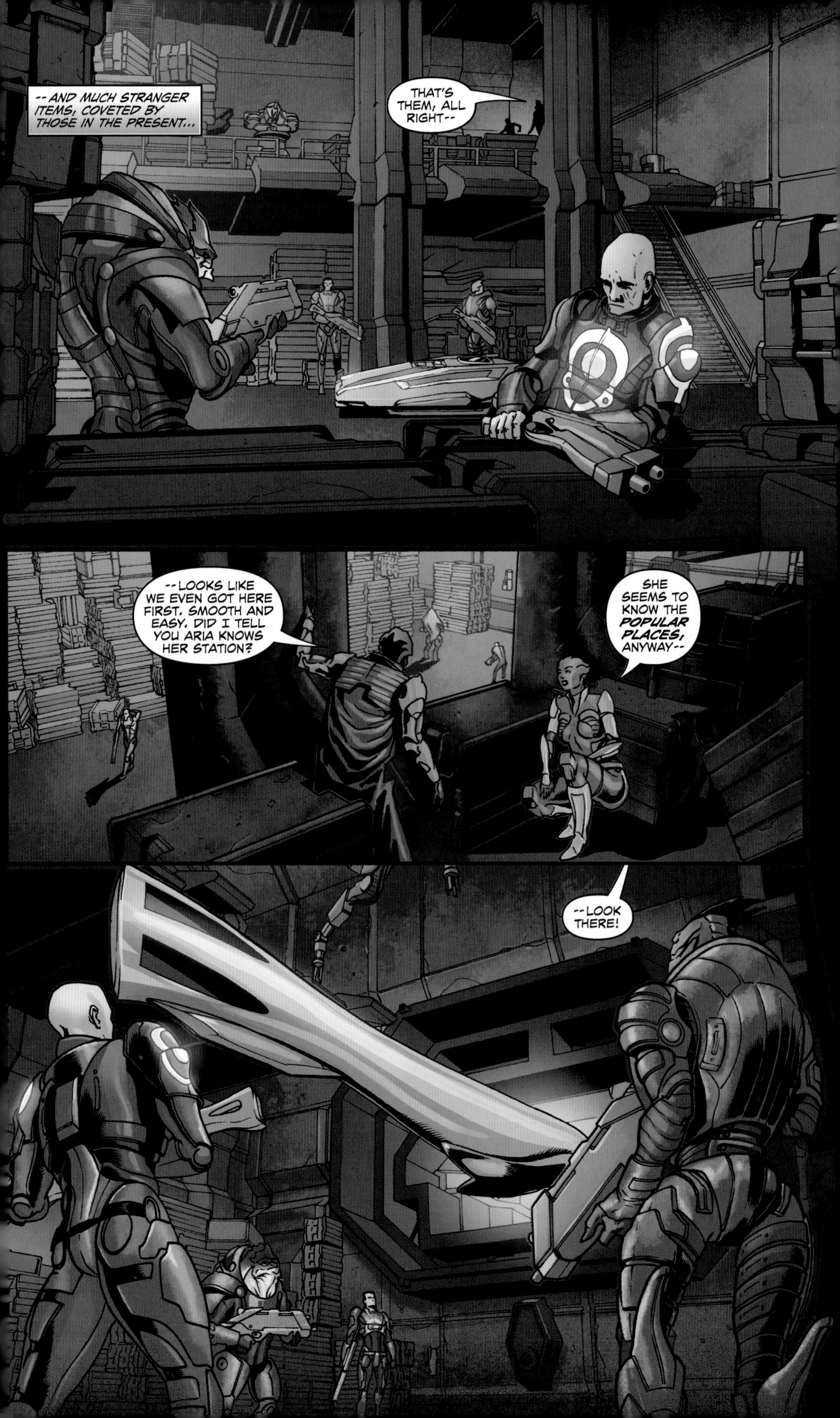
--AND MUCH STRANGER ITEMS, COVETED BY THOSE IN THE PRESENT...
THAT'S THEM, ALL RIGHT--
--LOOKS LIKE WE EVEN GOT HERE FIRST. SMOOTH AND EASY. DID I TELL YOU ARIA KNOWS HER STATION?
SHE SEEMS TO KNOW THE POPULAR PLACES, ANYWAY--
--LOOK THERE!

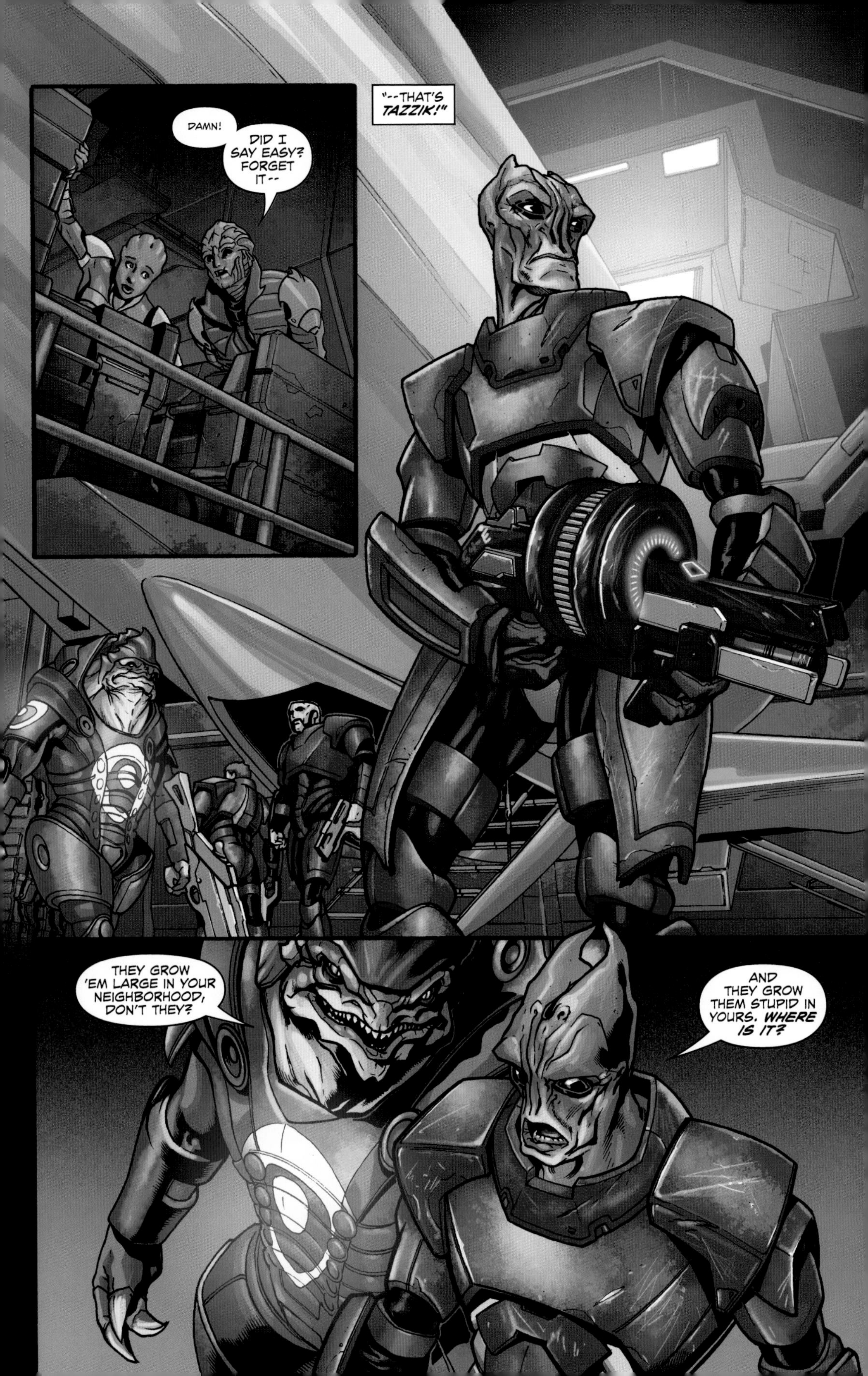
DAMN!
DID I SAY EASY? FORGET IT --
"--THAT'S *TAZZIK!*"
THEY GROW 'EM LARGE IN YOUR NEIGHBORHOOD, DON'T THEY?
AND THEY GROW THEM STUPID IN YOURS. ***WHERE IS IT?***

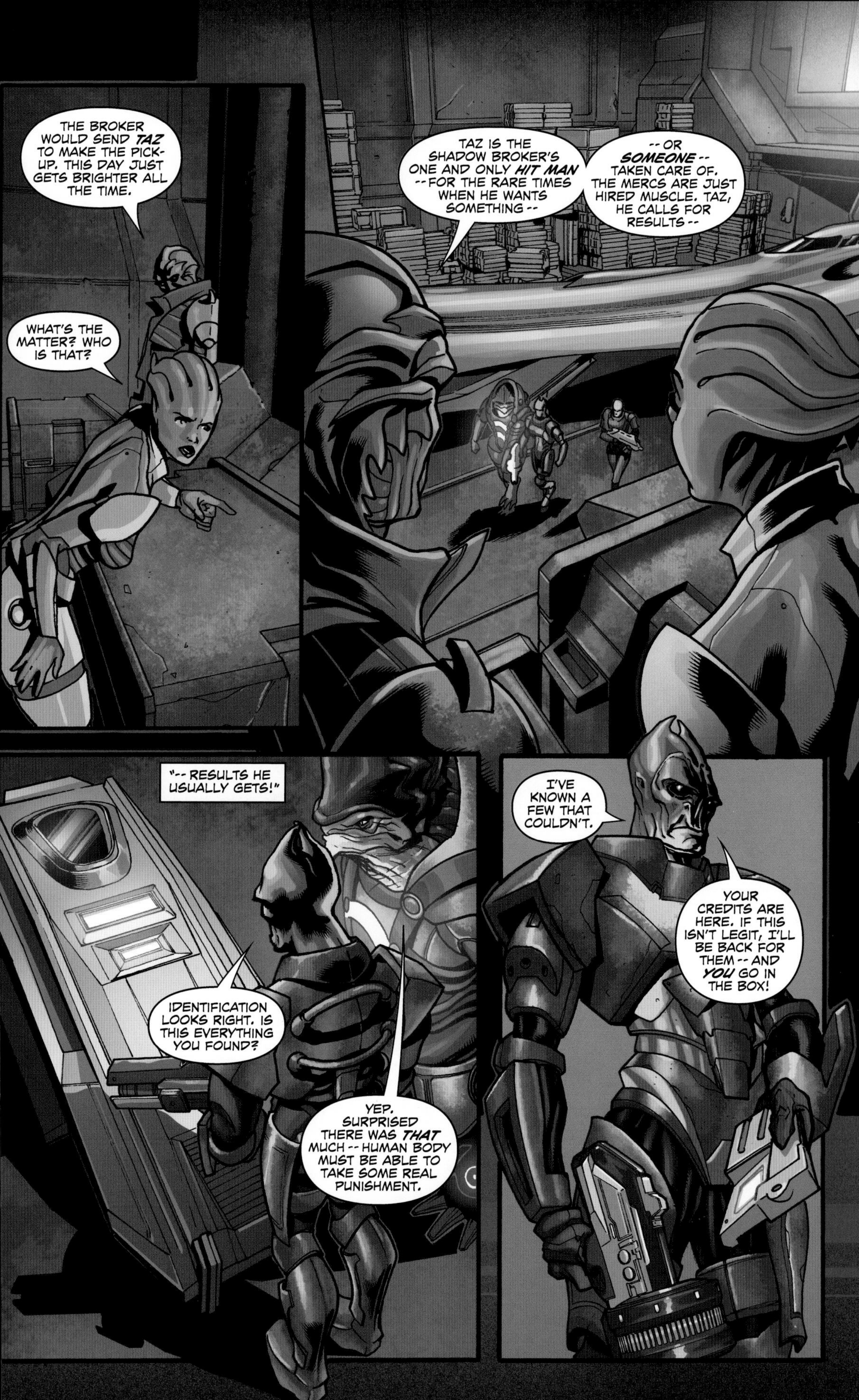
THE BROKER WOULD SEND *TAZ* TO MAKE THE PICK-UP. THIS DAY JUST GETS BRIGHTER ALL THE TIME.
WHAT'S THE MATTER? WHO IS THAT?
TAZ IS THE SHADOW BROKER'S ONE AND ONLY *HIT MAN* --FOR THE RARE TIMES WHEN HE WANTS SOMETHING--
--OR *SOMEONE*-- TAKEN CARE OF. THE MERCS ARE JUST HIRED MUSCLE. TAZ, HE CALLS FOR RESULTS--
"--RESULTS HE USUALLY GETS!"
IDENTIFICATION LOOKS RIGHT. IS THIS EVERYTHING YOU FOUND?
YEP. SURPRISED THERE WAS *THAT* MUCH--HUMAN BODY MUST BE ABLE TO TAKE SOME REAL PUNISHMENT.
I'VE KNOWN A FEW THAT COULDN'T.
YOUR CREDITS ARE HERE. IF THIS ISN'T LEGIT, I'LL BE BACK FOR THEM--AND *YOU* GO IN THE BOX!

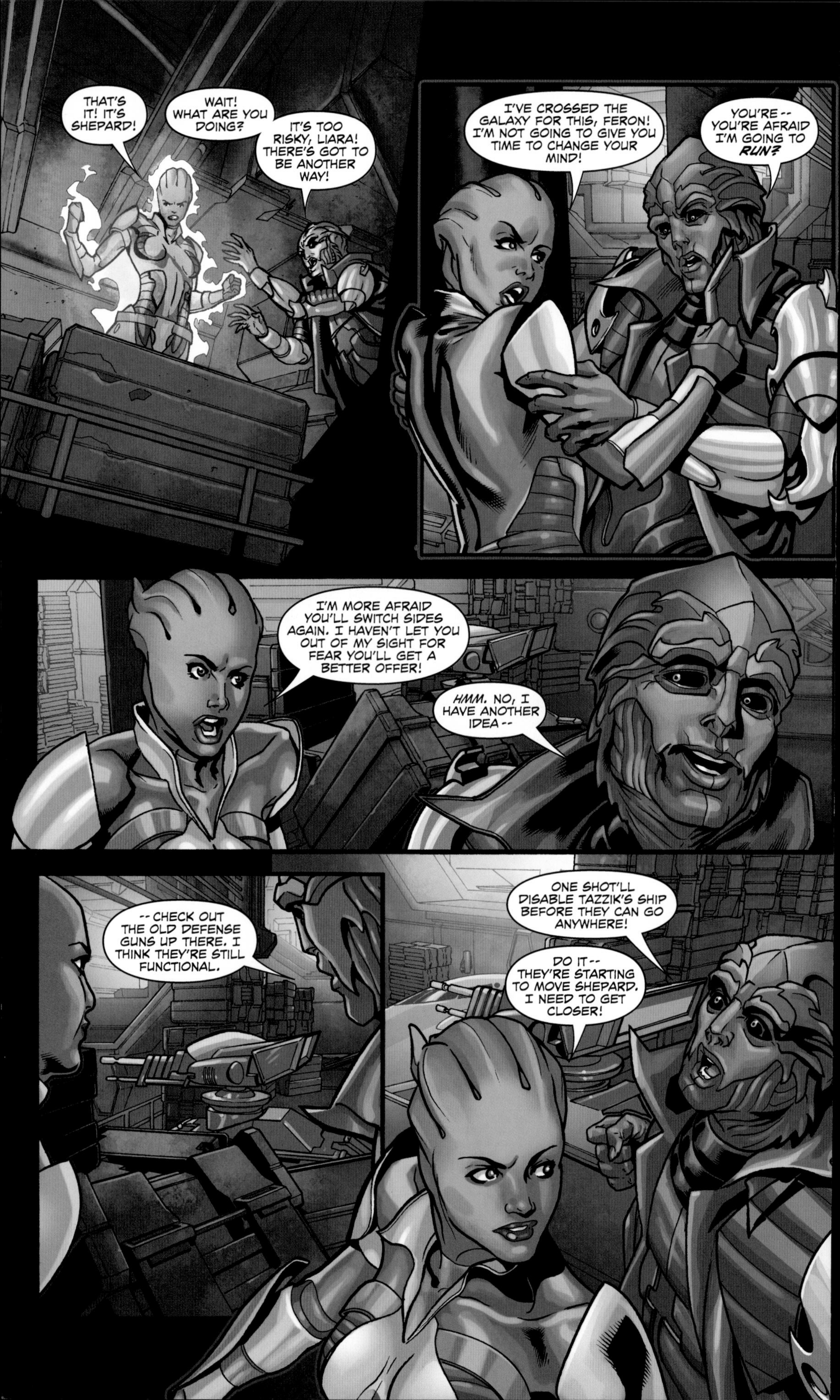
THAT'S IT! IT'S SHEPARD!
WAIT! WHAT ARE YOU DOING?
IT'S TOO RISKY, LIARA! THERE'S GOT TO BE ANOTHER WAY!
I'VE CROSSED THE GALAXY FOR THIS, FERON! I'M NOT GOING TO GIVE YOU TIME TO CHANGE YOUR MIND!
YOU'RE -- YOU'RE AFRAID I'M GOING TO RUN?
I'M MORE AFRAID YOU'LL SWITCH SIDES AGAIN. I HAVEN'T LET YOU OUT OF MY SIGHT FOR FEAR YOU'LL GET A BETTER OFFER!
HMM. NO, I HAVE ANOTHER IDEA --
-- CHECK OUT THE OLD DEFENSE GUNS UP THERE. I THINK THEY'RE STILL FUNCTIONAL.
ONE SHOT'LL DISABLE TAZZIK'S SHIP BEFORE THEY CAN GO ANYWHERE!
DO IT -- THEY'RE STARTING TO MOVE SHEPARD. I NEED TO GET CLOSER!

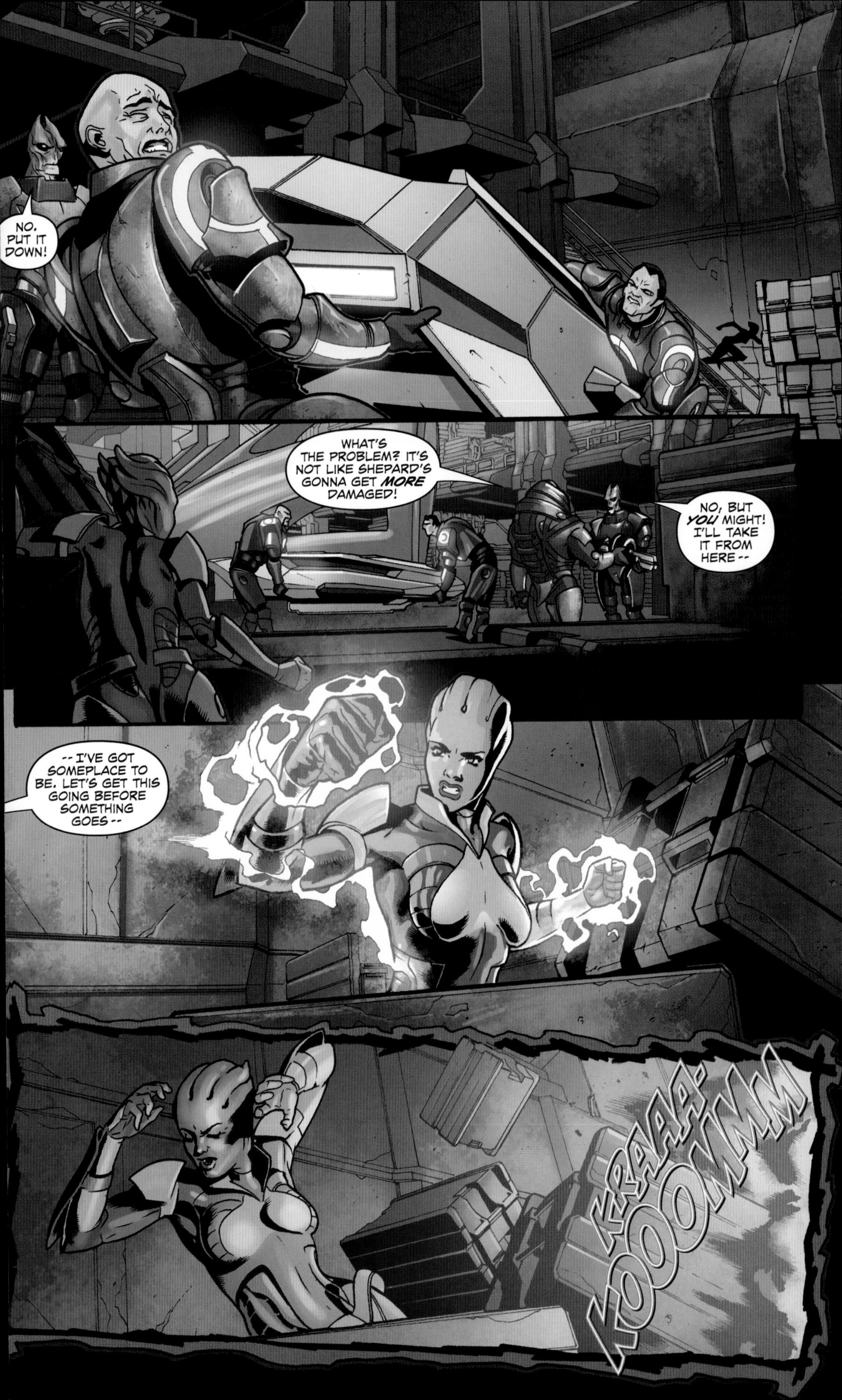
NO. PUT IT DOWN!
WHAT'S THE PROBLEM? IT'S NOT LIKE SHEPARD'S GONNA GET MORE DAMAGED!
NO, BUT YOU MIGHT! I'LL TAKE IT FROM HERE --
-- I'VE GOT SOMEPLACE TO BE. LET'S GET THIS GOING BEFORE SOMETHING GOES --
KRAAA-KOOOMMM

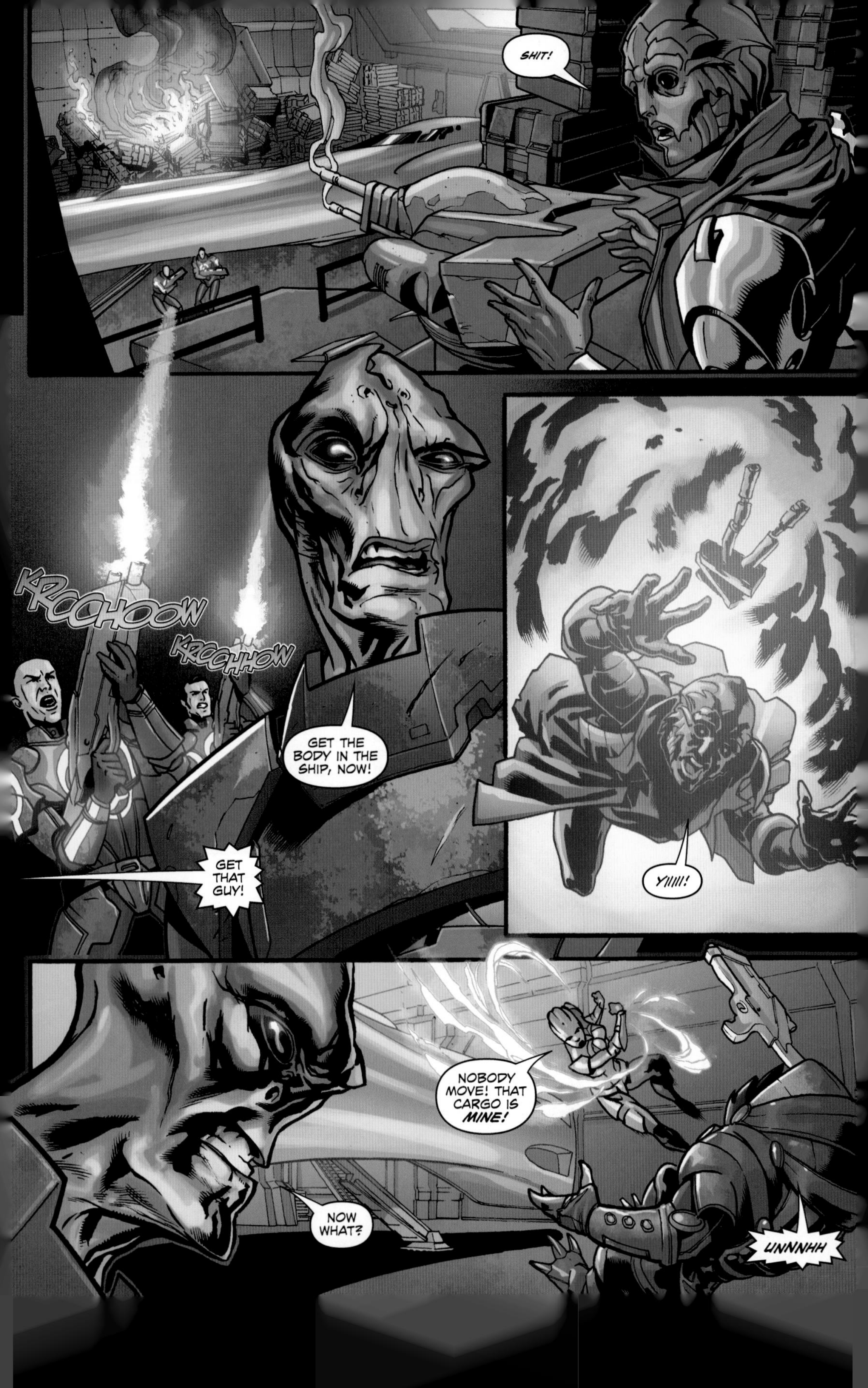
SHIT!
KROCHOOW
KROCHHOW
GET THE BODY IN THE SHIP, NOW!
GET THAT GUY!
YIIIII!
NOBODY MOVE! THAT CARGO IS MINE!
NOW WHAT?
UNNNHH

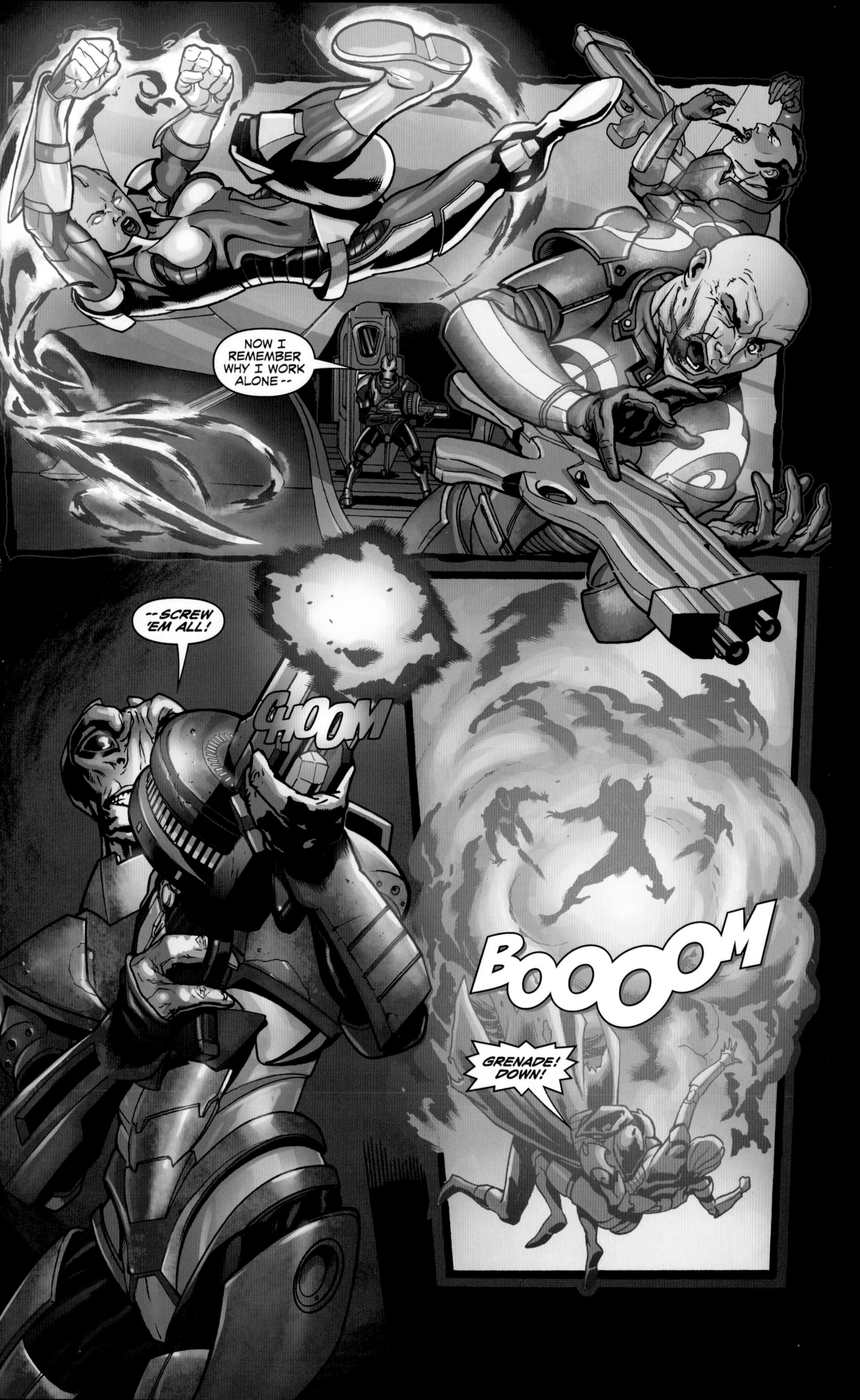
NOW I REMEMBER WHY I WORK ALONE--
--SCREW 'EM ALL!
CHOOM
BOOOOOM
GRENADE! DOWN!

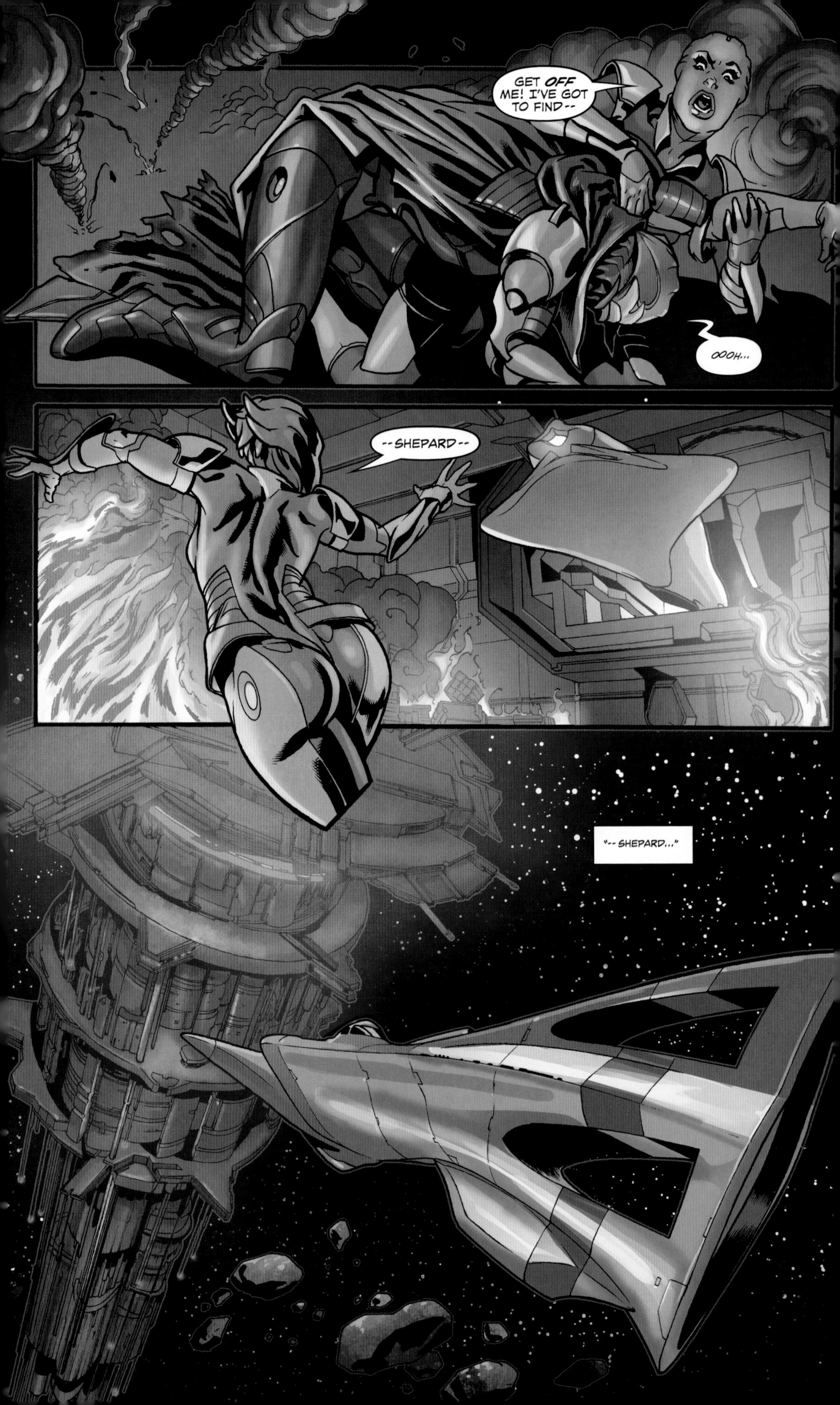
GET OFF ME! I'VE GOT TO FIND--
OOOH...
--SHEPARD--
"--SHEPARD..."

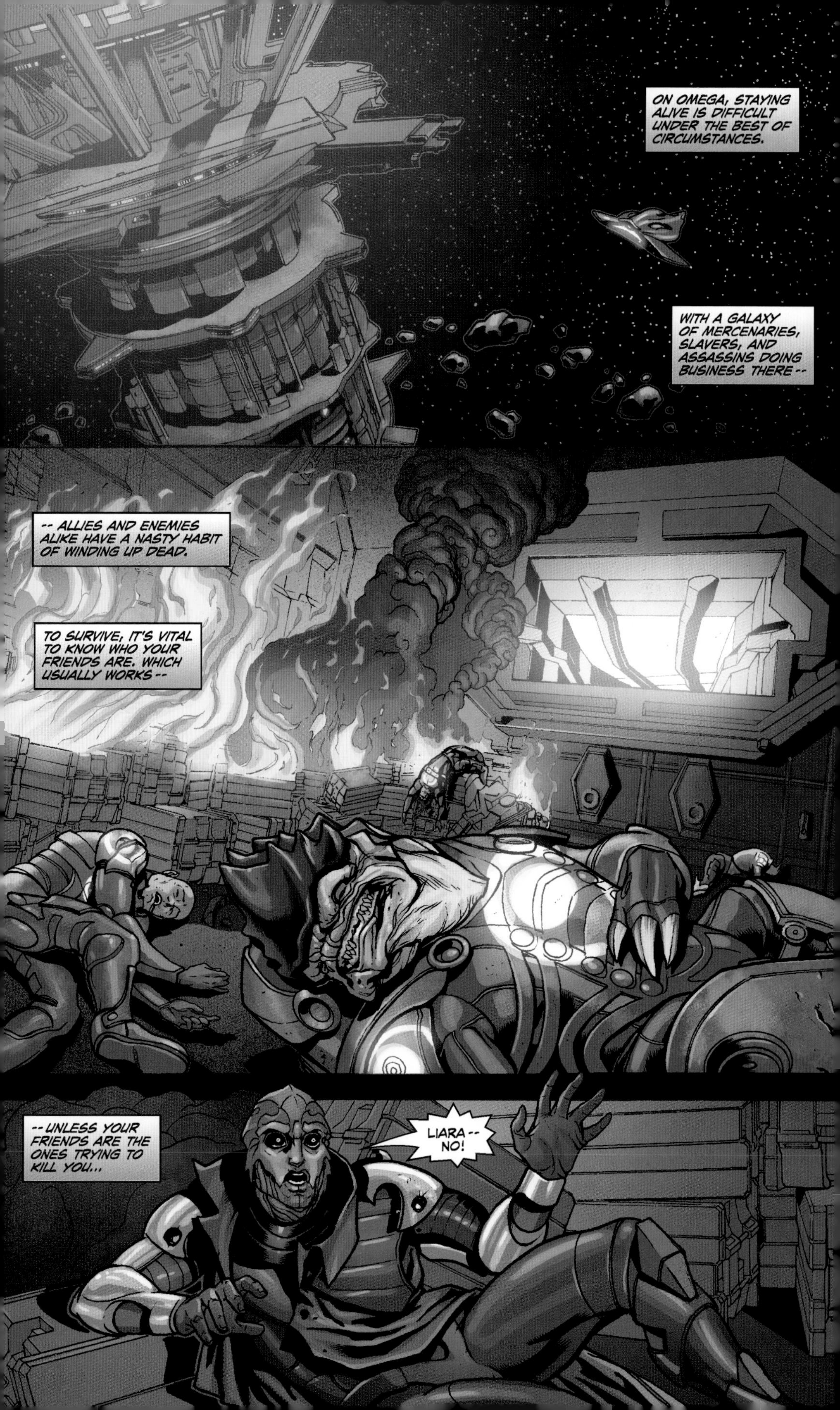
ON OMEGA, STAYING ALIVE IS DIFFICULT UNDER THE BEST OF CIRCUMSTANCES.
WITH A GALAXY OF MERCENARIES, SLAVERS, AND ASSASSINS DOING BUSINESS THERE --
-- ALLIES AND ENEMIES ALIKE HAVE A NASTY HABIT OF WINDING UP DEAD.
TO SURVIVE, IT'S VITAL TO KNOW WHO YOUR FRIENDS ARE. WHICH USUALLY WORKS --
-- UNLESS YOUR FRIENDS ARE THE ONES TRYING TO KILL YOU...
LIARA -- NO!

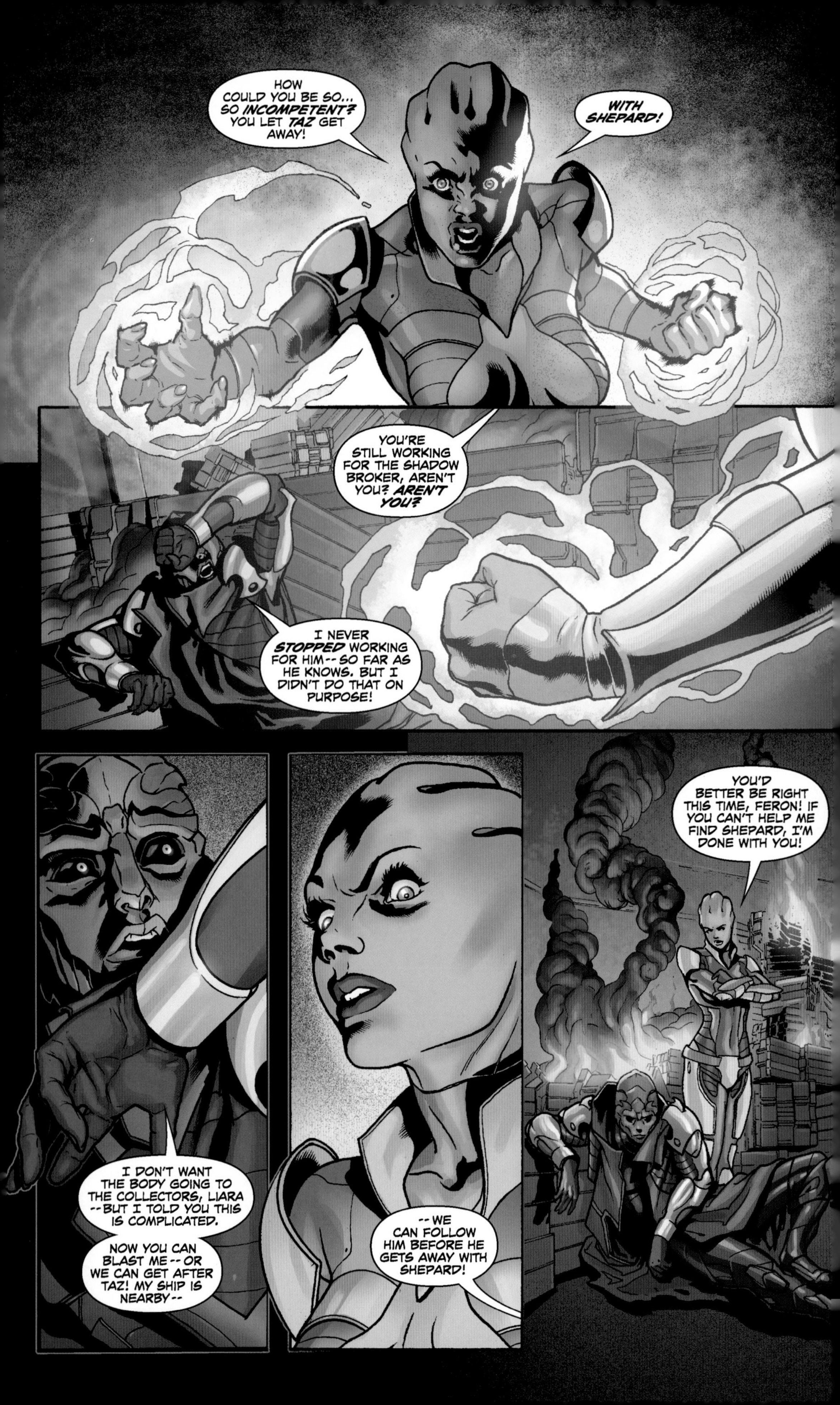
HOW COULD YOU BE SO... SO INCOMPETENT? YOU LET TAZ GET AWAY!
WITH SHEPARD!
YOU'RE STILL WORKING FOR THE SHADOW BROKER, AREN'T YOU? AREN'T YOU?
I NEVER STOPPED WORKING FOR HIM--SO FAR AS HE KNOWS. BUT I DIDN'T DO THAT ON PURPOSE!
I DON'T WANT THE BODY GOING TO THE COLLECTORS, LIARA--BUT I TOLD YOU THIS IS COMPLICATED.
NOW YOU CAN BLAST ME--OR WE CAN GET AFTER TAZ! MY SHIP IS NEARBY--
--WE CAN FOLLOW HIM BEFORE HE GETS AWAY WITH SHEPARD!
YOU'D BETTER BE RIGHT THIS TIME, FERON! IF YOU CAN'T HELP ME FIND SHEPARD, I'M DONE WITH YOU!

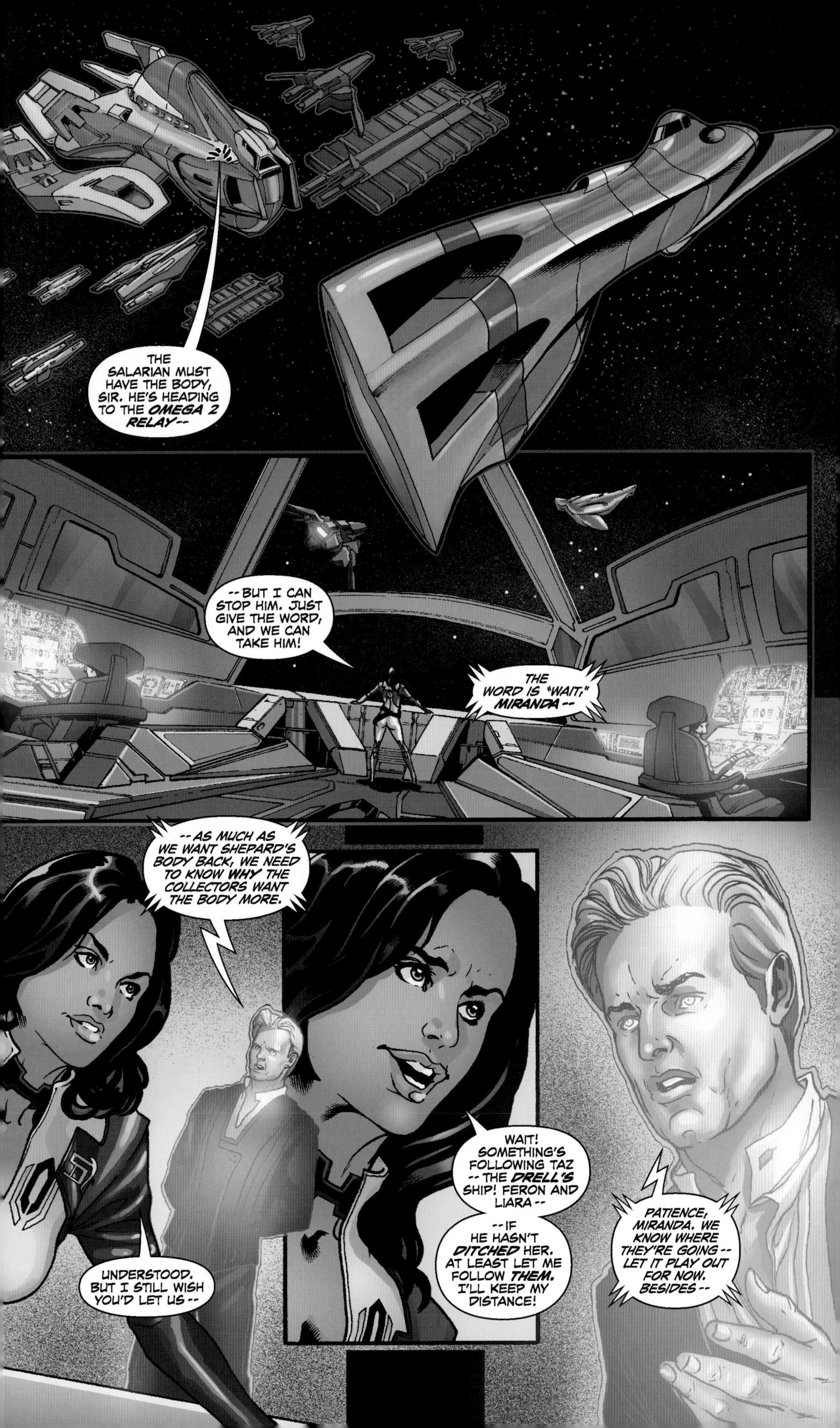
THE SALARIAN MUST HAVE THE BODY, SIR. HE'S HEADING TO THE OMEGA 2 RELAY--
--BUT I CAN STOP HIM. JUST GIVE THE WORD, AND WE CAN TAKE HIM!
THE WORD IS "WAIT," MIRANDA--
--AS MUCH AS WE WANT SHEPARD'S BODY BACK, WE NEED TO KNOW WHY THE COLLECTORS WANT THE BODY MORE.
UNDERSTOOD. BUT I STILL WISH YOU'D LET US--
WAIT! SOMETHING'S FOLLOWING TAZ--THE DRELL'S SHIP! FERON AND LIARA--
--IF HE HASN'T DITCHED HER. AT LEAST LET ME FOLLOW THEM. I'LL KEEP MY DISTANCE!
PATIENCE, MIRANDA. WE KNOW WHERE THEY'RE GOING--LET IT PLAY OUT FOR NOW. BESIDES--

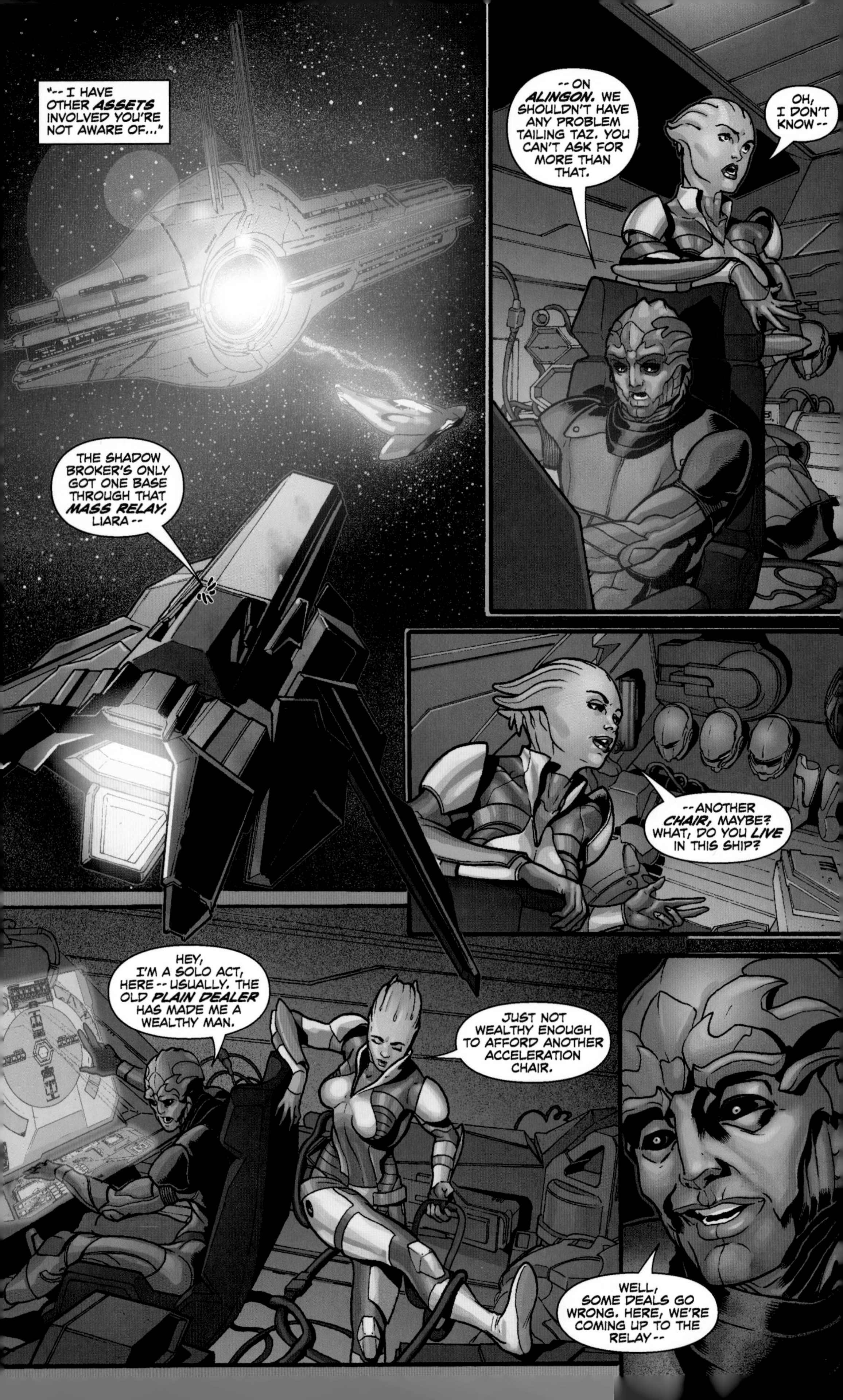
"-- I HAVE OTHER ASSETS INVOLVED YOU'RE NOT AWARE OF..."
THE SHADOW BROKER'S ONLY GOT ONE BASE THROUGH THAT MASS RELAY, LIARA --
-- ON ALINGON. WE SHOULDN'T HAVE ANY PROBLEM TAILING TAZ. YOU CAN'T ASK FOR MORE THAN THAT.
OH, I DON'T KNOW --
-- ANOTHER CHAIR, MAYBE? WHAT, DO YOU LIVE IN THIS SHIP?
HEY, I'M A SOLO ACT, HERE -- USUALLY. THE OLD PLAIN DEALER HAS MADE ME A WEALTHY MAN.
JUST NOT WEALTHY ENOUGH TO AFFORD ANOTHER ACCELERATION CHAIR.
WELL, SOME DEALS GO WRONG. HERE, WE'RE COMING UP TO THE RELAY --

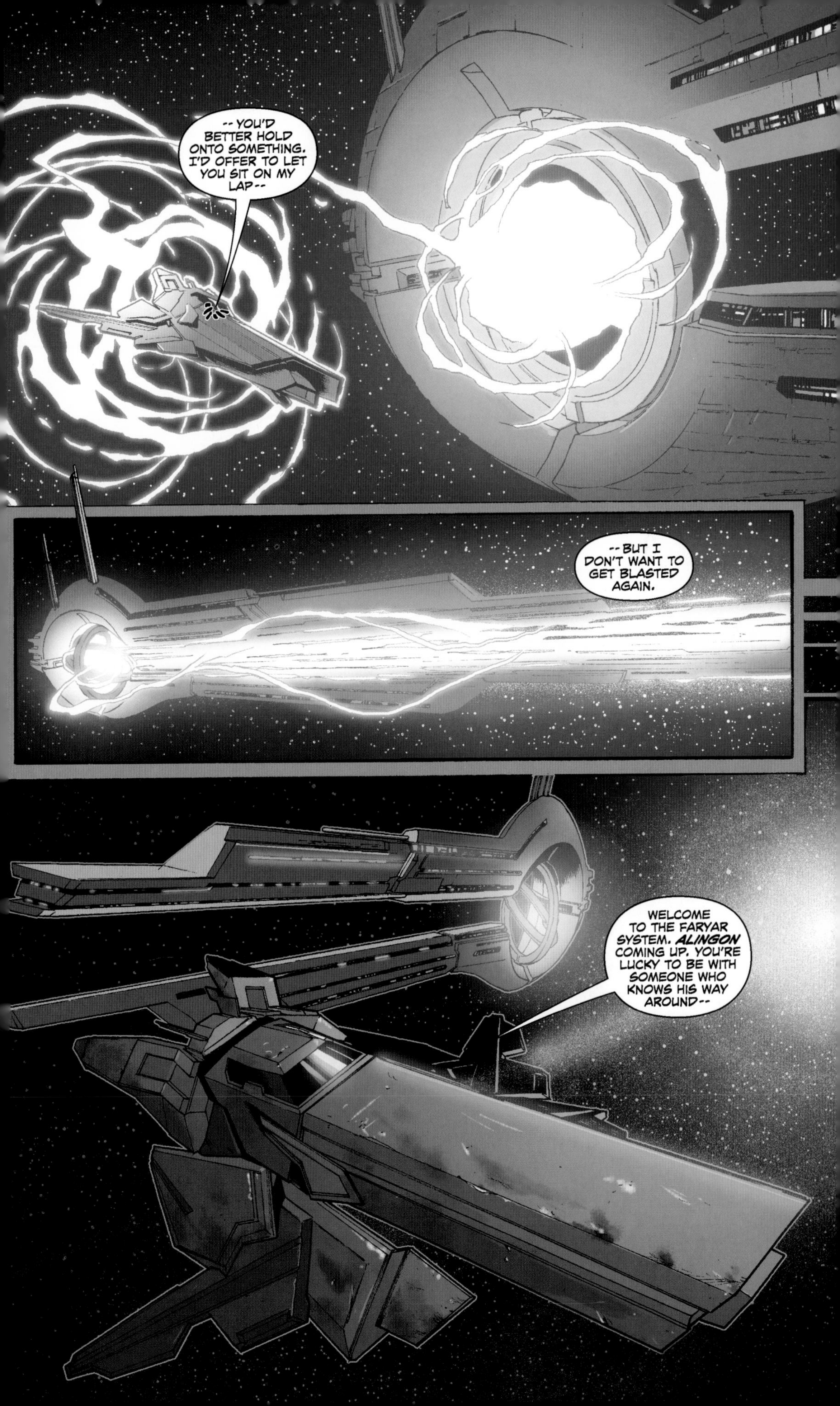
--YOU'D BETTER HOLD ONTO SOMETHING. I'D OFFER TO LET YOU SIT ON MY LAP--
--BUT I DON'T WANT TO GET BLASTED AGAIN.
WELCOME TO THE FARYAR SYSTEM. ALINGON COMING UP. YOU'RE LUCKY TO BE WITH SOMEONE WHO KNOWS HIS WAY AROUND--

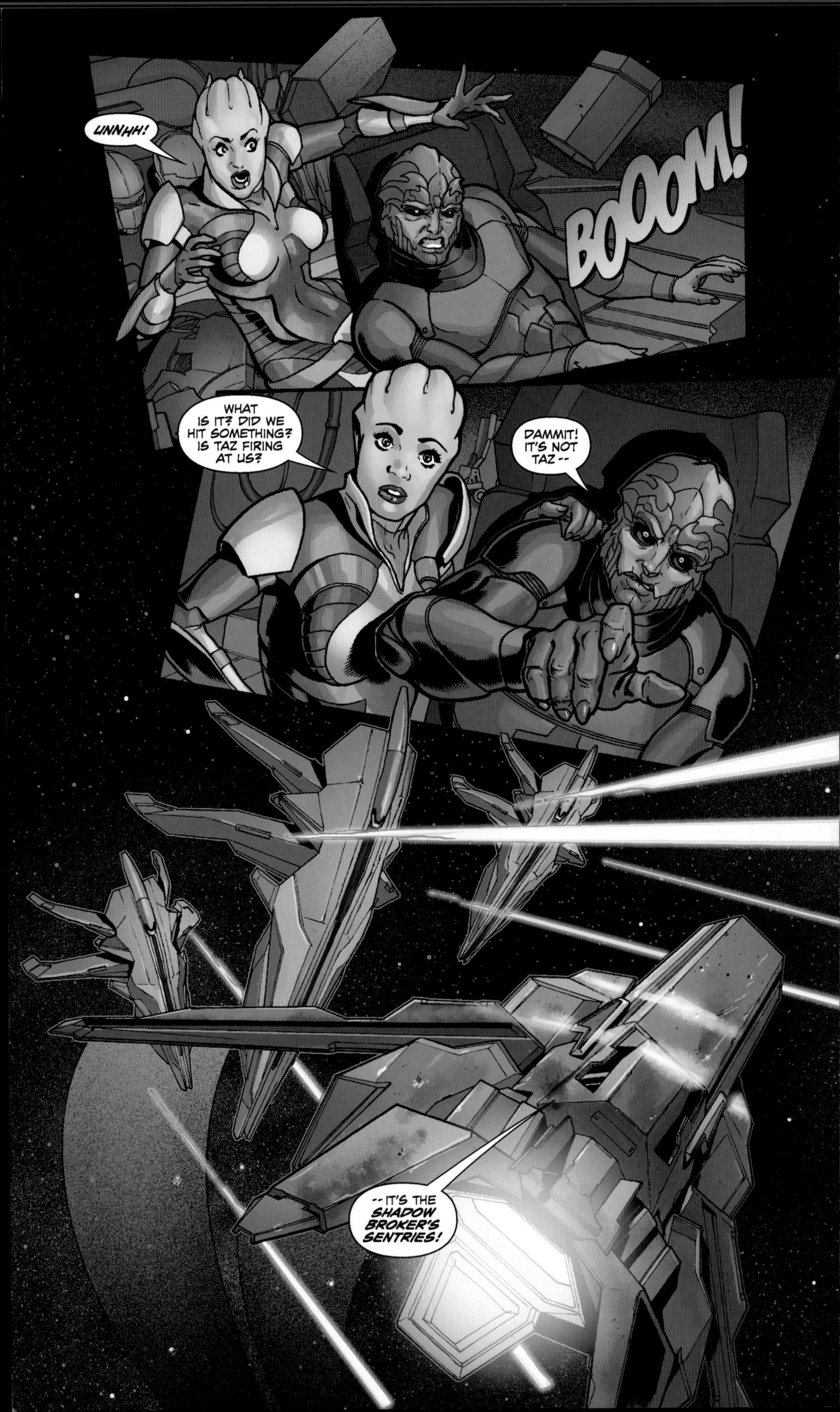
UNNHH!
BOOOM!
WHAT IS IT? DID WE HIT SOMETHING? IS TAZ FIRING AT US?
DAMMIT! IT'S NOT TAZ --
-- IT'S THE SHADOW BROKER'S SENTRIES!

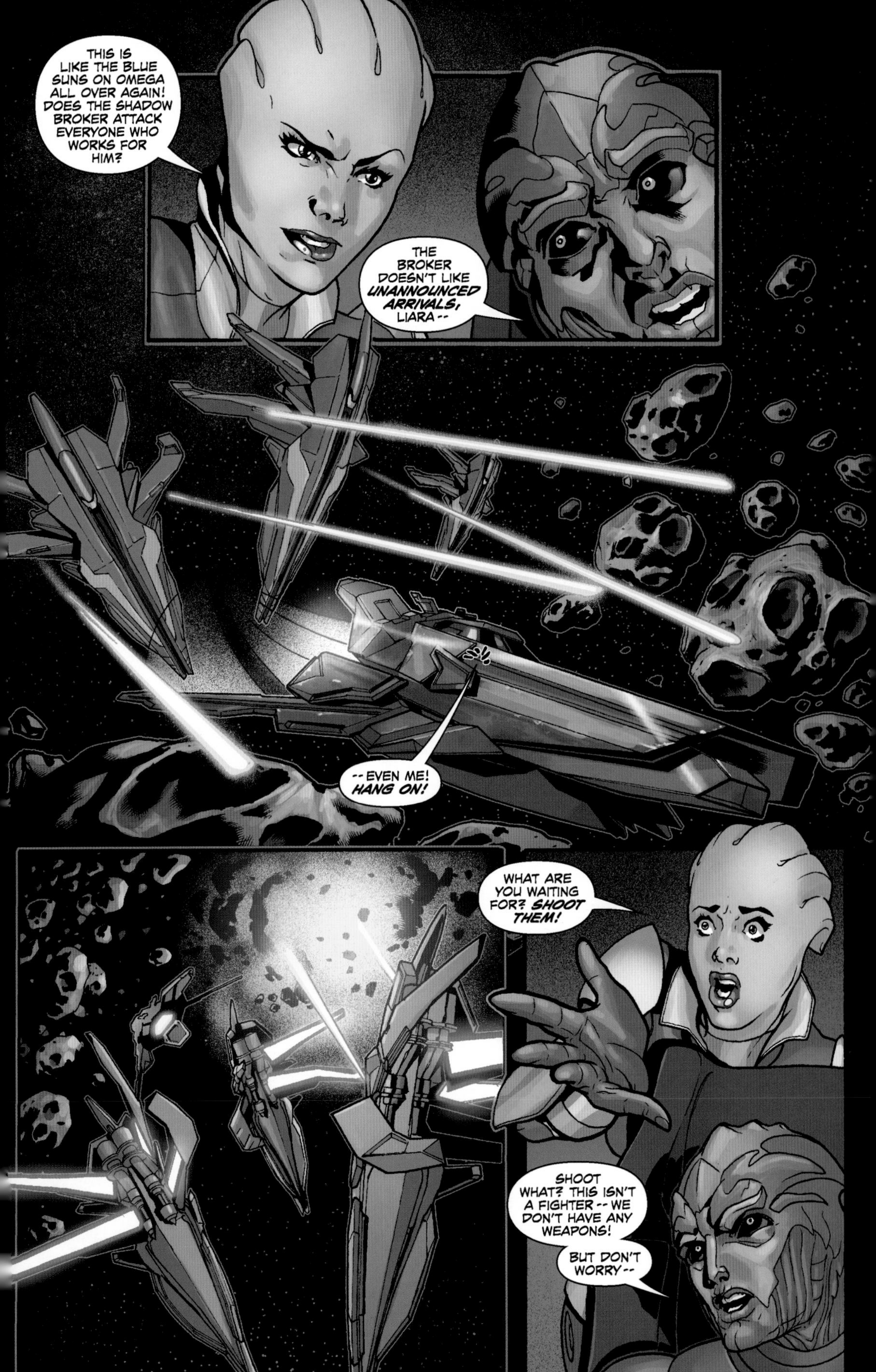
THIS IS LIKE THE BLUE SUNS ON OMEGA ALL OVER AGAIN! DOES THE SHADOW BROKER ATTACK EVERYONE WHO WORKS FOR HIM?
THE BROKER DOESN'T LIKE *UNANNOUNCED ARRIVALS,* LIARA --
-- EVEN ME! *HANG ON!*
WHAT ARE YOU WAITING FOR? *SHOOT THEM!*
SHOOT WHAT? THIS ISN'T A FIGHTER -- WE DON'T HAVE ANY WEAPONS!
BUT DON'T WORRY --

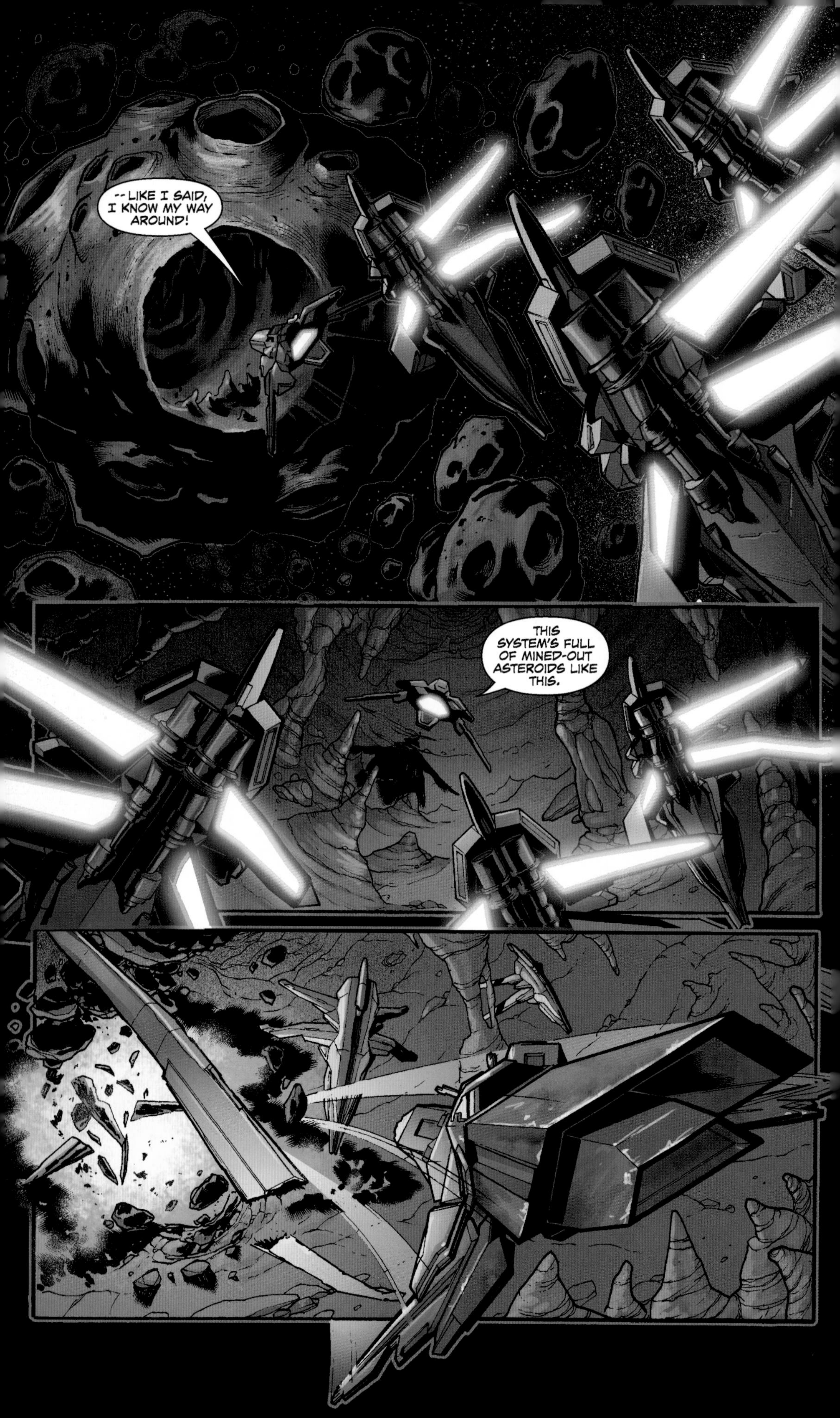
--LIKE I SAID, I KNOW MY WAY AROUND!
THIS SYSTEM'S FULL OF MINED-OUT ASTEROIDS LIKE THIS.

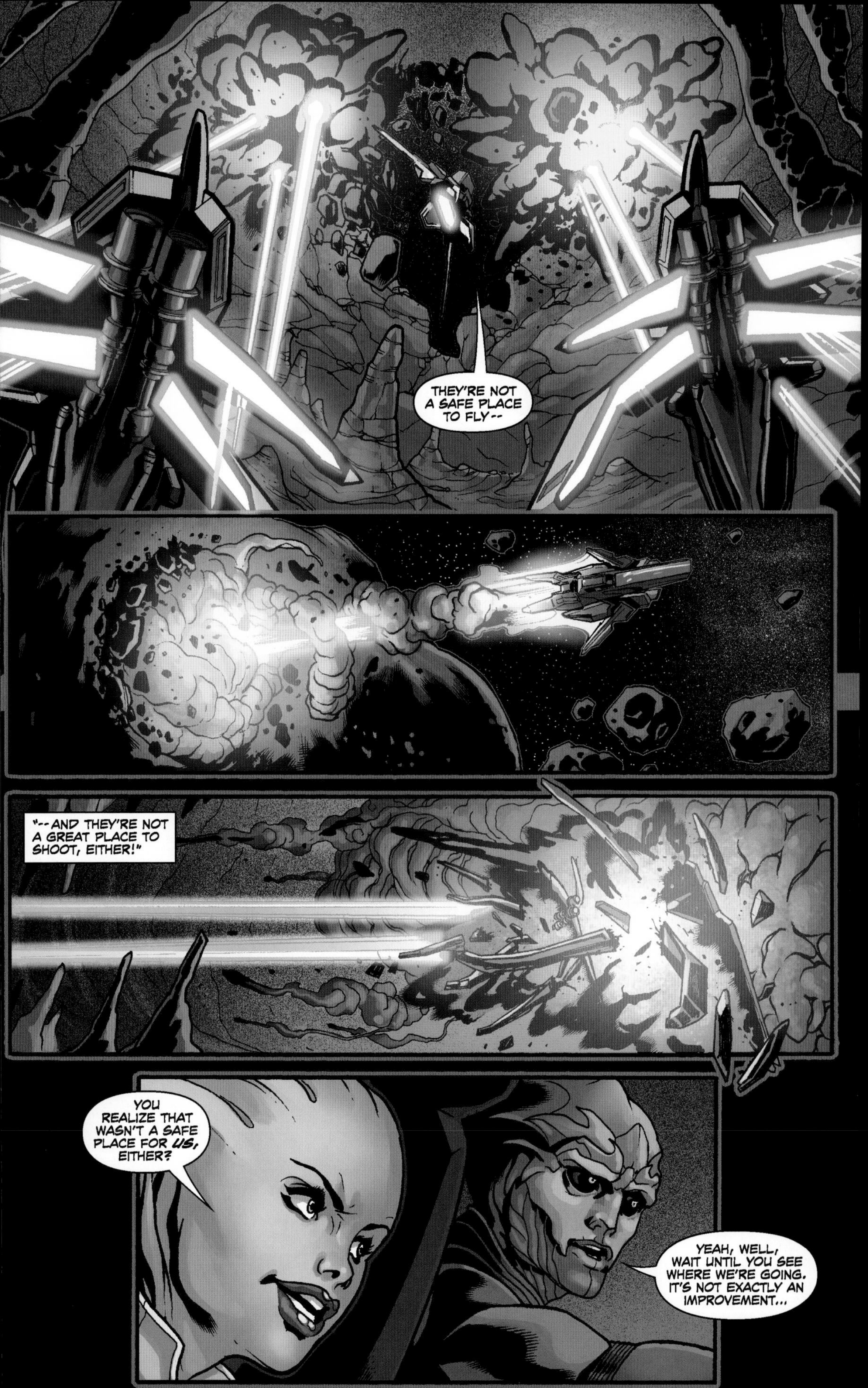
THEY'RE NOT A SAFE PLACE TO FLY--
"--AND THEY'RE NOT A GREAT PLACE TO SHOOT, EITHER!"
YOU REALIZE THAT WASN'T A SAFE PLACE FOR *US*, EITHER?
YEAH, WELL, WAIT UNTIL YOU SEE WHERE WE'RE GOING. IT'S NOT EXACTLY AN IMPROVEMENT...

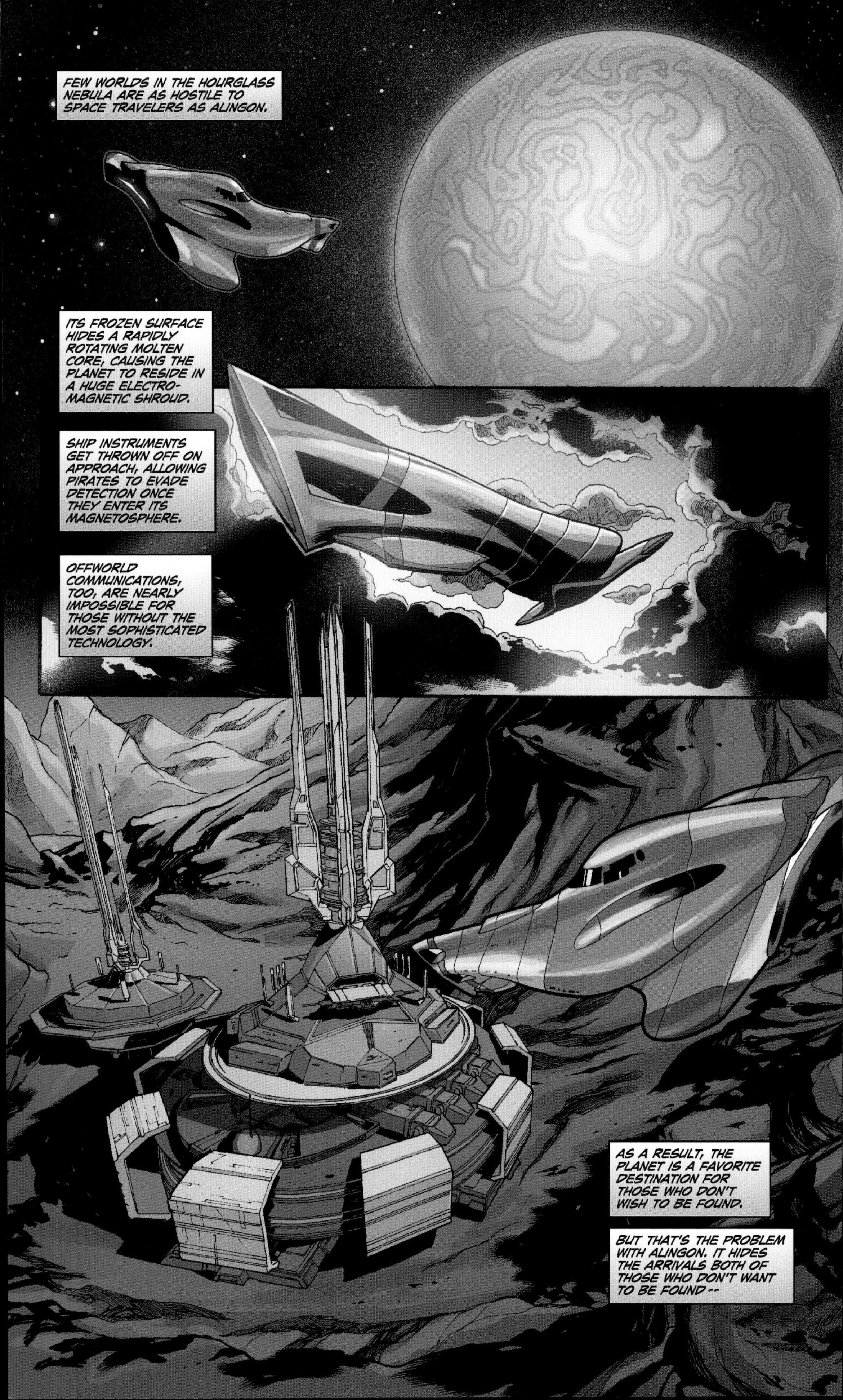
FEW WORLDS IN THE HOURGLASS NEBULA ARE AS HOSTILE TO SPACE TRAVELERS AS ALINGON.
ITS FROZEN SURFACE HIDES A RAPIDLY ROTATING MOLTEN CORE, CAUSING THE PLANET TO RESIDE IN A HUGE ELECTRO-MAGNETIC SHROUD.
SHIP INSTRUMENTS GET THROWN OFF ON APPROACH, ALLOWING PIRATES TO EVADE DETECTION ONCE THEY ENTER ITS MAGNETOSPHERE.
OFFWORLD COMMUNICATIONS, TOO, ARE NEARLY IMPOSSIBLE FOR THOSE WITHOUT THE MOST SOPHISTICATED TECHNOLOGY.
AS A RESULT, THE PLANET IS A FAVORITE DESTINATION FOR THOSE WHO DON'T WISH TO BE FOUND.
BUT THAT'S THE PROBLEM WITH ALINGON. IT HIDES THE ARRIVALS BOTH OF THOSE WHO DON'T WANT TO BE FOUND--

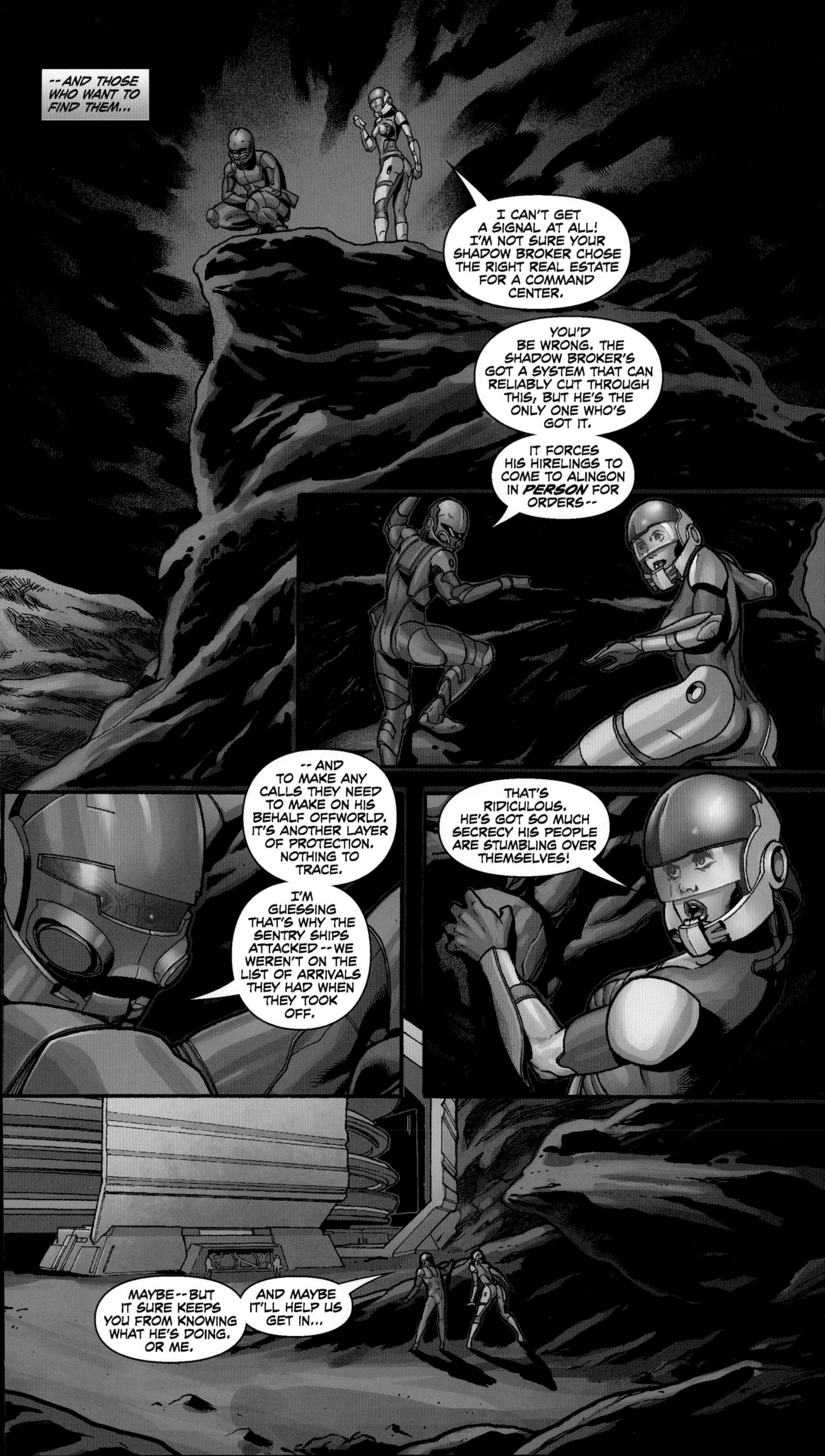
--AND THOSE WHO WANT TO FIND THEM...
I CAN'T GET A SIGNAL AT ALL! I'M NOT SURE YOUR SHADOW BROKER CHOSE THE RIGHT REAL ESTATE FOR A COMMAND CENTER.
YOU'D BE WRONG. THE SHADOW BROKER'S GOT A SYSTEM THAT CAN RELIABLY CUT THROUGH THIS, BUT HE'S THE ONLY ONE WHO'S GOT IT.
IT FORCES HIS HIRELINGS TO COME TO ALINGON IN *PERSON* FOR ORDERS--
--AND TO MAKE ANY CALLS THEY NEED TO MAKE ON HIS BEHALF OFFWORLD. IT'S ANOTHER LAYER OF PROTECTION. NOTHING TO TRACE.
I'M GUESSING THAT'S WHY THE SENTRY SHIPS ATTACKED--WE WEREN'T ON THE LIST OF ARRIVALS THEY HAD WHEN THEY TOOK OFF.
THAT'S RIDICULOUS. HE'S GOT SO MUCH SECRECY HIS PEOPLE ARE STUMBLING OVER THEMSELVES!
MAYBE--BUT IT SURE KEEPS YOU FROM KNOWING WHAT HE'S DOING. OR ME.
AND MAYBE IT'LL HELP US GET IN...

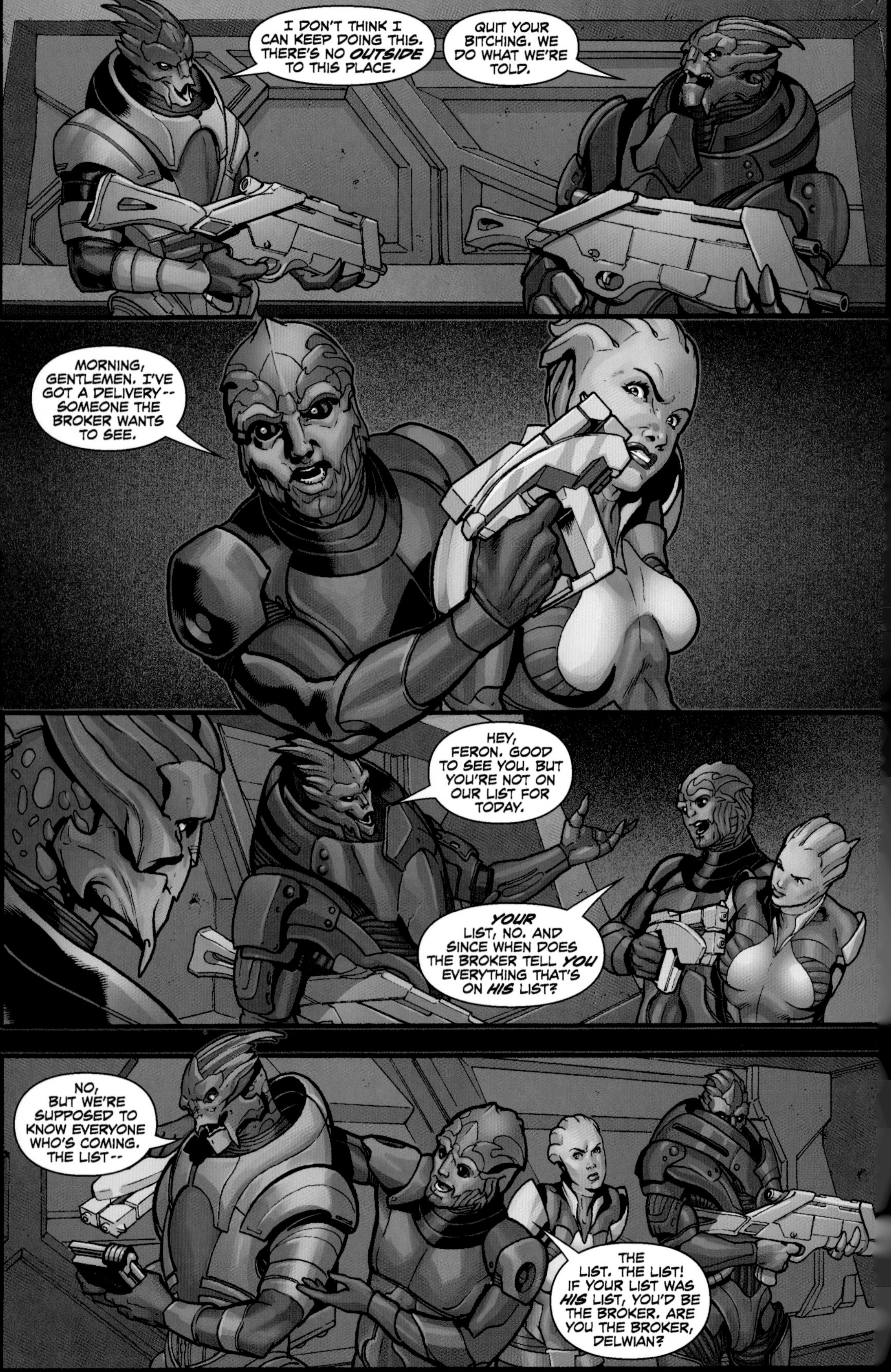
I DON'T THINK I CAN KEEP DOING THIS. THERE'S NO *OUTSIDE* TO THIS PLACE.
QUIT YOUR BITCHING. WE DO WHAT WE'RE TOLD.
MORNING, GENTLEMEN. I'VE GOT A DELIVERY-- SOMEONE THE BROKER WANTS TO SEE.
HEY, FERON. GOOD TO SEE YOU. BUT YOU'RE NOT ON OUR LIST FOR TODAY.
YOUR LIST, NO. AND SINCE WHEN DOES THE BROKER TELL *YOU* EVERYTHING THAT'S ON *HIS* LIST?
NO, BUT WE'RE SUPPOSED TO KNOW EVERYONE WHO'S COMING. THE LIST--
THE LIST. THE LIST! IF YOUR LIST WAS *HIS* LIST, YOU'D BE THE BROKER. ARE YOU THE BROKER, DELWIAN?

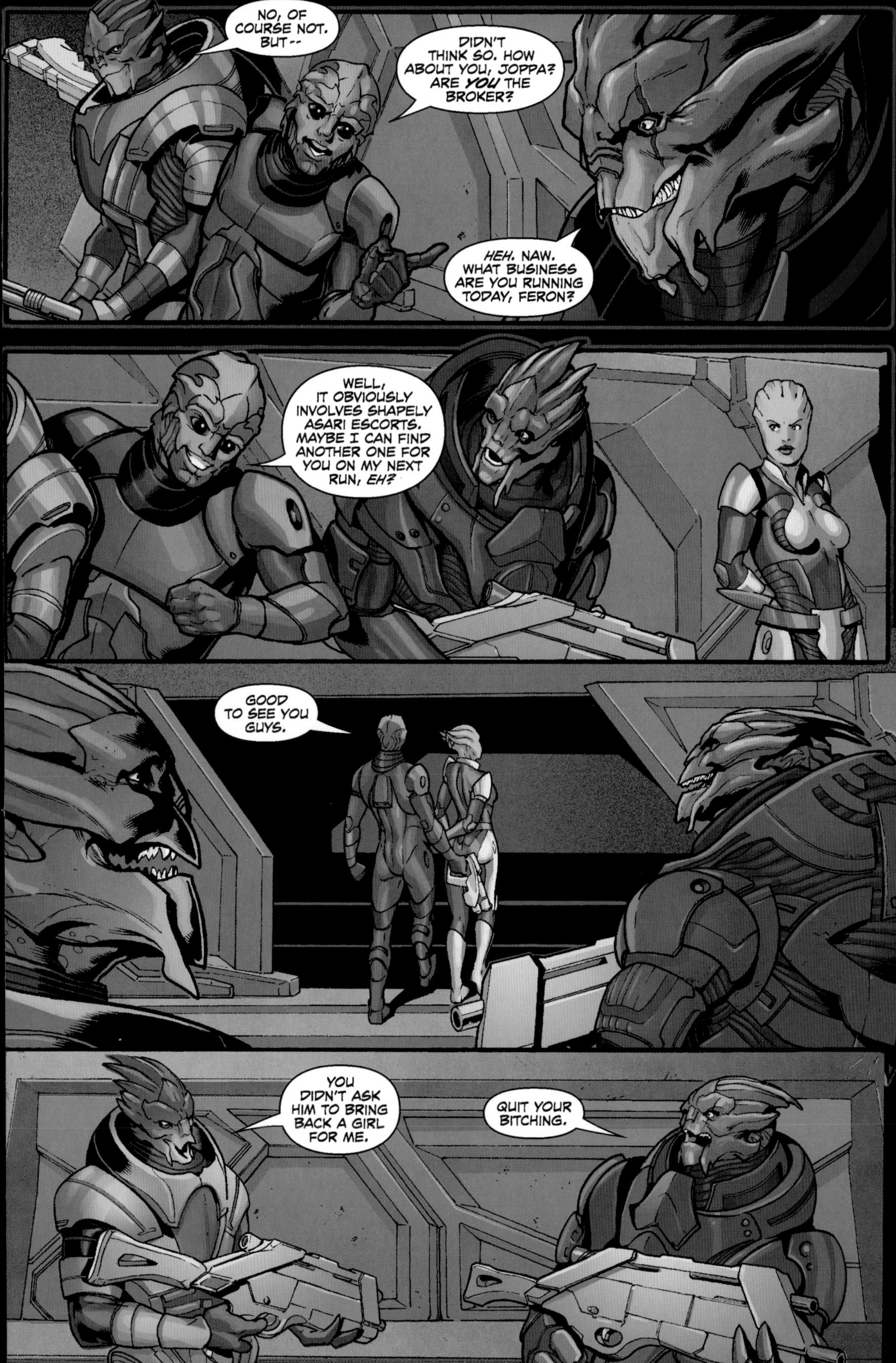
NO, OF COURSE NOT. BUT--
DIDN'T THINK SO. HOW ABOUT YOU, JOPPA? ARE *YOU* THE BROKER?
HEH. NAW. WHAT BUSINESS ARE YOU RUNNING TODAY, FERON?
WELL, IT OBVIOUSLY INVOLVES SHAPELY ASARI ESCORTS. MAYBE I CAN FIND ANOTHER ONE FOR YOU ON MY NEXT RUN, *EH?*
GOOD TO SEE YOU GUYS.
YOU DIDN'T ASK HIM TO BRING BACK A GIRL FOR ME.
QUIT YOUR BITCHING.

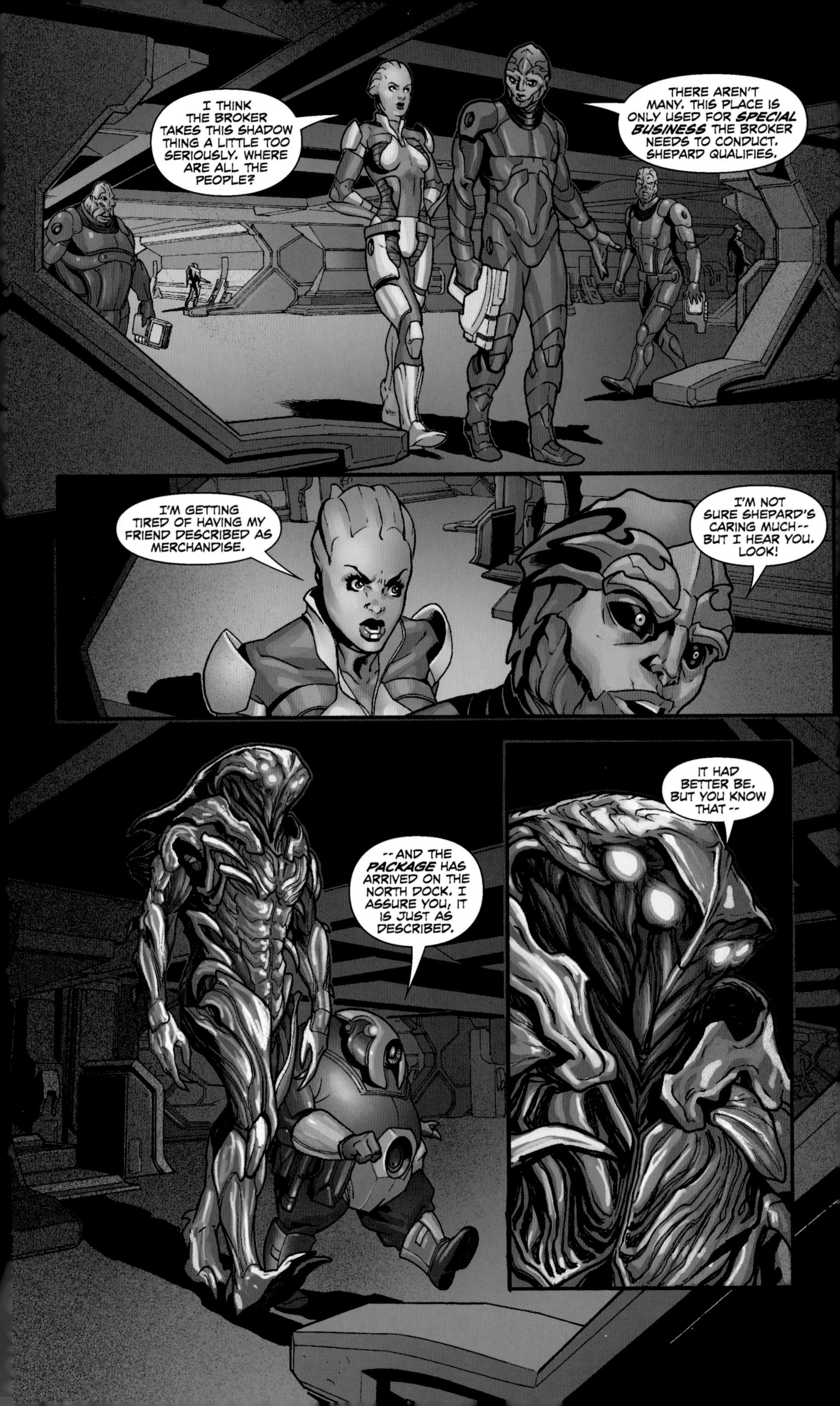

I THINK THE BROKER TAKES THIS SHADOW THING A LITTLE TOO SERIOUSLY. WHERE ARE ALL THE PEOPLE?
THERE AREN'T MANY. THIS PLACE IS ONLY USED FOR SPECIAL BUSINESS THE BROKER NEEDS TO CONDUCT. SHEPARD QUALIFIES.
I'M GETTING TIRED OF HAVING MY FRIEND DESCRIBED AS MERCHANDISE.
I'M NOT SURE SHEPARD'S CARING MUCH-- BUT I HEAR YOU. LOOK!
--AND THE PACKAGE HAS ARRIVED ON THE NORTH DOCK. I ASSURE YOU, IT IS JUST AS DESCRIBED.
IT HAD BETTER BE. BUT YOU KNOW THAT --

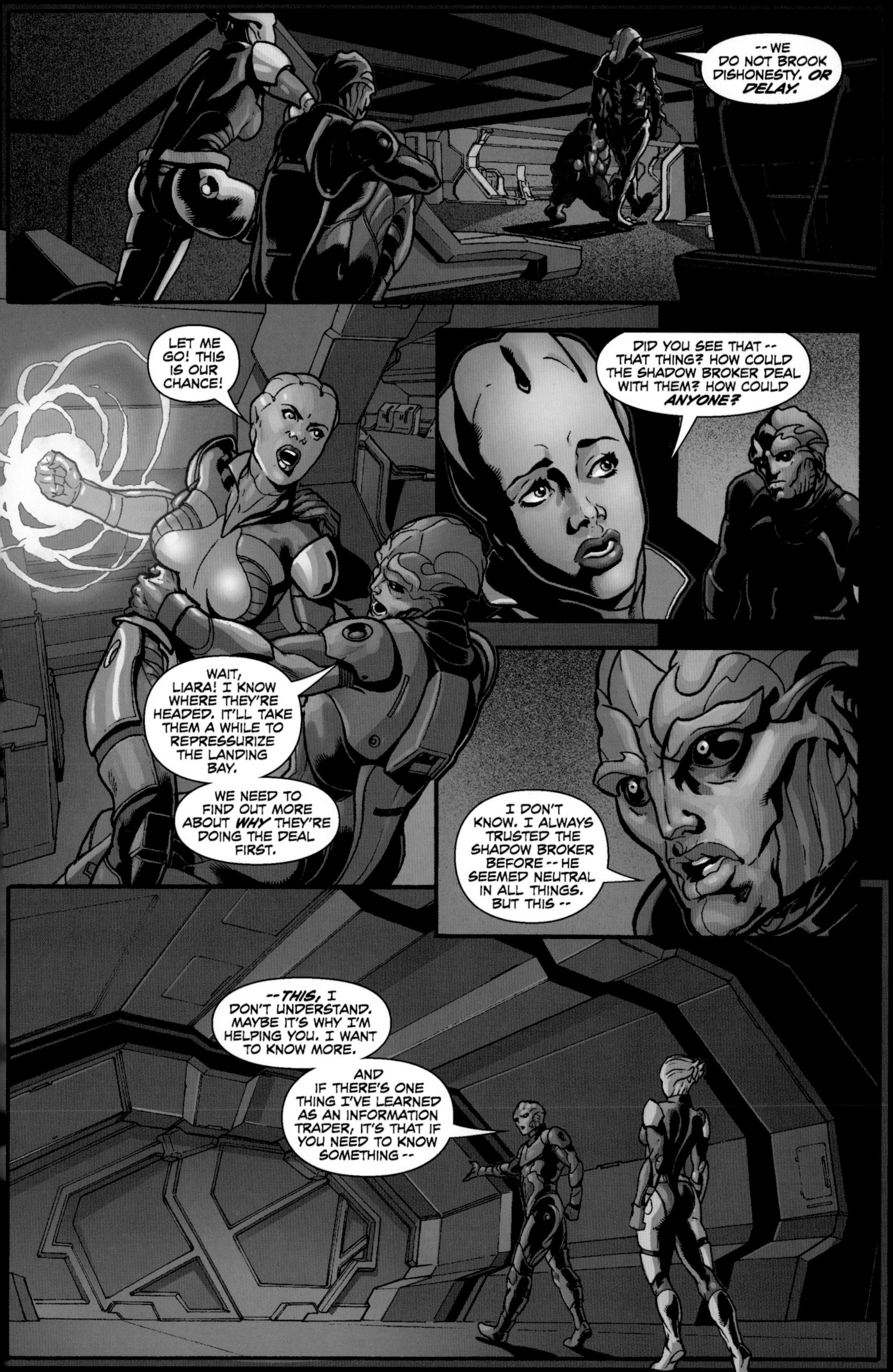
--WE DO NOT BROOK DISHONESTY. OR DELAY.
LET ME GO! THIS IS OUR CHANCE!
DID YOU SEE THAT -- THAT THING? HOW COULD THE SHADOW BROKER DEAL WITH THEM? HOW COULD ANYONE?
WAIT, LIARA! I KNOW WHERE THEY'RE HEADED. IT'LL TAKE THEM A WHILE TO REPRESSURIZE THE LANDING BAY.
WE NEED TO FIND OUT MORE ABOUT WHY THEY'RE DOING THE DEAL FIRST.
I DON'T KNOW. I ALWAYS TRUSTED THE SHADOW BROKER BEFORE -- HE SEEMED NEUTRAL IN ALL THINGS. BUT THIS --
--THIS, I DON'T UNDERSTAND. MAYBE IT'S WHY I'M HELPING YOU. I WANT TO KNOW MORE.
AND IF THERE'S ONE THING I'VE LEARNED AS AN INFORMATION TRADER, IT'S THAT IF YOU NEED TO KNOW SOMETHING --

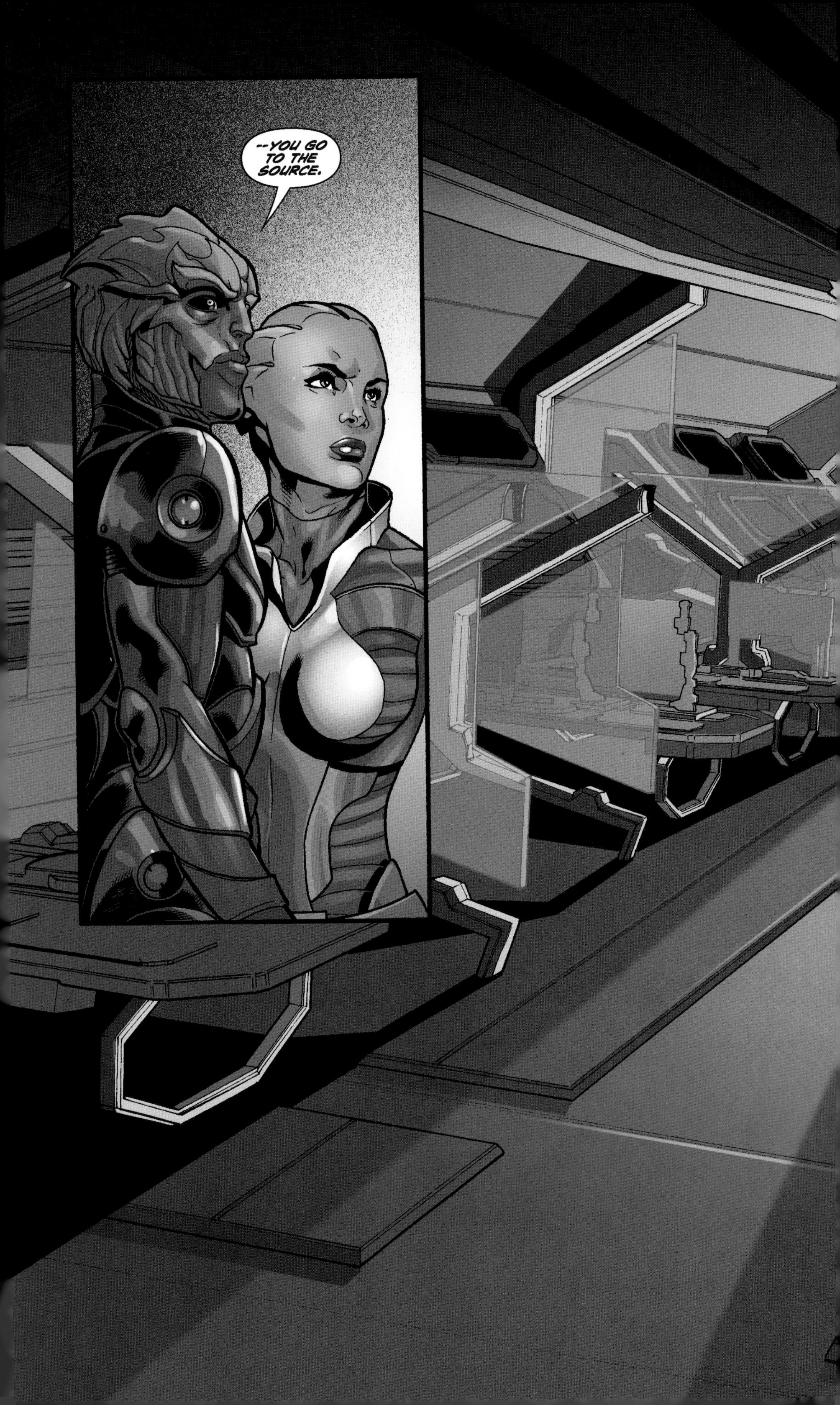
--YOU GO TO THE SOURCE.

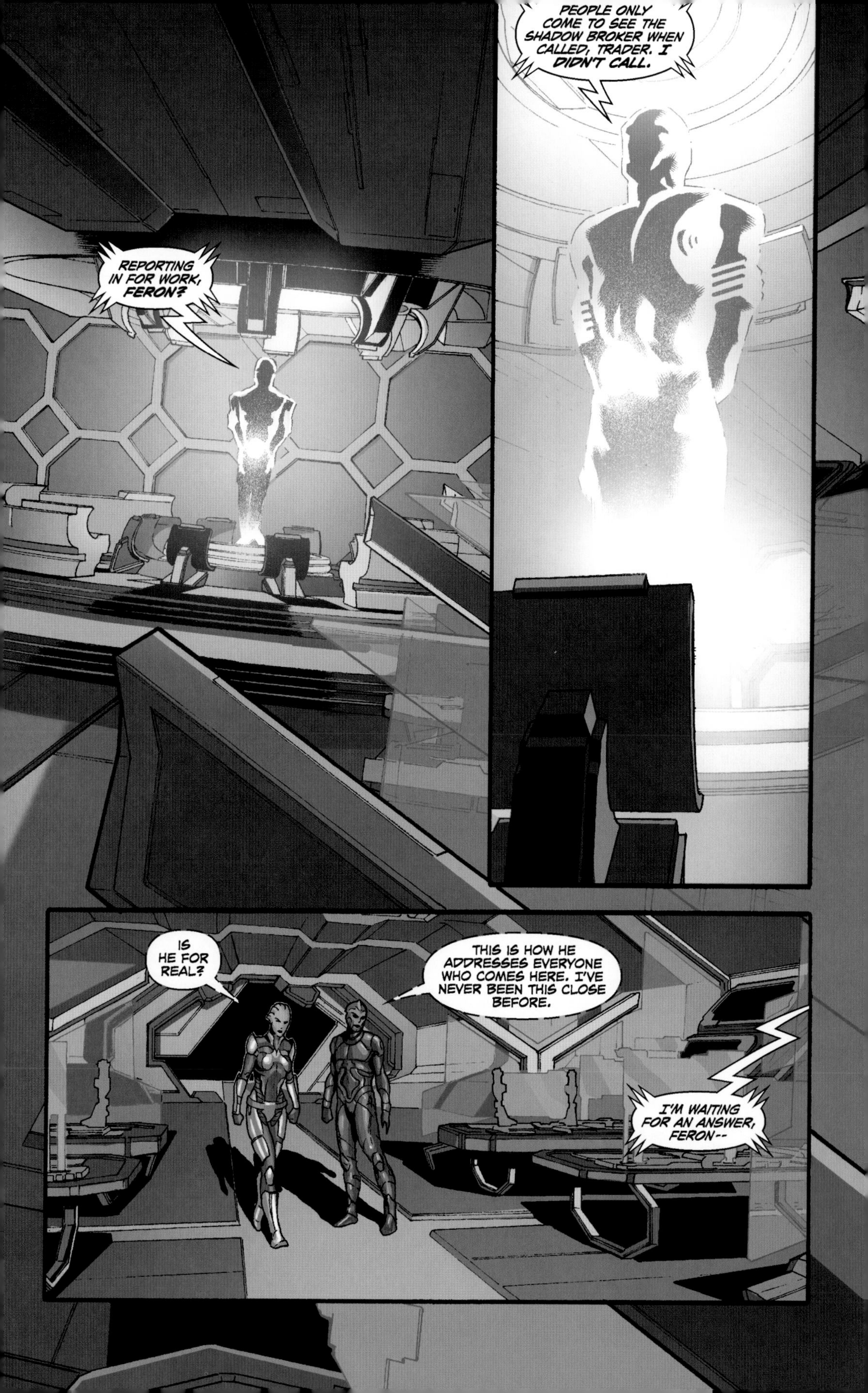
REPORTING IN FOR WORK, FERON?
PEOPLE ONLY COME TO SEE THE SHADOW BROKER WHEN CALLED, TRADER. I DIDN'T CALL.
IS HE FOR REAL?
THIS IS HOW HE ADDRESSES EVERYONE WHO COMES HERE. I'VE NEVER BEEN THIS CLOSE BEFORE.
I'M WAITING FOR AN ANSWER, FERON--

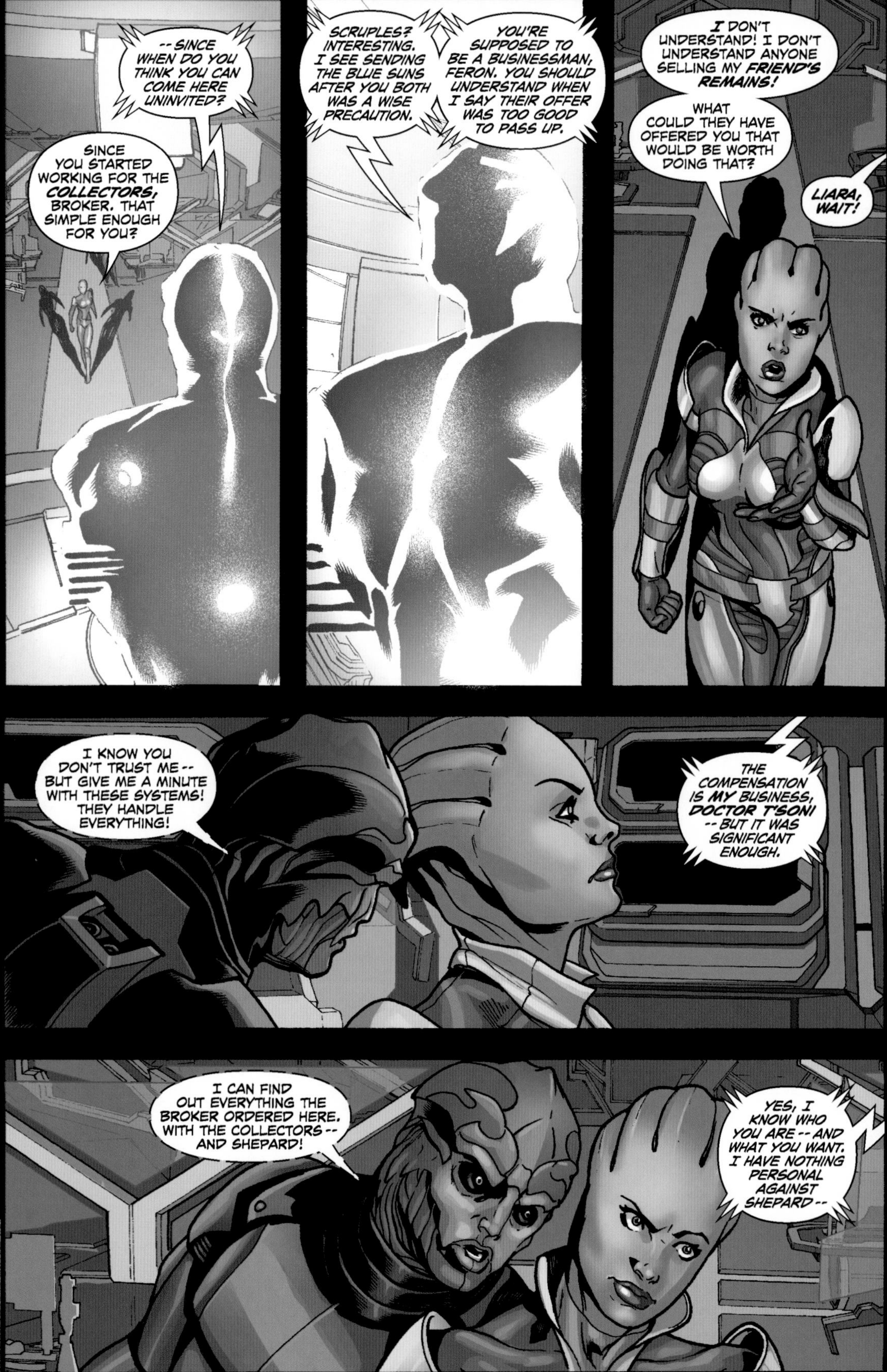
-- SINCE WHEN DO YOU THINK YOU CAN COME HERE UNINVITED?
SINCE YOU STARTED WORKING FOR THE COLLECTORS, BROKER. THAT SIMPLE ENOUGH FOR YOU?
SCRUPLES? INTERESTING. I SEE SENDING THE BLUE SUNS AFTER YOU BOTH WAS A WISE PRECAUTION.
YOU'RE SUPPOSED TO BE A BUSINESSMAN, FERON. YOU SHOULD UNDERSTAND WHEN I SAY THEIR OFFER WAS TOO GOOD TO PASS UP.
I DON'T UNDERSTAND! I DON'T UNDERSTAND ANYONE SELLING MY FRIEND'S REMAINS!
WHAT COULD THEY HAVE OFFERED YOU THAT WOULD BE WORTH DOING THAT?
LIARA, WAIT!
I KNOW YOU DON'T TRUST ME -- BUT GIVE ME A MINUTE WITH THESE SYSTEMS! THEY HANDLE EVERYTHING!
THE COMPENSATION IS MY BUSINESS, DOCTOR T'SONI -- BUT IT WAS SIGNIFICANT ENOUGH.
I CAN FIND OUT EVERYTHING THE BROKER ORDERED HERE. WITH THE COLLECTORS -- AND SHEPARD!
YES, I KNOW WHO YOU ARE -- AND WHAT YOU WANT. I HAVE NOTHING PERSONAL AGAINST SHEPARD --

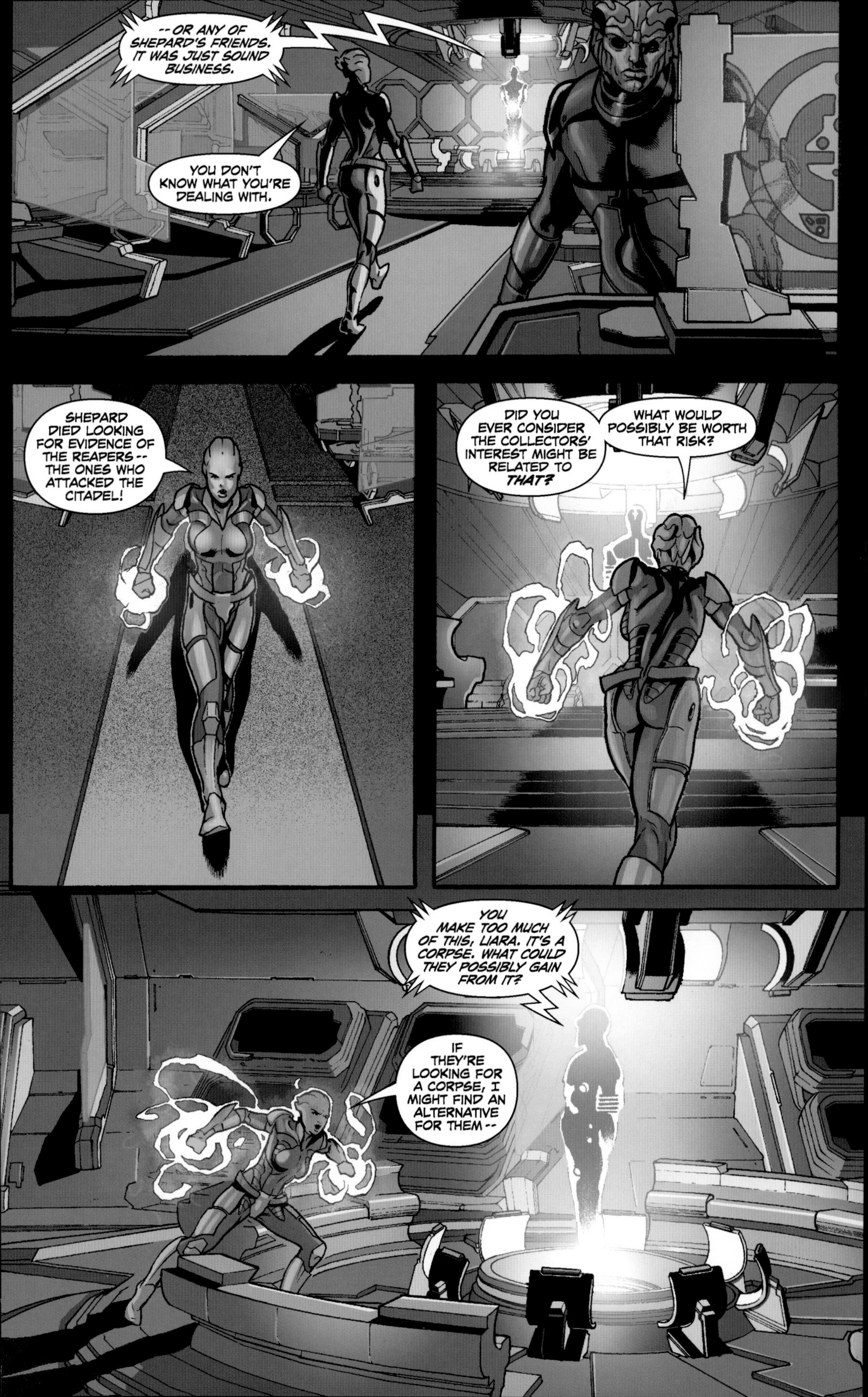
--OR ANY OF SHEPARD'S FRIENDS. IT WAS JUST SOUND BUSINESS.
YOU DON'T KNOW WHAT YOU'RE DEALING WITH.
SHEPARD DIED LOOKING FOR EVIDENCE OF THE REAPERS-- THE ONES WHO ATTACKED THE CITADEL!
WHAT WOULD POSSIBLY BE WORTH THAT RISK?
DID YOU EVER CONSIDER THE COLLECTORS' INTEREST MIGHT BE RELATED TO *THAT?*
YOU MAKE TOO MUCH OF THIS, LIARA. IT'S A CORPSE. WHAT COULD THEY POSSIBLY GAIN FROM IT?
IF THEY'RE LOOKING FOR A CORPSE, I MIGHT FIND AN ALTERNATIVE FOR THEM--

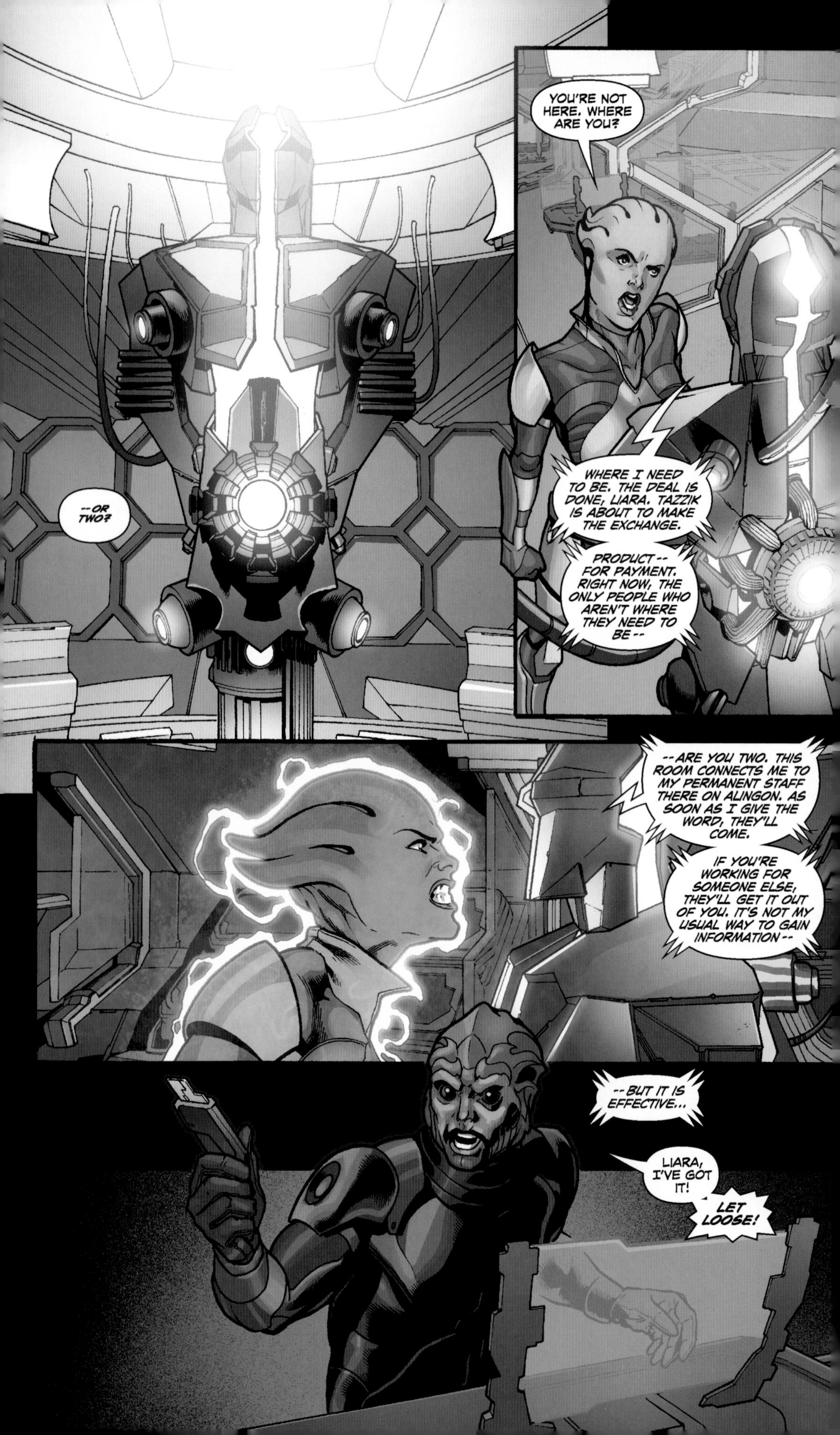
YOU'RE NOT HERE. WHERE ARE YOU?
--OR TWO?
WHERE I NEED TO BE. THE DEAL IS DONE, LIARA. TAZZIK IS ABOUT TO MAKE THE EXCHANGE.
PRODUCT-- FOR PAYMENT. RIGHT NOW, THE ONLY PEOPLE WHO AREN'T WHERE THEY NEED TO BE--
--ARE YOU TWO. THIS ROOM CONNECTS ME TO MY PERMANENT STAFF THERE ON ALINGON. AS SOON AS I GIVE THE WORD, THEY'LL COME.
IF YOU'RE WORKING FOR SOMEONE ELSE, THEY'LL GET IT OUT OF YOU. IT'S NOT MY USUAL WAY TO GAIN INFORMATION--
--BUT IT IS EFFECTIVE...
LIARA, I'VE GOT IT!
LET LOOSE!

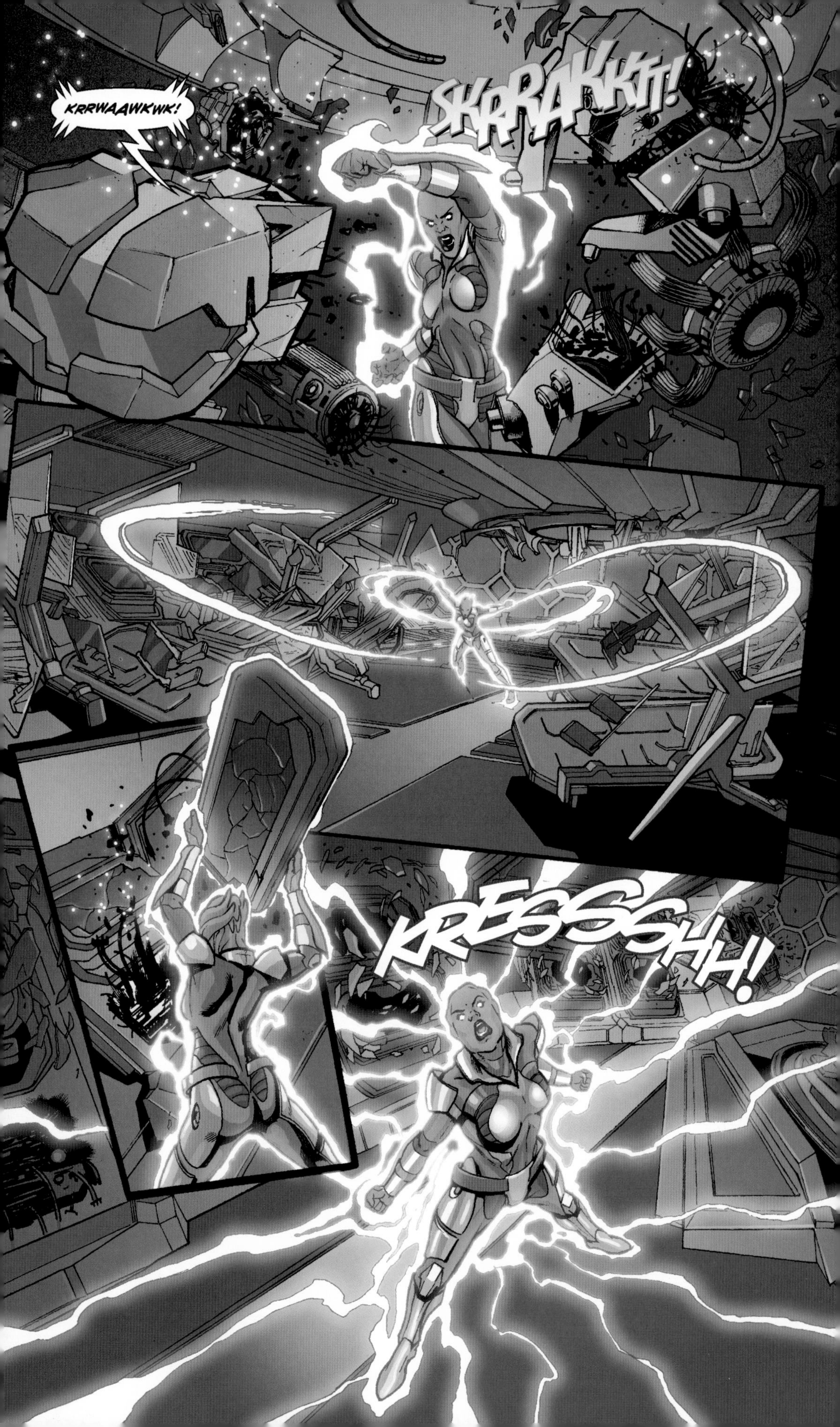
KRRWAAWKWK!
SKRRAKKTT!
KRESSSHH!

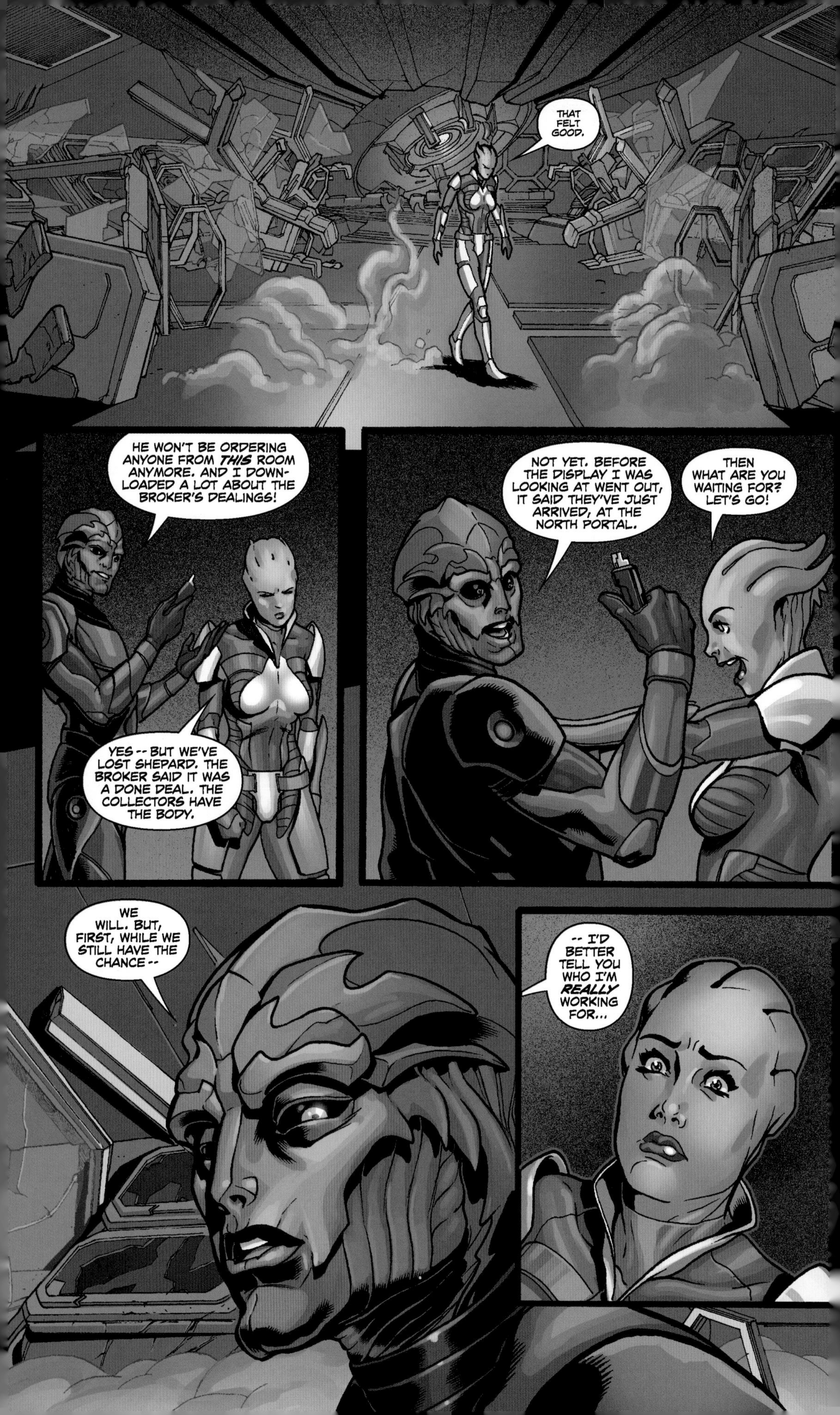
THAT FELT GOOD.
HE WON'T BE ORDERING ANYONE FROM THIS ROOM ANYMORE. AND I DOWN-LOADED A LOT ABOUT THE BROKER'S DEALINGS!
YES -- BUT WE'VE LOST SHEPARD. THE BROKER SAID IT WAS A DONE DEAL. THE COLLECTORS HAVE THE BODY.
NOT YET. BEFORE THE DISPLAY I WAS LOOKING AT WENT OUT, IT SAID THEY'VE JUST ARRIVED, AT THE NORTH PORTAL.
THEN WHAT ARE YOU WAITING FOR? LET'S GO!
WE WILL. BUT, FIRST, WHILE WE STILL HAVE THE CHANCE --
-- I'D BETTER TELL YOU WHO I'M REALLY WORKING FOR...

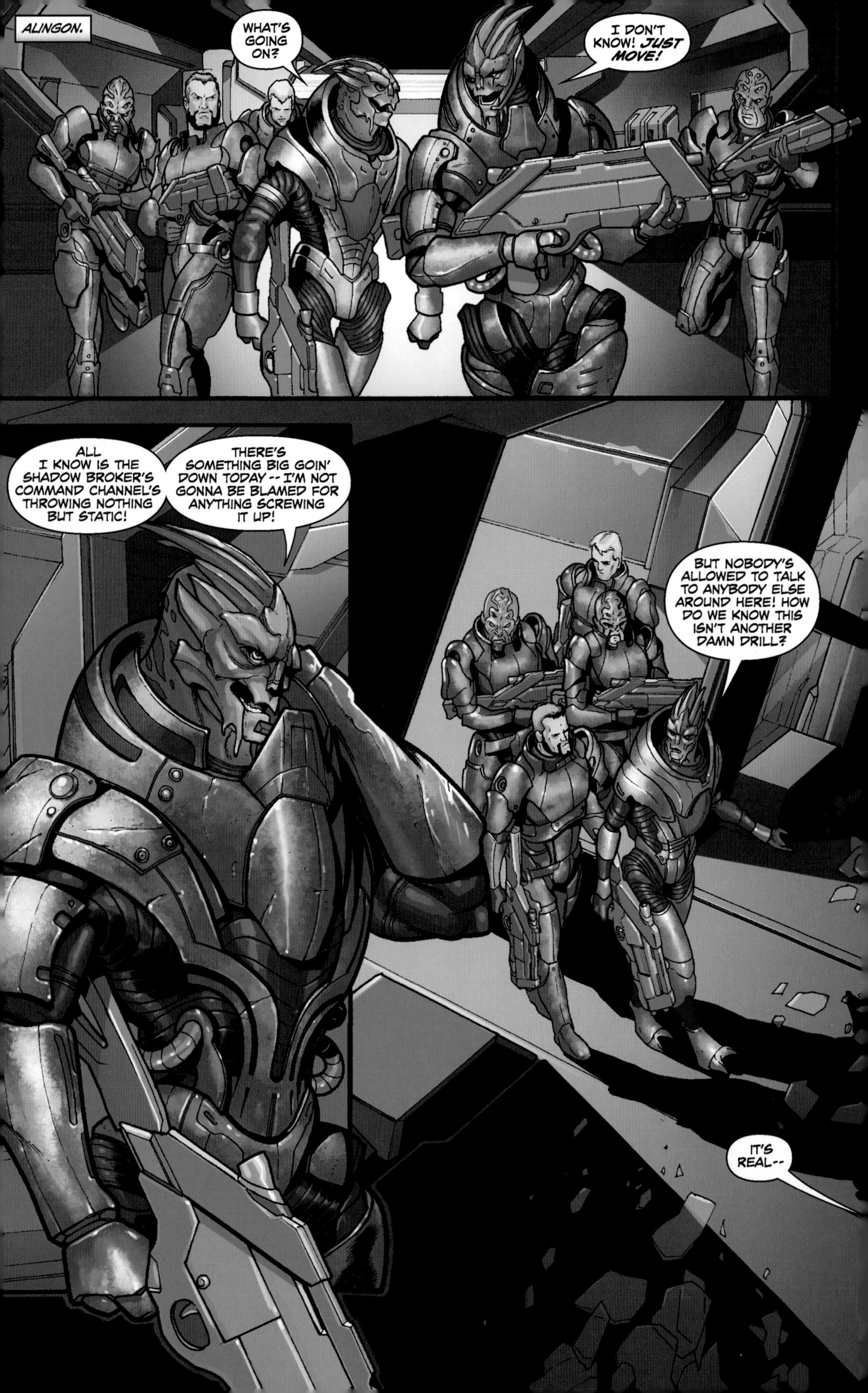
ALINGON.
WHAT'S GOING ON?
I DON'T KNOW! JUST MOVE!
ALL I KNOW IS THE SHADOW BROKER'S COMMAND CHANNEL'S THROWING NOTHING BUT STATIC!
THERE'S SOMETHING BIG GOIN' DOWN TODAY -- I'M NOT GONNA BE BLAMED FOR ANYTHING SCREWING IT UP!
BUT NOBODY'S ALLOWED TO TALK TO ANYBODY ELSE AROUND HERE! HOW DO WE KNOW THIS ISN'T ANOTHER DAMN DRILL?
IT'S REAL--

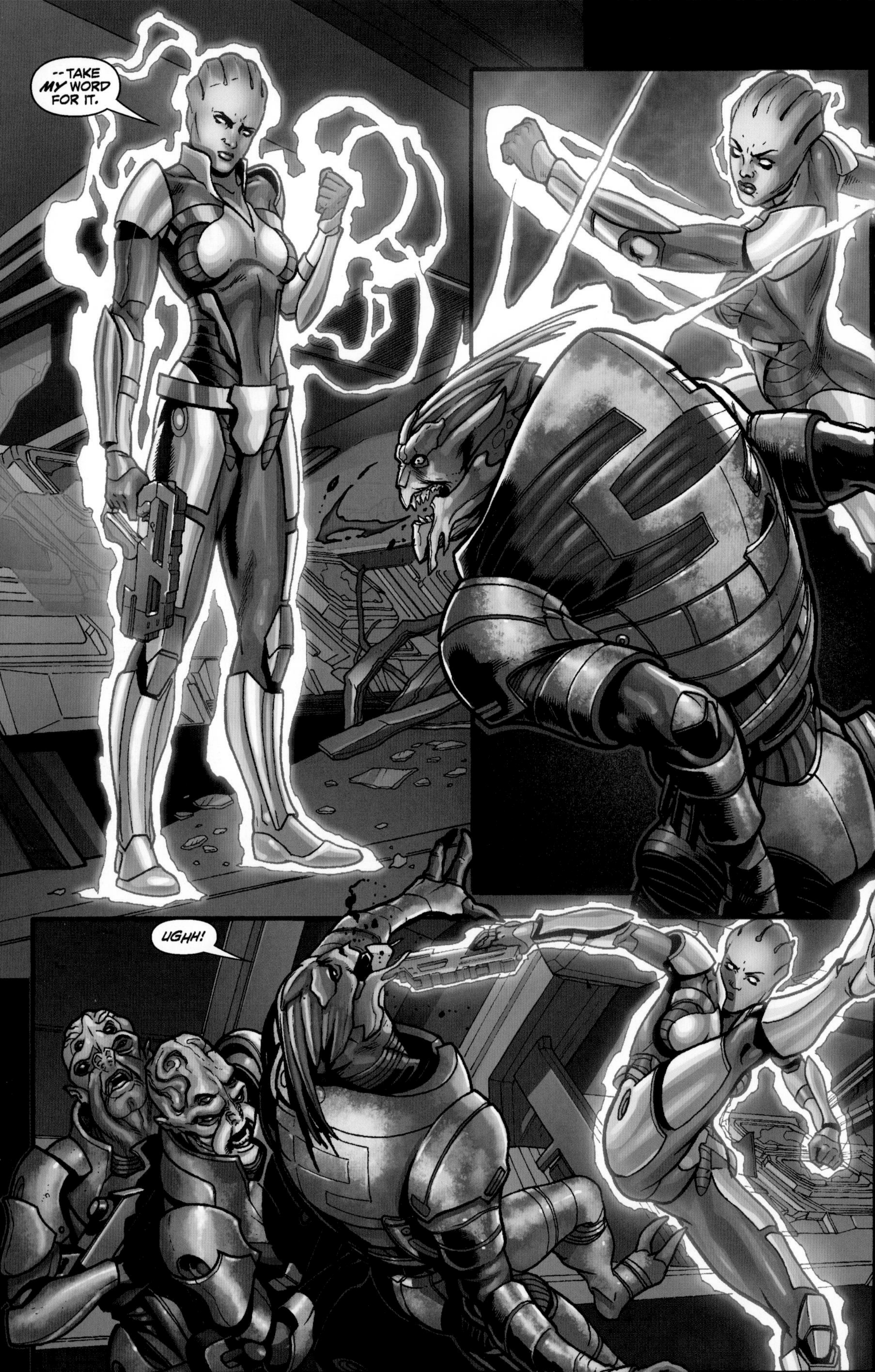
--TAKE MY WORD FOR IT.
UGHH!

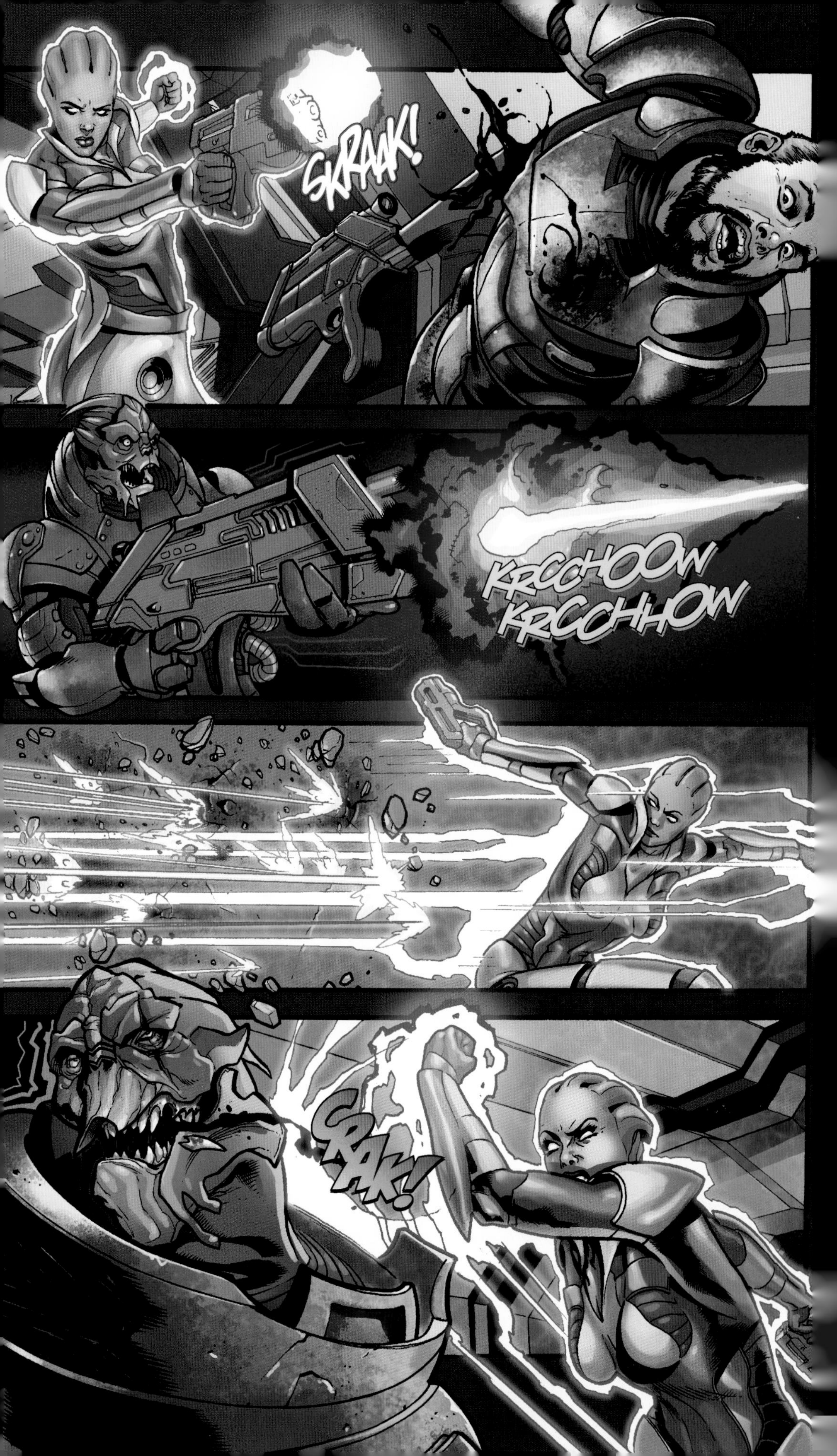
SKRAAK!
KRCCHOOW
KRCCHHOW
CRAAK!

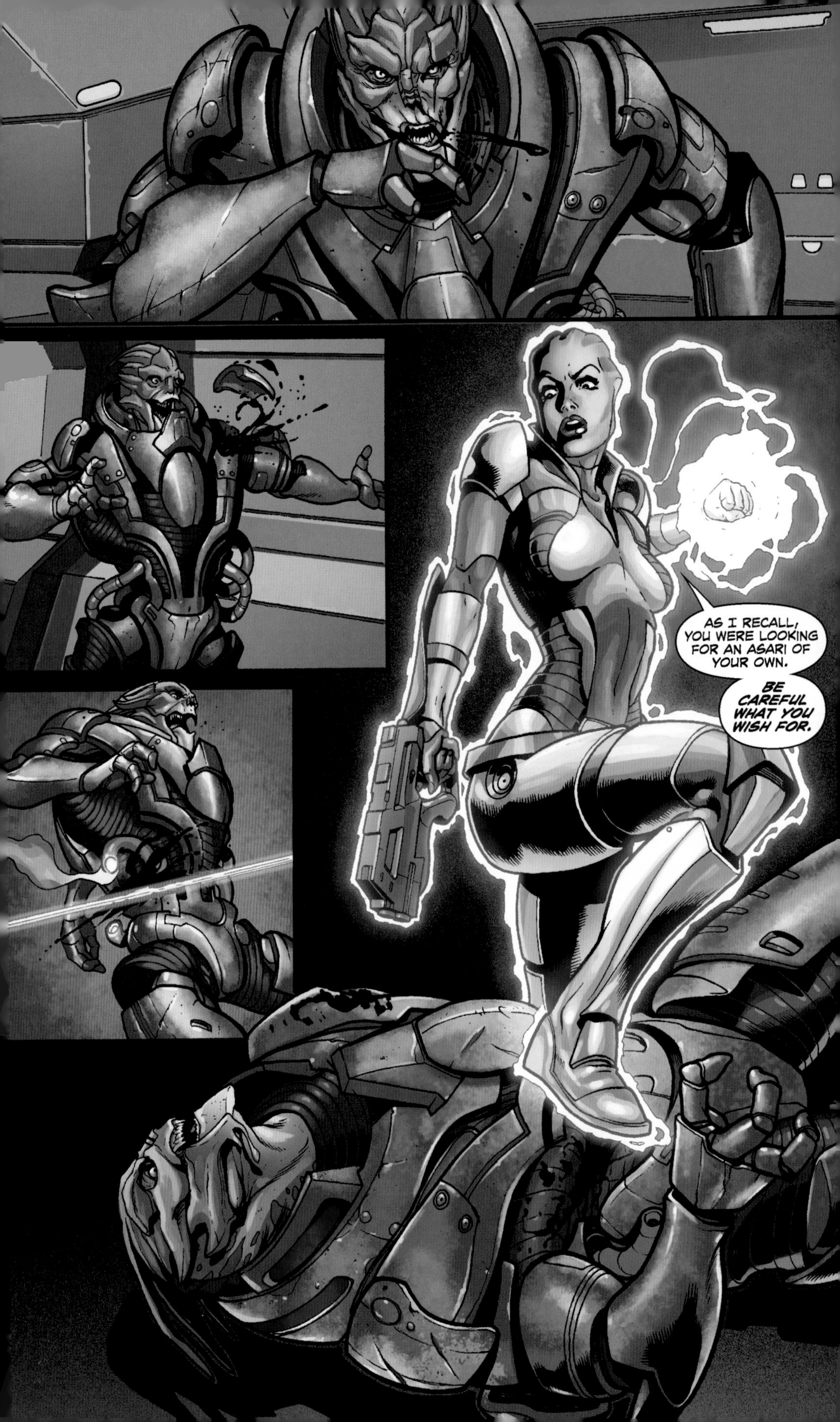
AS I RECALL, YOU WERE LOOKING FOR AN ASARI OF YOUR OWN.
BE CAREFUL WHAT YOU WISH FOR.

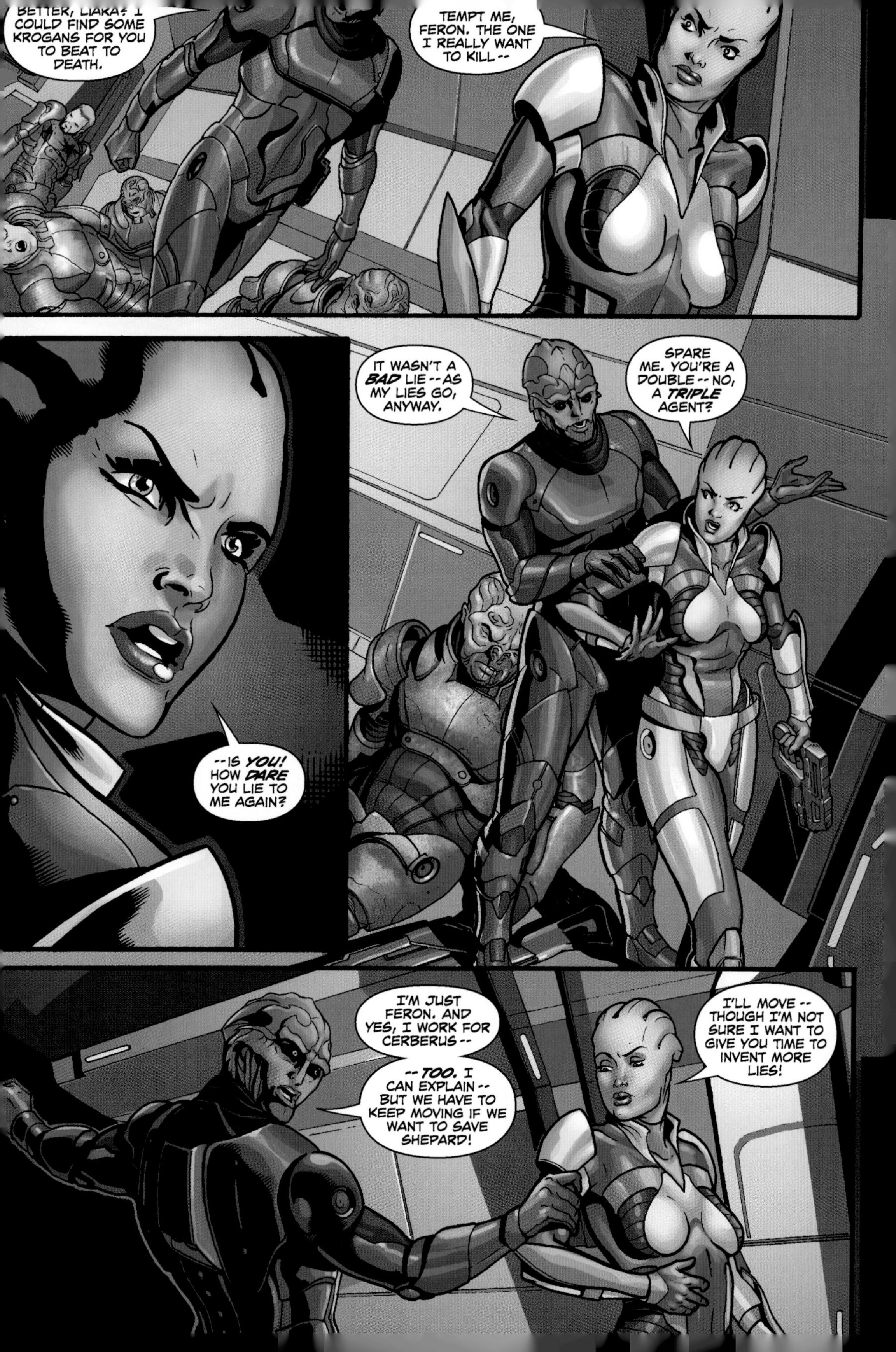
BETTER, LIARA? I COULD FIND SOME KROGANS FOR YOU TO BEAT TO DEATH.
TEMPT ME, FERON. THE ONE I REALLY WANT TO KILL --
--IS YOU! HOW DARE YOU LIE TO ME AGAIN?
IT WASN'T A BAD LIE -- AS MY LIES GO, ANYWAY.
SPARE ME. YOU'RE A DOUBLE -- NO, A TRIPLE AGENT?
I'M JUST FERON. AND YES, I WORK FOR CERBERUS --
-- TOO. I CAN EXPLAIN -- BUT WE HAVE TO KEEP MOVING IF WE WANT TO SAVE SHEPARD!
I'LL MOVE -- THOUGH I'M NOT SURE I WANT TO GIVE YOU TIME TO INVENT MORE LIES!

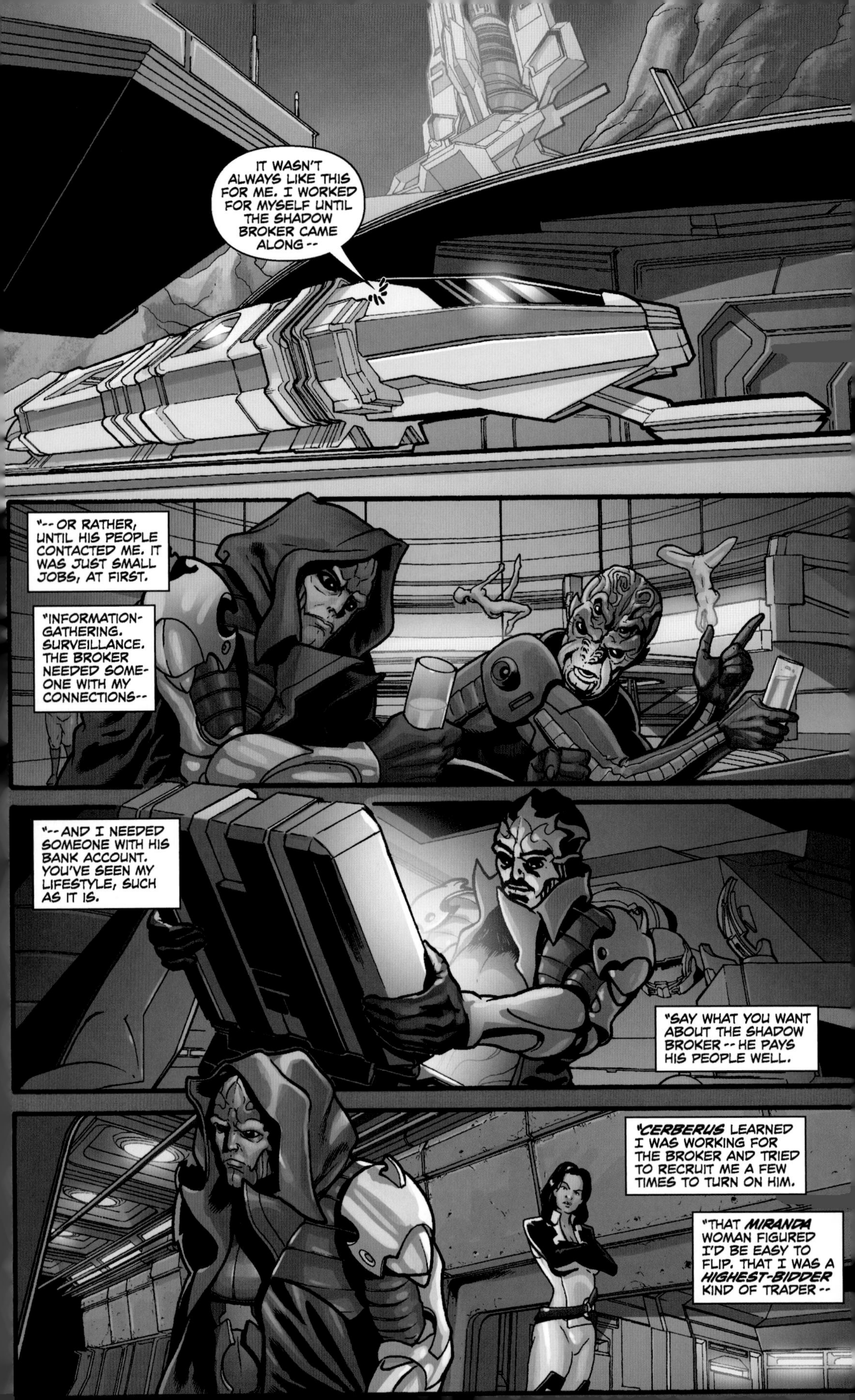
IT WASN'T ALWAYS LIKE THIS FOR ME. I WORKED FOR MYSELF UNTIL THE SHADOW BROKER CAME ALONG--
"--OR RATHER, UNTIL HIS PEOPLE CONTACTED ME. IT WAS JUST SMALL JOBS, AT FIRST.
"INFORMATION-GATHERING. SURVEILLANCE. THE BROKER NEEDED SOME-ONE WITH MY CONNECTIONS--
"--AND I NEEDED SOMEONE WITH HIS BANK ACCOUNT. YOU'VE SEEN MY LIFESTYLE, SUCH AS IT IS.
"SAY WHAT YOU WANT ABOUT THE SHADOW BROKER--HE PAYS HIS PEOPLE WELL.
"CERBERUS LEARNED I WAS WORKING FOR THE BROKER AND TRIED TO RECRUIT ME A FEW TIMES TO TURN ON HIM.
"THAT MIRANDA WOMAN FIGURED I'D BE EASY TO FLIP. THAT I WAS A HIGHEST-BIDDER KIND OF TRADER--

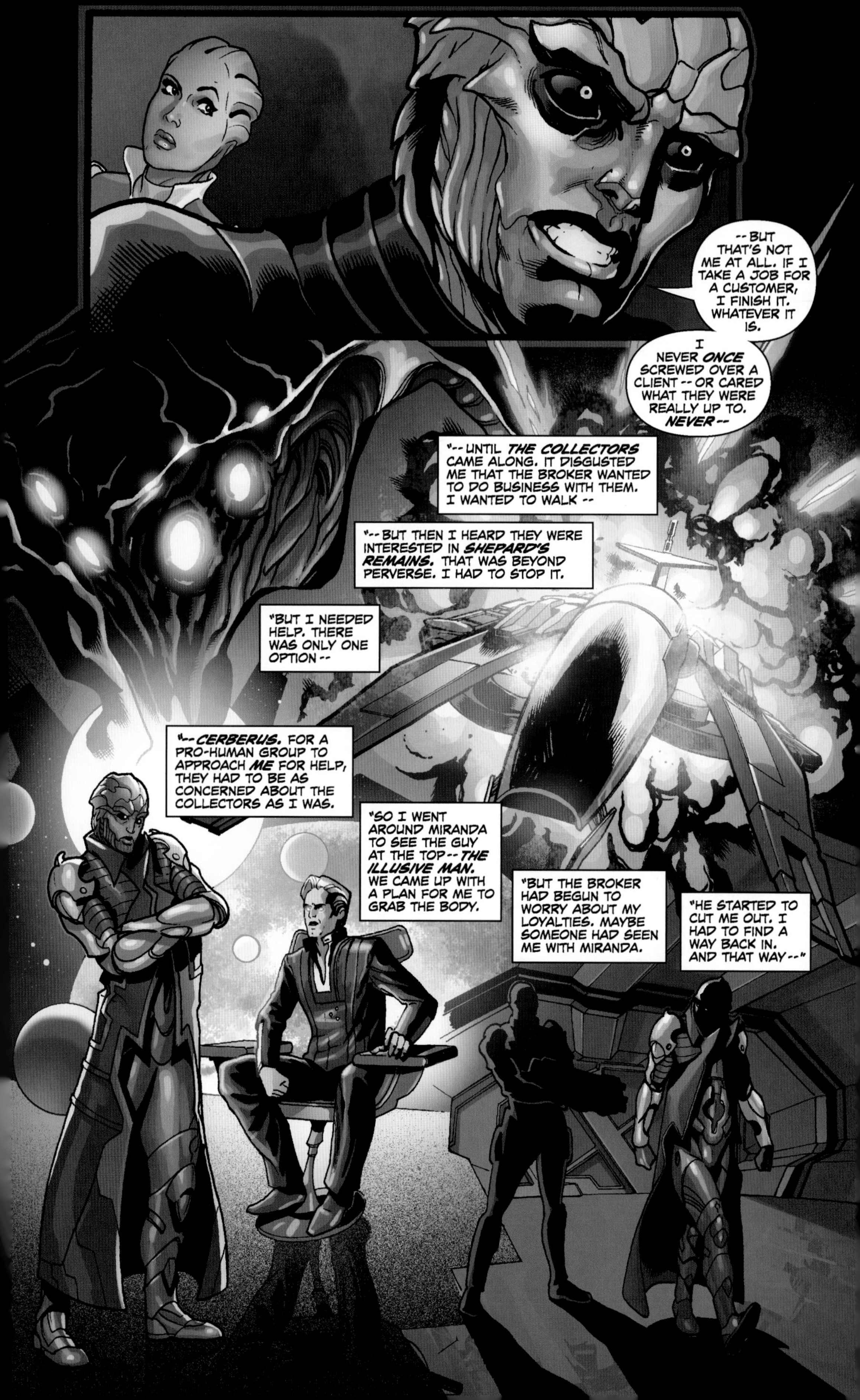
--BUT THAT'S NOT ME AT ALL. IF I TAKE A JOB FOR A CUSTOMER, I FINISH IT. WHATEVER IT IS.
I NEVER ONCE SCREWED OVER A CLIENT--OR CARED WHAT THEY WERE REALLY UP TO. NEVER--
"--UNTIL THE COLLECTORS CAME ALONG. IT DISGUSTED ME THAT THE BROKER WANTED TO DO BUSINESS WITH THEM. I WANTED TO WALK--
"--BUT THEN I HEARD THEY WERE INTERESTED IN SHEPARD'S REMAINS. THAT WAS BEYOND PERVERSE. I HAD TO STOP IT.
"BUT I NEEDED HELP. THERE WAS ONLY ONE OPTION--
"--CERBERUS. FOR A PRO-HUMAN GROUP TO APPROACH ME FOR HELP, THEY HAD TO BE AS CONCERNED ABOUT THE COLLECTORS AS I WAS.
"SO I WENT AROUND MIRANDA TO SEE THE GUY AT THE TOP--THE ILLUSIVE MAN. WE CAME UP WITH A PLAN FOR ME TO GRAB THE BODY.
"BUT THE BROKER HAD BEGUN TO WORRY ABOUT MY LOYALTIES. MAYBE SOMEONE HAD SEEN ME WITH MIRANDA.
"HE STARTED TO CUT ME OUT. I HAD TO FIND A WAY BACK IN. AND THAT WAY--"

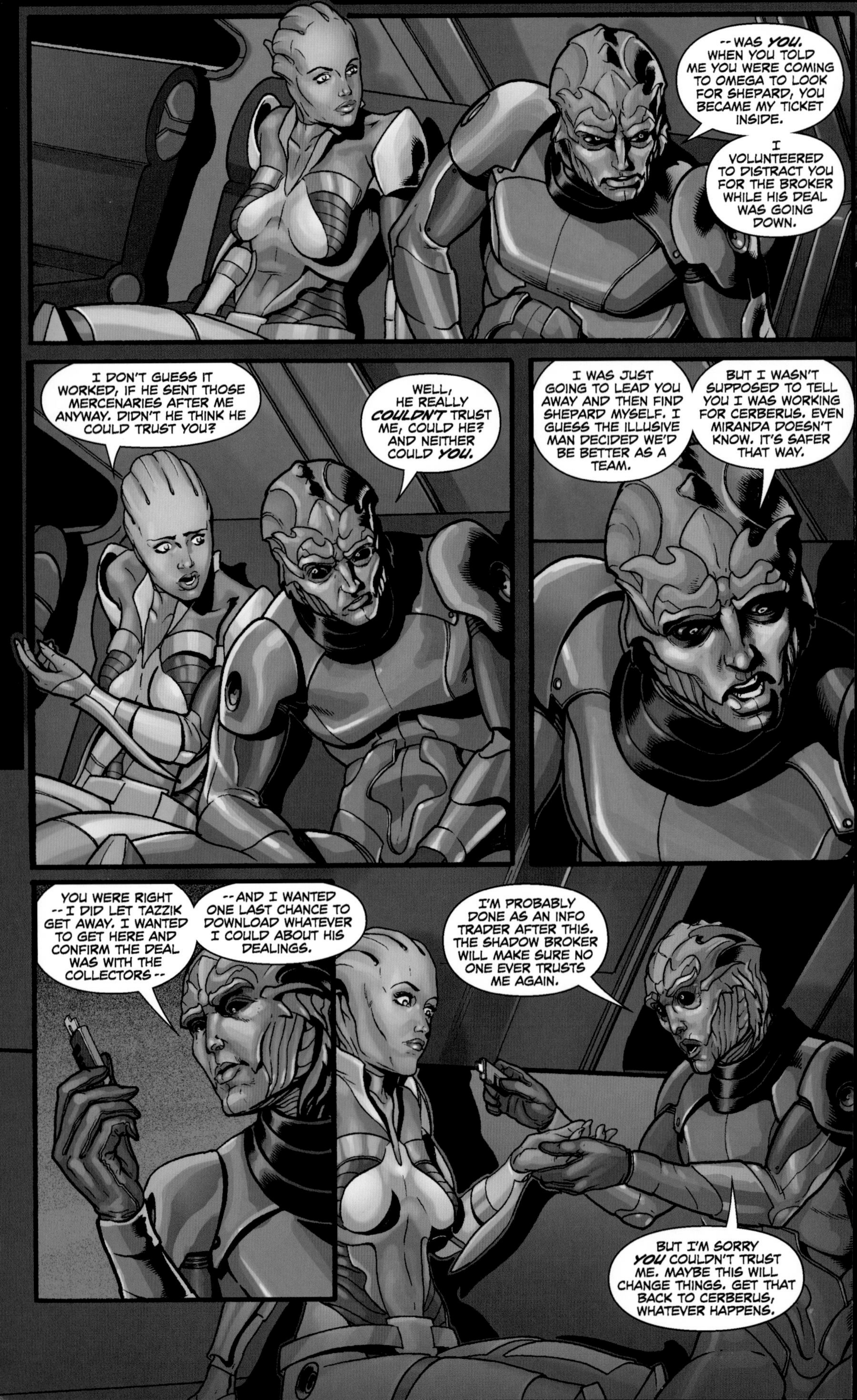

--WAS YOU. WHEN YOU TOLD ME YOU WERE COMING TO OMEGA TO LOOK FOR SHEPARD, YOU BECAME MY TICKET INSIDE.
I VOLUNTEERED TO DISTRACT YOU FOR THE BROKER WHILE HIS DEAL WAS GOING DOWN.
I DON'T GUESS IT WORKED, IF HE SENT THOSE MERCENARIES AFTER ME ANYWAY. DIDN'T HE THINK HE COULD TRUST YOU?
WELL, HE REALLY COULDN'T TRUST ME, COULD HE? AND NEITHER COULD YOU.
I WAS JUST GOING TO LEAD YOU AWAY AND THEN FIND SHEPARD MYSELF. I GUESS THE ILLUSIVE MAN DECIDED WE'D BE BETTER AS A TEAM.
BUT I WASN'T SUPPOSED TO TELL YOU I WAS WORKING FOR CERBERUS. EVEN MIRANDA DOESN'T KNOW. IT'S SAFER THAT WAY.
YOU WERE RIGHT --I DID LET TAZZIK GET AWAY. I WANTED TO GET HERE AND CONFIRM THE DEAL WAS WITH THE COLLECTORS--
--AND I WANTED ONE LAST CHANCE TO DOWNLOAD WHATEVER I COULD ABOUT HIS DEALINGS.
I'M PROBABLY DONE AS AN INFO TRADER AFTER THIS. THE SHADOW BROKER WILL MAKE SURE NO ONE EVER TRUSTS ME AGAIN.
BUT I'M SORRY YOU COULDN'T TRUST ME. MAYBE THIS WILL CHANGE THINGS. GET THAT BACK TO CERBERUS, WHATEVER HAPPENS.

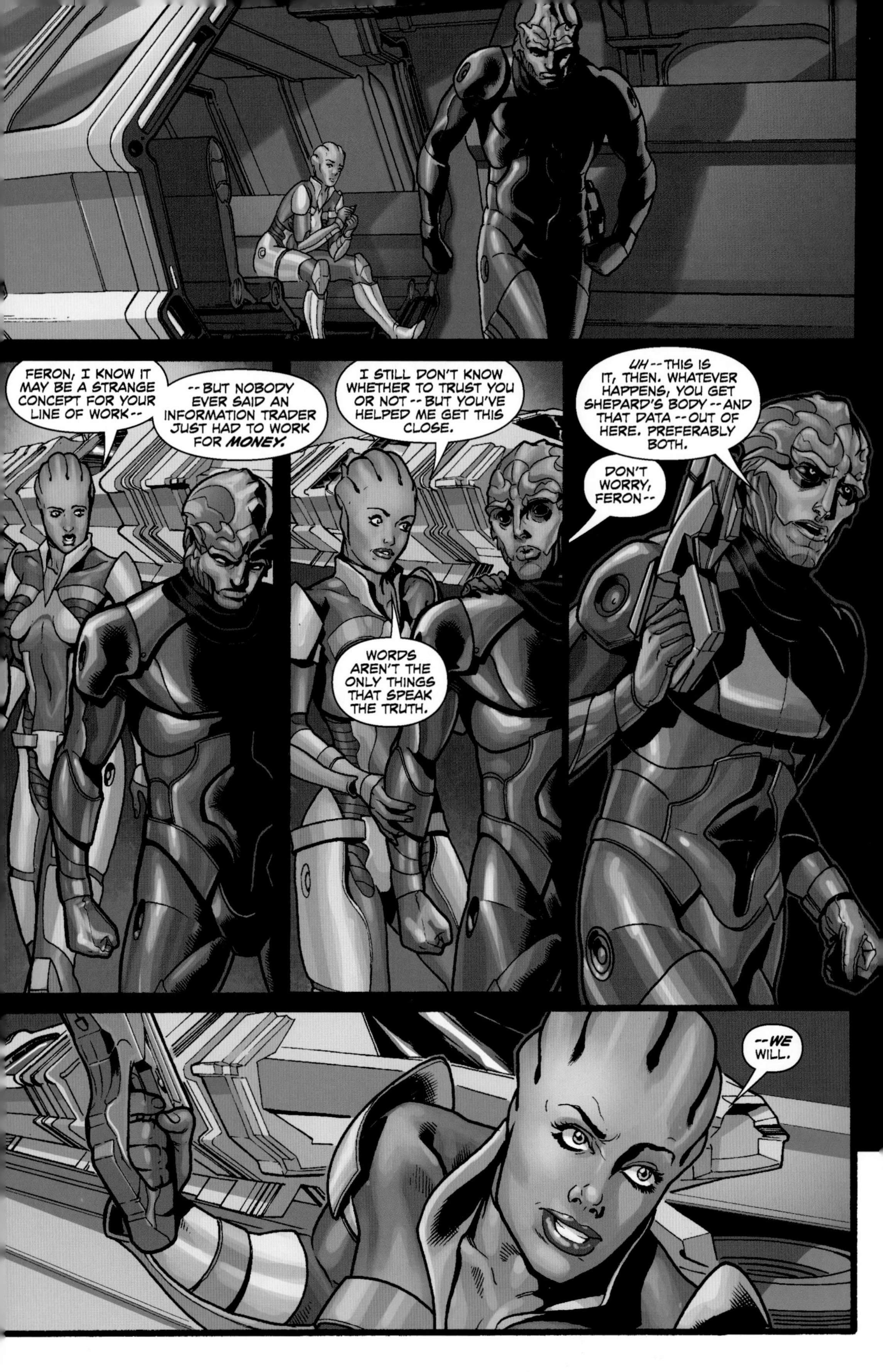
FERON, I KNOW IT MAY BE A STRANGE CONCEPT FOR YOUR LINE OF WORK--
--BUT NOBODY EVER SAID AN INFORMATION TRADER JUST HAD TO WORK FOR *MONEY.*
I STILL DON'T KNOW WHETHER TO TRUST YOU OR NOT--BUT YOU'VE HELPED ME GET THIS CLOSE.
WORDS AREN'T THE ONLY THINGS THAT SPEAK THE TRUTH.
UH--THIS IS IT, THEN. WHATEVER HAPPENS, YOU GET SHEPARD'S BODY--AND THAT DATA--OUT OF HERE. PREFERABLY BOTH.
DON'T WORRY, FERON--
--*WE* WILL.

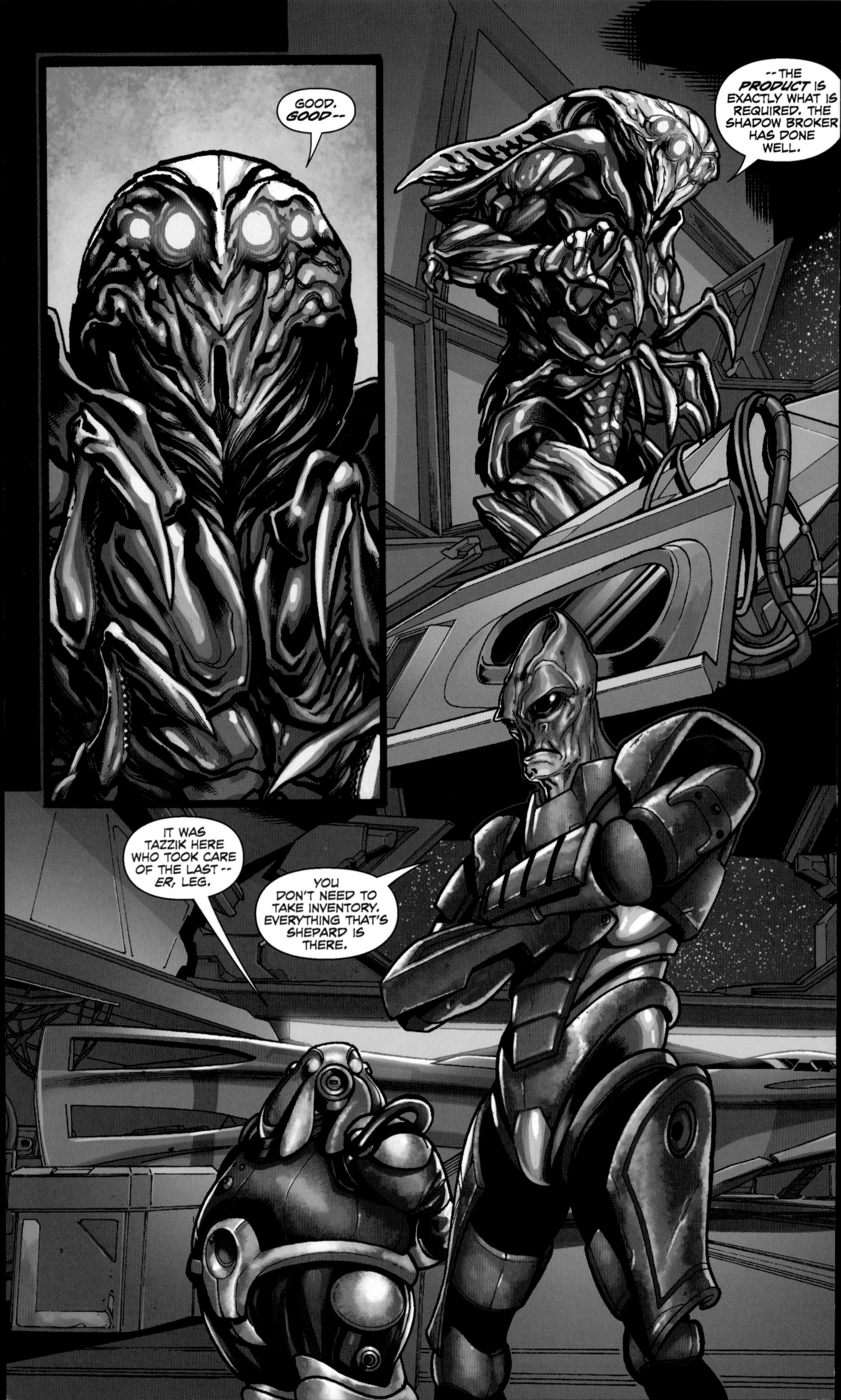
GOOD. GOOD--
--THE PRODUCT IS EXACTLY WHAT IS REQUIRED. THE SHADOW BROKER HAS DONE WELL.
IT WAS TAZZIK HERE WHO TOOK CARE OF THE LAST-- ER, LEG.
YOU DON'T NEED TO TAKE INVENTORY. EVERYTHING THAT'S SHEPARD IS THERE.

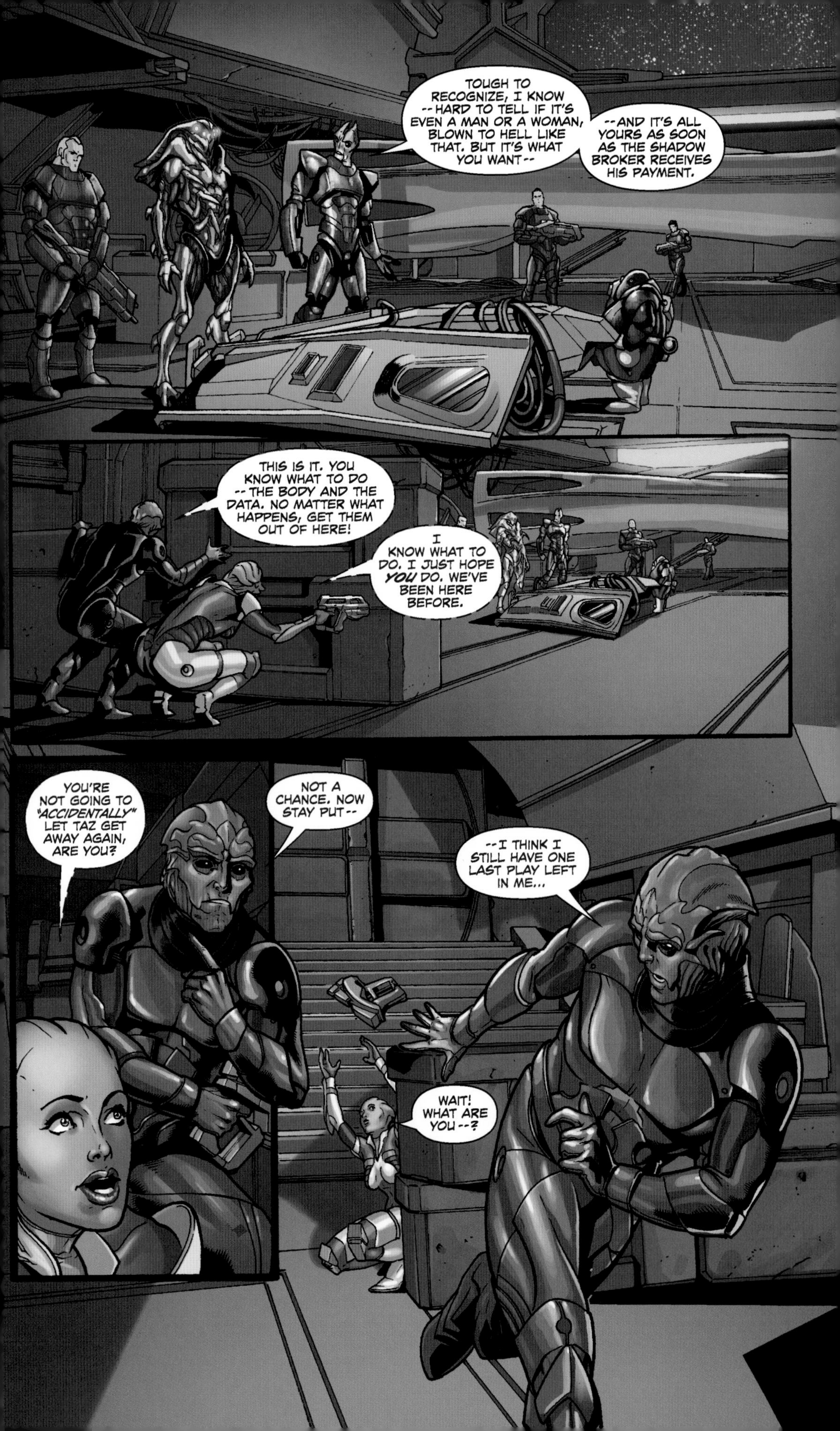
TOUGH TO RECOGNIZE, I KNOW --HARD TO TELL IF IT'S EVEN A MAN OR A WOMAN, BLOWN TO HELL LIKE THAT. BUT IT'S WHAT YOU WANT--
--AND IT'S ALL YOURS AS SOON AS THE SHADOW BROKER RECEIVES HIS PAYMENT.
THIS IS IT. YOU KNOW WHAT TO DO --THE BODY AND THE DATA. NO MATTER WHAT HAPPENS, GET THEM OUT OF HERE!
I KNOW WHAT TO DO. I JUST HOPE *YOU* DO. WE'VE BEEN HERE BEFORE.
YOU'RE NOT GOING TO *"ACCIDENTALLY"* LET TAZ GET AWAY AGAIN, ARE YOU?
NOT A CHANCE. NOW STAY PUT--
--I THINK I STILL HAVE ONE LAST PLAY LEFT IN ME...
WAIT! WHAT ARE YOU--?

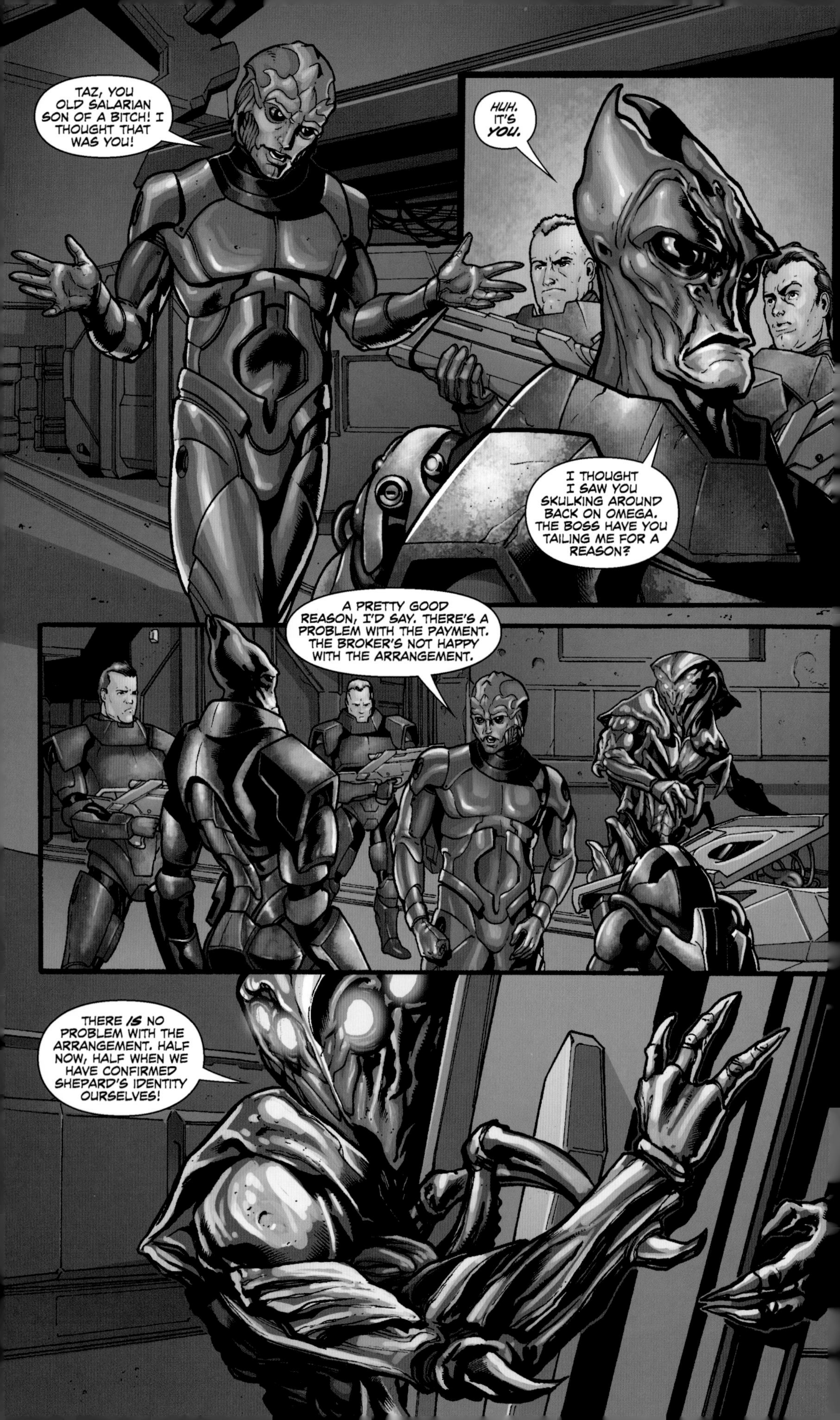
TAZ, YOU OLD SALARIAN SON OF A BITCH! I THOUGHT THAT WAS YOU!
HUH. IT'S *YOU.*
I THOUGHT I SAW YOU SKULKING AROUND BACK ON OMEGA. THE BOSS HAVE YOU TAILING ME FOR A REASON?
A PRETTY GOOD REASON, I'D SAY. THERE'S A PROBLEM WITH THE PAYMENT. THE BROKER'S NOT HAPPY WITH THE ARRANGEMENT.
THERE *IS* NO PROBLEM WITH THE ARRANGEMENT. HALF NOW, HALF WHEN WE HAVE CONFIRMED SHEPARD'S IDENTITY OURSELVES!

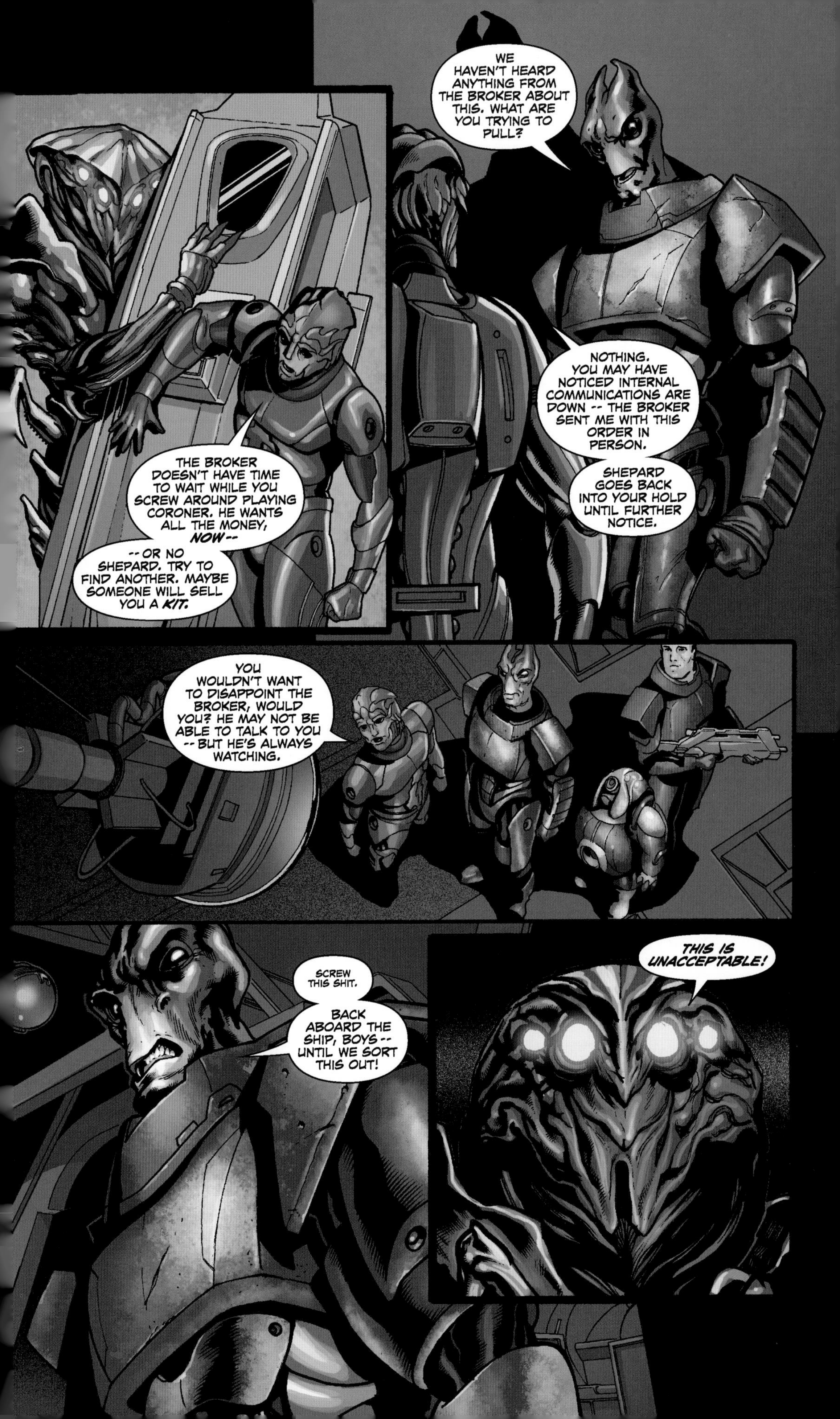
WE HAVEN'T HEARD ANYTHING FROM THE BROKER ABOUT THIS. WHAT ARE YOU TRYING TO PULL?
THE BROKER DOESN'T HAVE TIME TO WAIT WHILE YOU SCREW AROUND PLAYING CORONER. HE WANTS ALL THE MONEY, NOW--
--OR NO SHEPARD. TRY TO FIND ANOTHER. MAYBE SOMEONE WILL SELL YOU A KIT.
NOTHING. YOU MAY HAVE NOTICED INTERNAL COMMUNICATIONS ARE DOWN -- THE BROKER SENT ME WITH THIS ORDER IN PERSON.
SHEPARD GOES BACK INTO YOUR HOLD UNTIL FURTHER NOTICE.
YOU WOULDN'T WANT TO DISAPPOINT THE BROKER, WOULD YOU? HE MAY NOT BE ABLE TO TALK TO YOU --BUT HE'S ALWAYS WATCHING.
SCREW THIS SHIT.
BACK ABOARD THE SHIP, BOYS-- UNTIL WE SORT THIS OUT!
THIS IS UNACCEPTABLE!

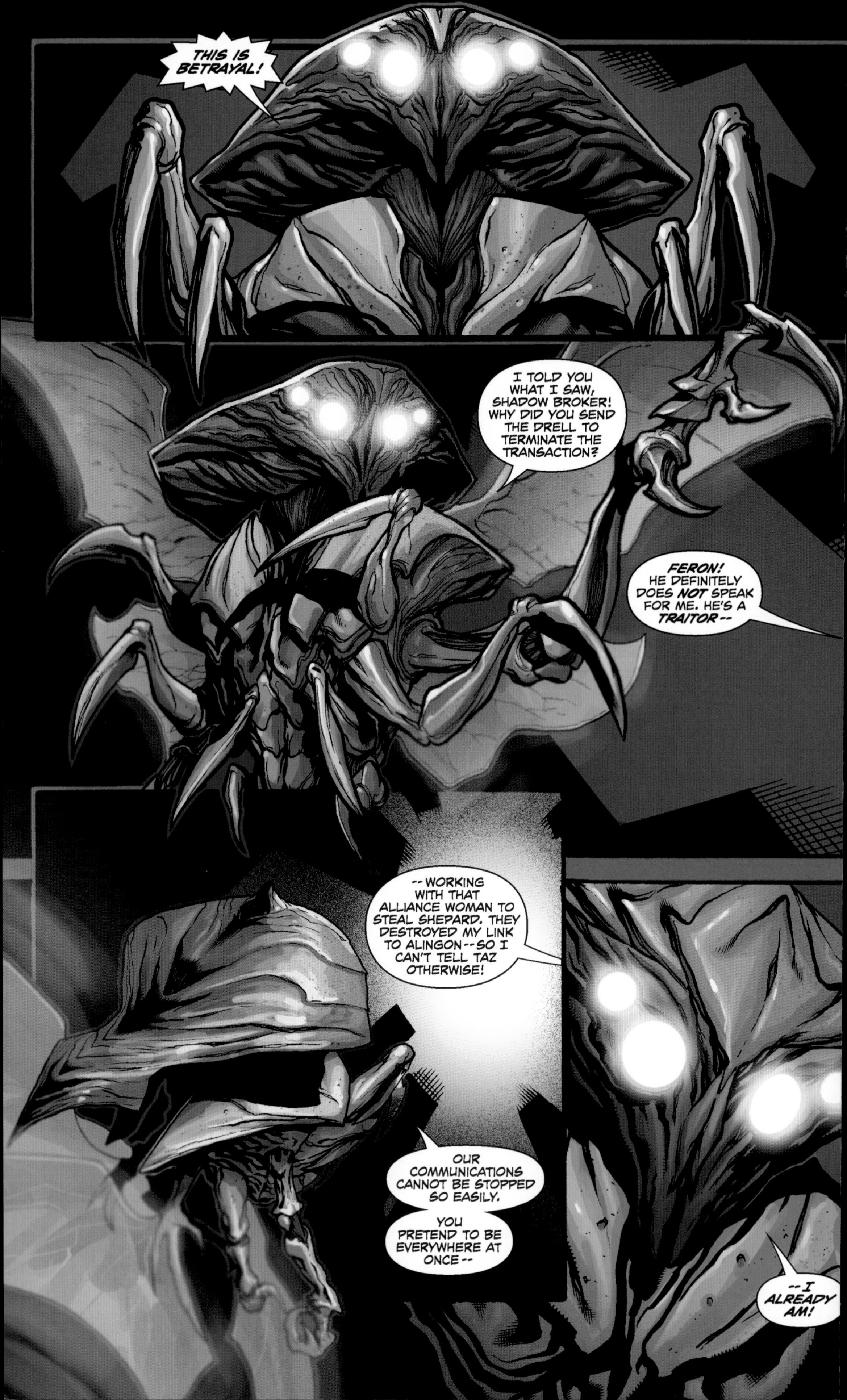
THIS IS BETRAYAL!
I TOLD YOU WHAT I SAW, SHADOW BROKER! WHY DID YOU SEND THE DRELL TO TERMINATE THE TRANSACTION?
FERON! HE DEFINITELY DOES NOT SPEAK FOR ME. HE'S A TRAITOR--
--WORKING WITH THAT ALLIANCE WOMAN TO STEAL SHEPARD. THEY DESTROYED MY LINK TO ALINGON--SO I CAN'T TELL TAZ OTHERWISE!
OUR COMMUNICATIONS CANNOT BE STOPPED SO EASILY.
YOU PRETEND TO BE EVERYWHERE AT ONCE--
--I ALREADY AM!

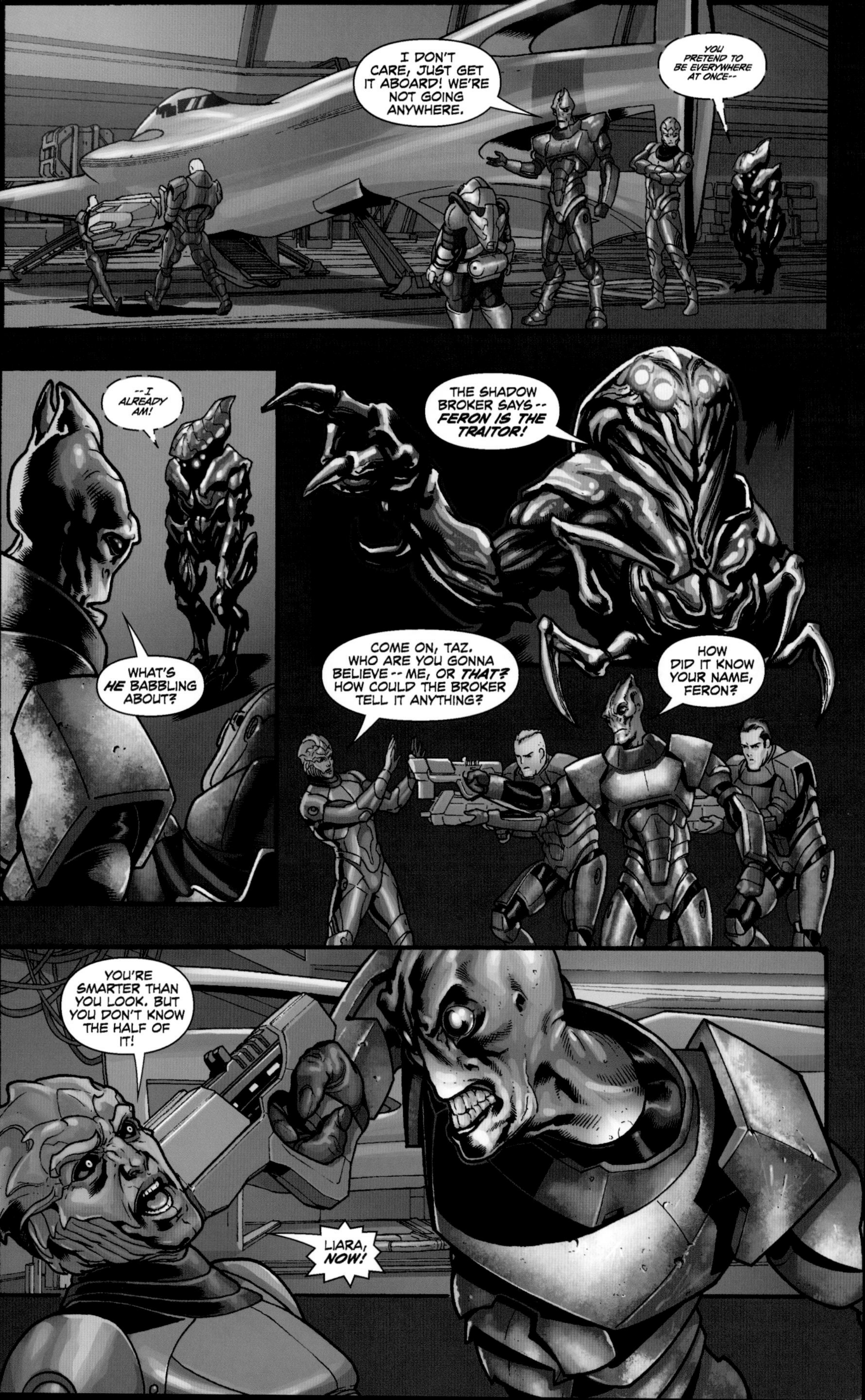
I DON'T CARE, JUST GET IT ABOARD! WE'RE NOT GOING ANYWHERE.
YOU PRETEND TO BE EVERYWHERE AT ONCE--
--I ALREADY AM!
WHAT'S *HE* BABBLING ABOUT?
THE SHADOW BROKER SAYS-- *FERON IS THE TRAITOR!*
COME ON, TAZ. WHO ARE YOU GONNA BELIEVE--ME, OR *THAT?* HOW COULD THE BROKER TELL IT ANYTHING?
HOW DID IT KNOW YOUR NAME, FERON?
YOU'RE SMARTER THAN YOU LOOK. BUT YOU DON'T KNOW THE HALF OF IT!
LIARA, *NOW!*

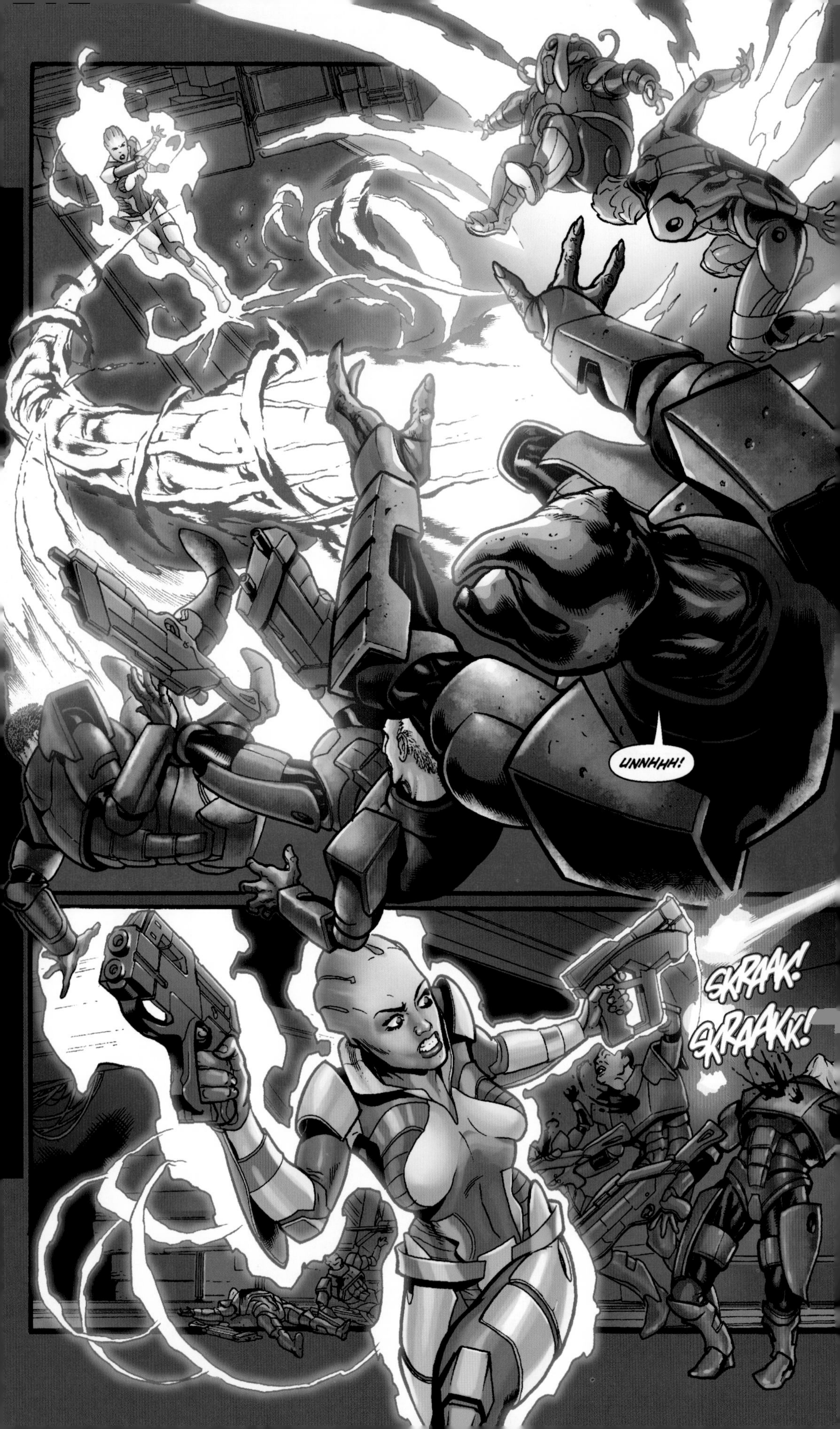
UNNHHH!
SKRAAK!
SKRAAKK!

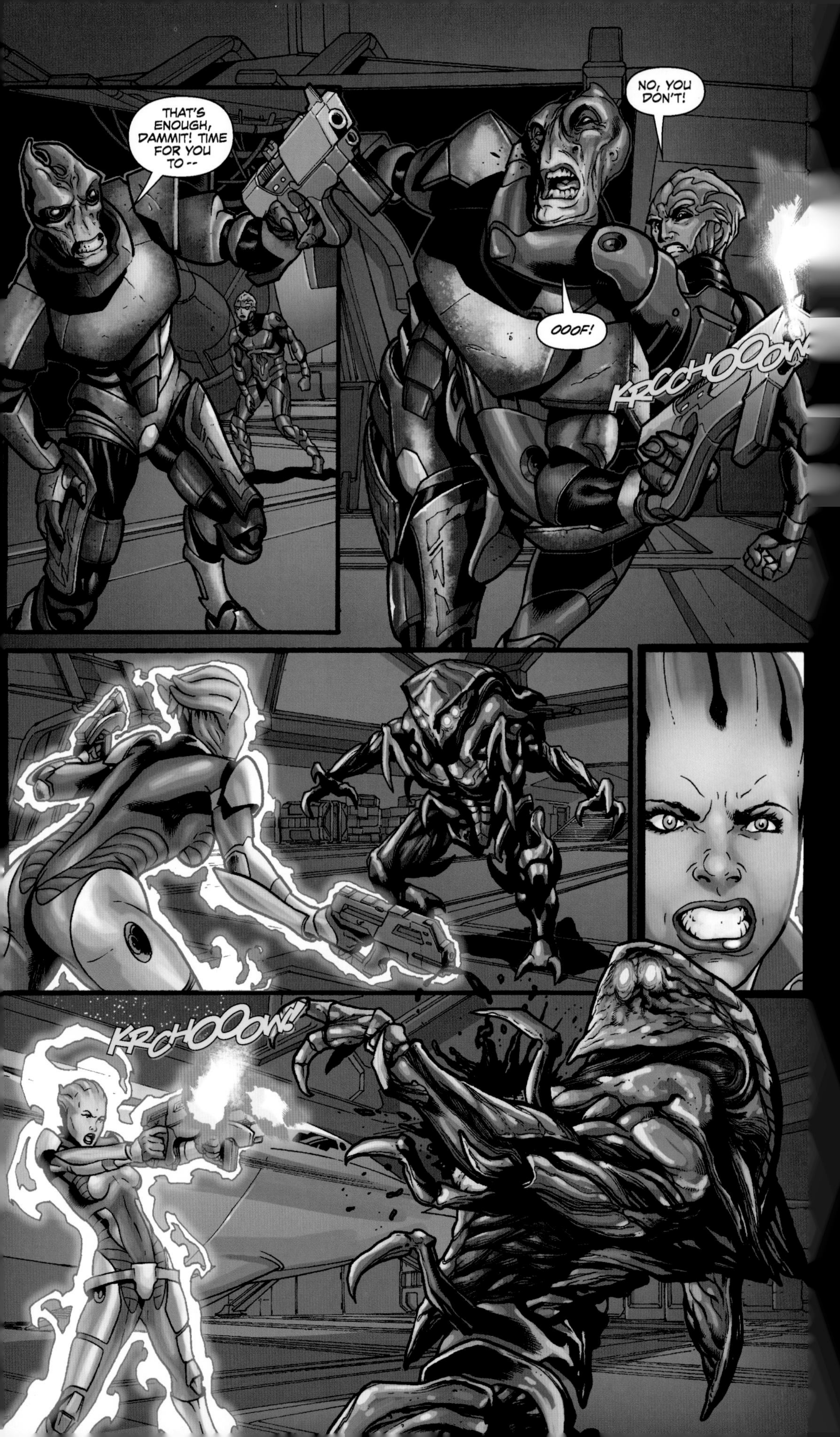
THAT'S ENOUGH, DAMMIT! TIME FOR YOU TO --
NO, YOU DON'T!
OOOF!
KRCCHOOOOW!
KRCHOOOOW!

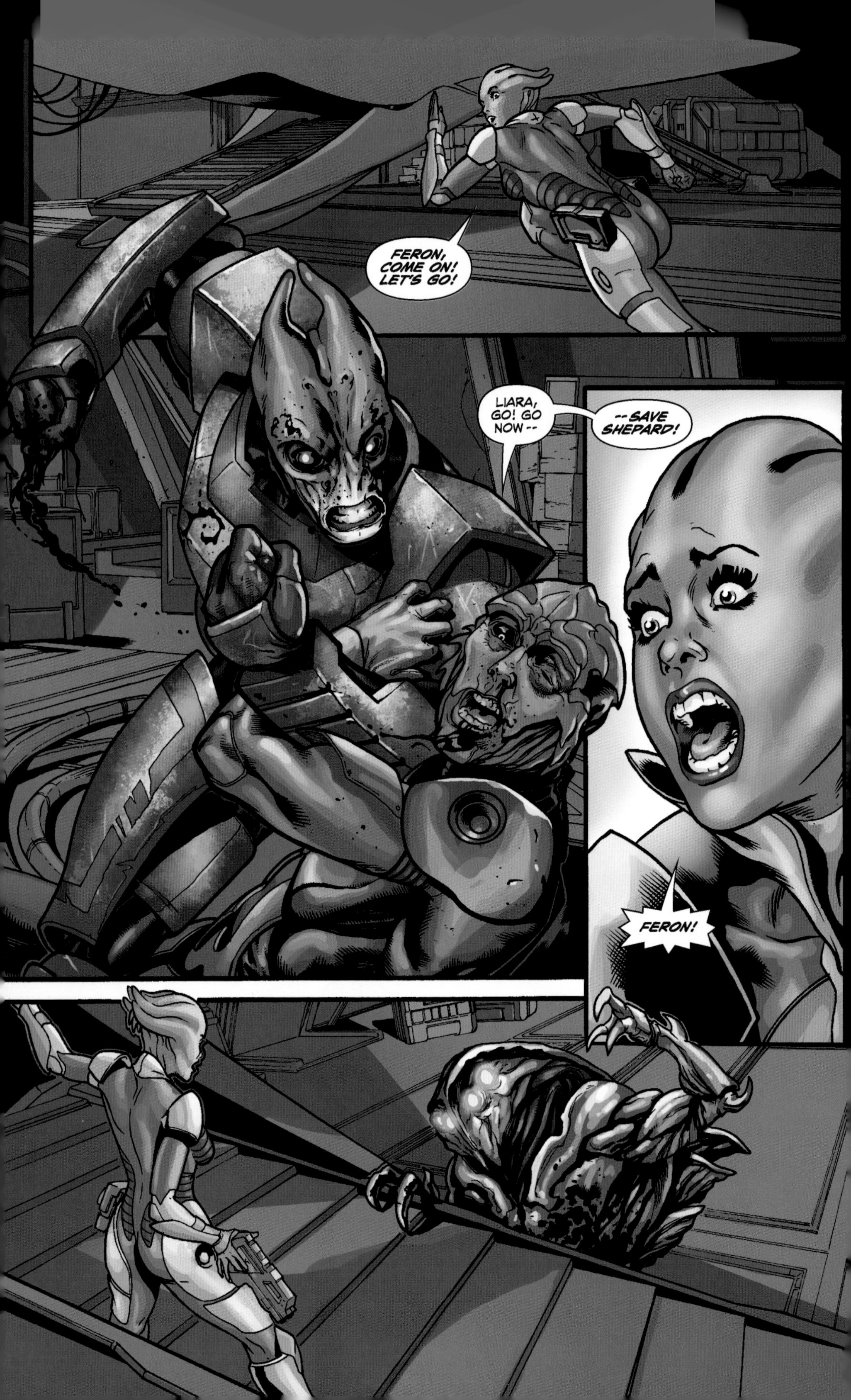
FERON, COME ON! LET'S GO!
LIARA, GO! GO NOW --
-- SAVE SHEPARD!
FERON!

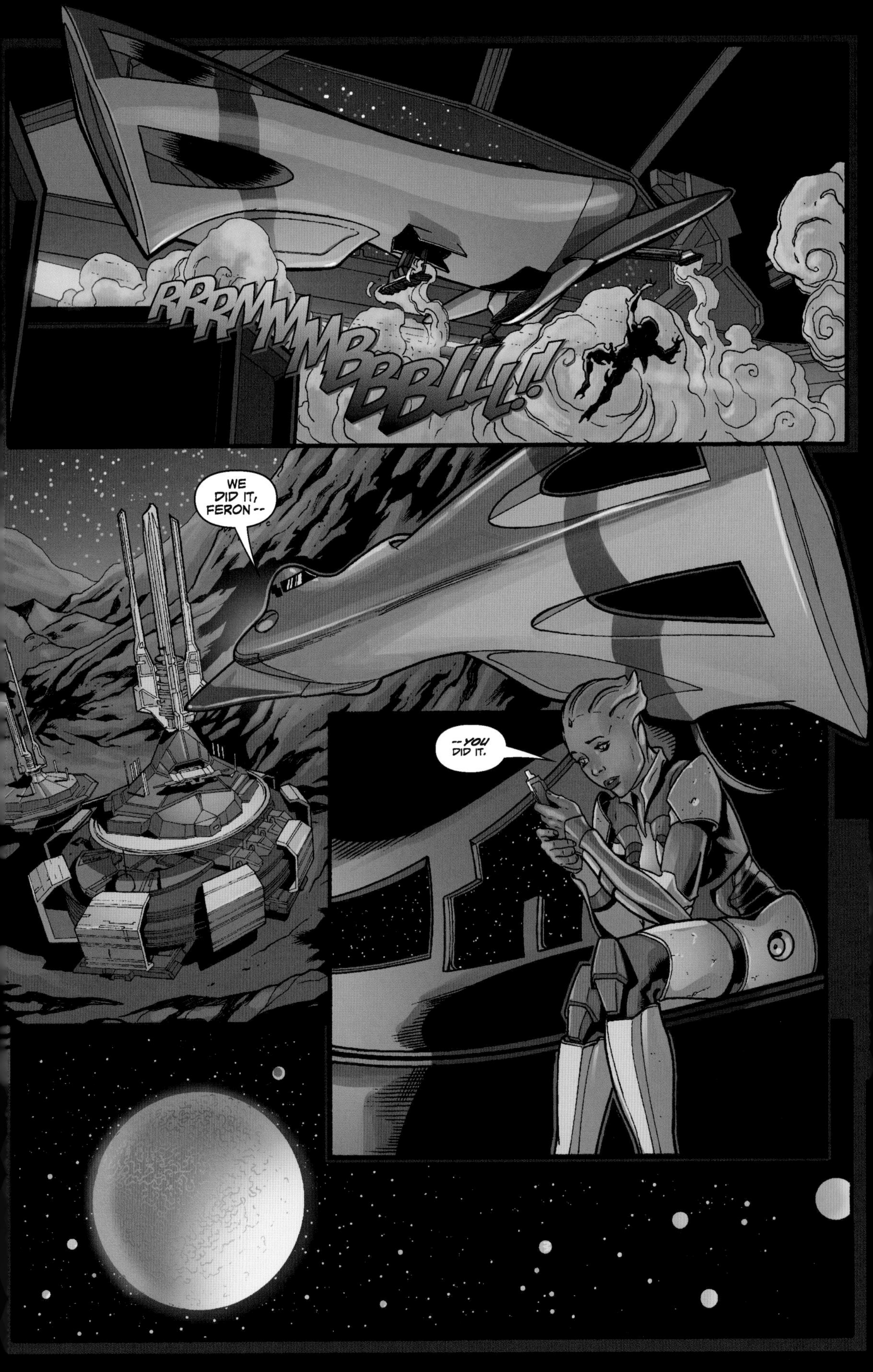
RRRMMMBBBLLL!!
WE DID IT, FERON --
-- YOU DID IT.

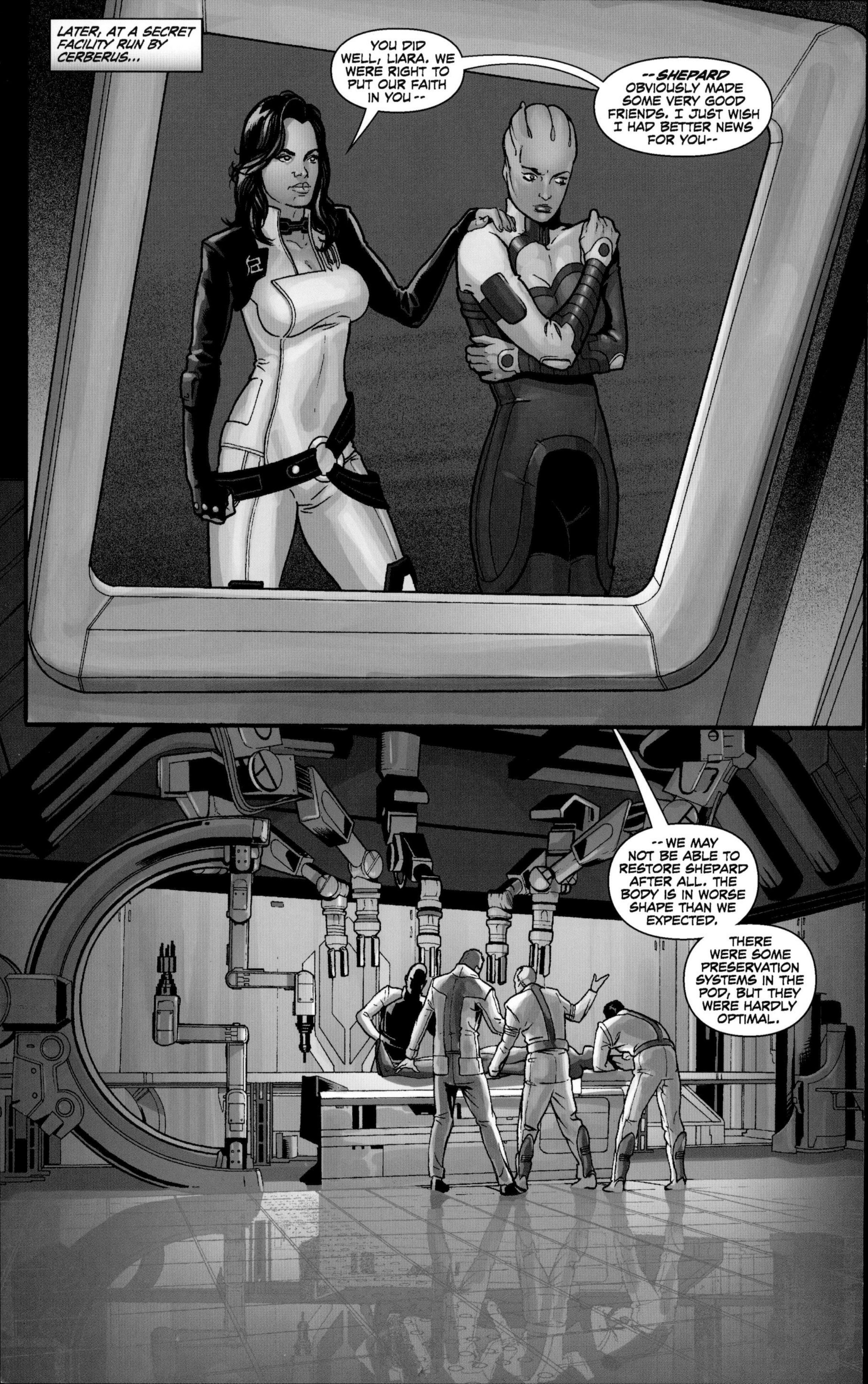
LATER, AT A SECRET FACILITY RUN BY CERBERUS...
YOU DID WELL, LIARA. WE WERE RIGHT TO PUT OUR FAITH IN YOU --
--SHEPARD OBVIOUSLY MADE SOME VERY GOOD FRIENDS. I JUST WISH I HAD BETTER NEWS FOR YOU--
--WE MAY NOT BE ABLE TO RESTORE SHEPARD AFTER ALL. THE BODY IS IN WORSE SHAPE THAN WE EXPECTED.
THERE WERE SOME PRESERVATION SYSTEMS IN THE POD, BUT THEY WERE HARDLY OPTIMAL.

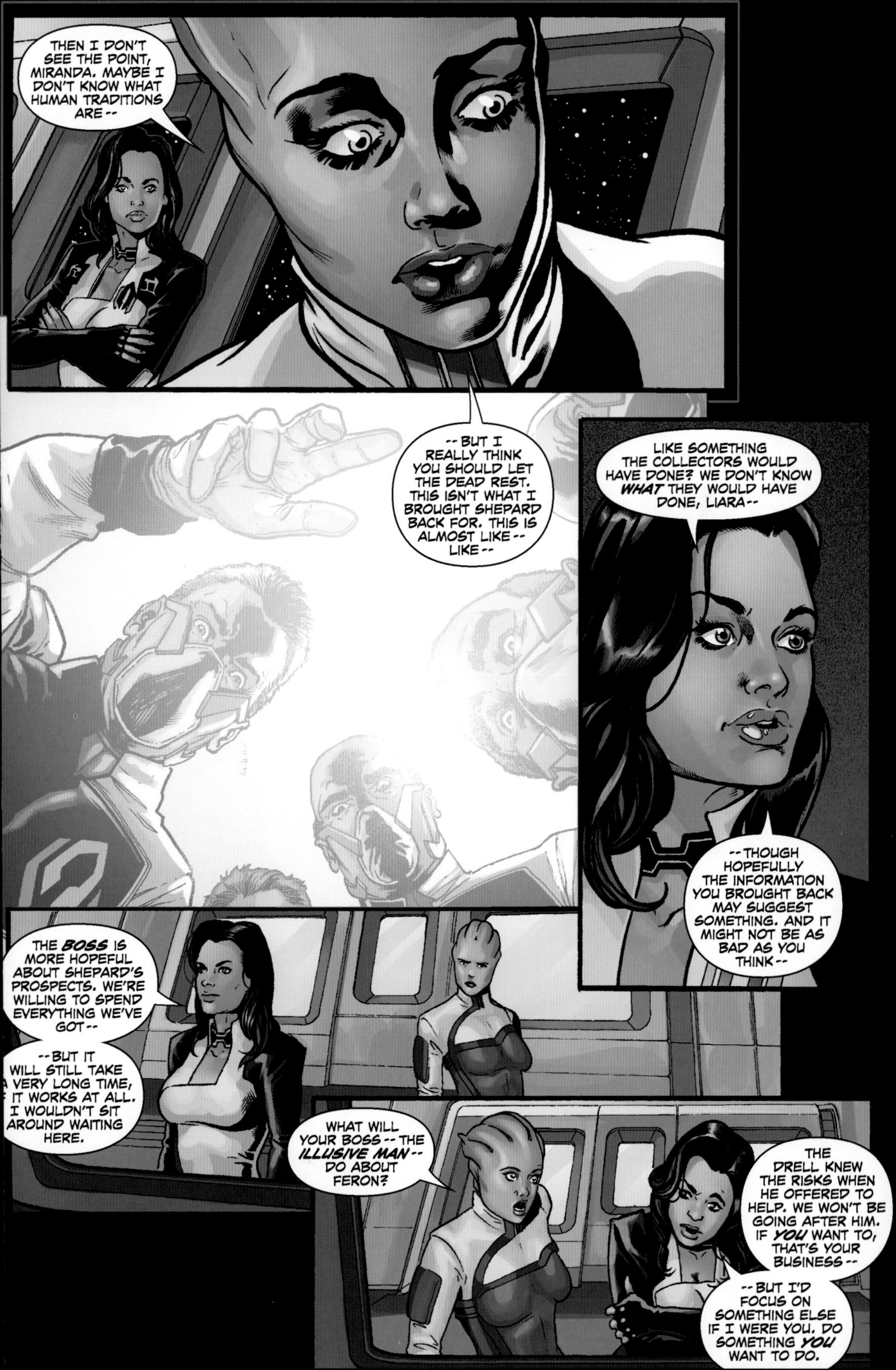
THEN I DON'T SEE THE POINT, MIRANDA. MAYBE I DON'T KNOW WHAT HUMAN TRADITIONS ARE--
--BUT I REALLY THINK YOU SHOULD LET THE DEAD REST. THIS ISN'T WHAT I BROUGHT SHEPARD BACK FOR. THIS IS ALMOST LIKE-- LIKE--
LIKE SOMETHING THE COLLECTORS WOULD HAVE DONE? WE DON'T KNOW *WHAT* THEY WOULD HAVE DONE, LIARA--
--THOUGH HOPEFULLY THE INFORMATION YOU BROUGHT BACK MAY SUGGEST SOMETHING. AND IT MIGHT NOT BE AS BAD AS YOU THINK--
THE *BOSS* IS MORE HOPEFUL ABOUT SHEPARD'S PROSPECTS. WE'RE WILLING TO SPEND EVERYTHING WE'VE GOT--
--BUT IT WILL STILL TAKE A VERY LONG TIME, IF IT WORKS AT ALL. I WOULDN'T SIT AROUND WAITING HERE.
WHAT WILL YOUR BOSS-- THE *ILLUSIVE MAN*-- DO ABOUT FERON?
THE DRELL KNEW THE RISKS WHEN HE OFFERED TO HELP. WE WON'T BE GOING AFTER HIM. IF *YOU* WANT TO, THAT'S YOUR BUSINESS--
--BUT I'D FOCUS ON SOMETHING ELSE IF I WERE YOU. DO SOMETHING *YOU* WANT TO DO.

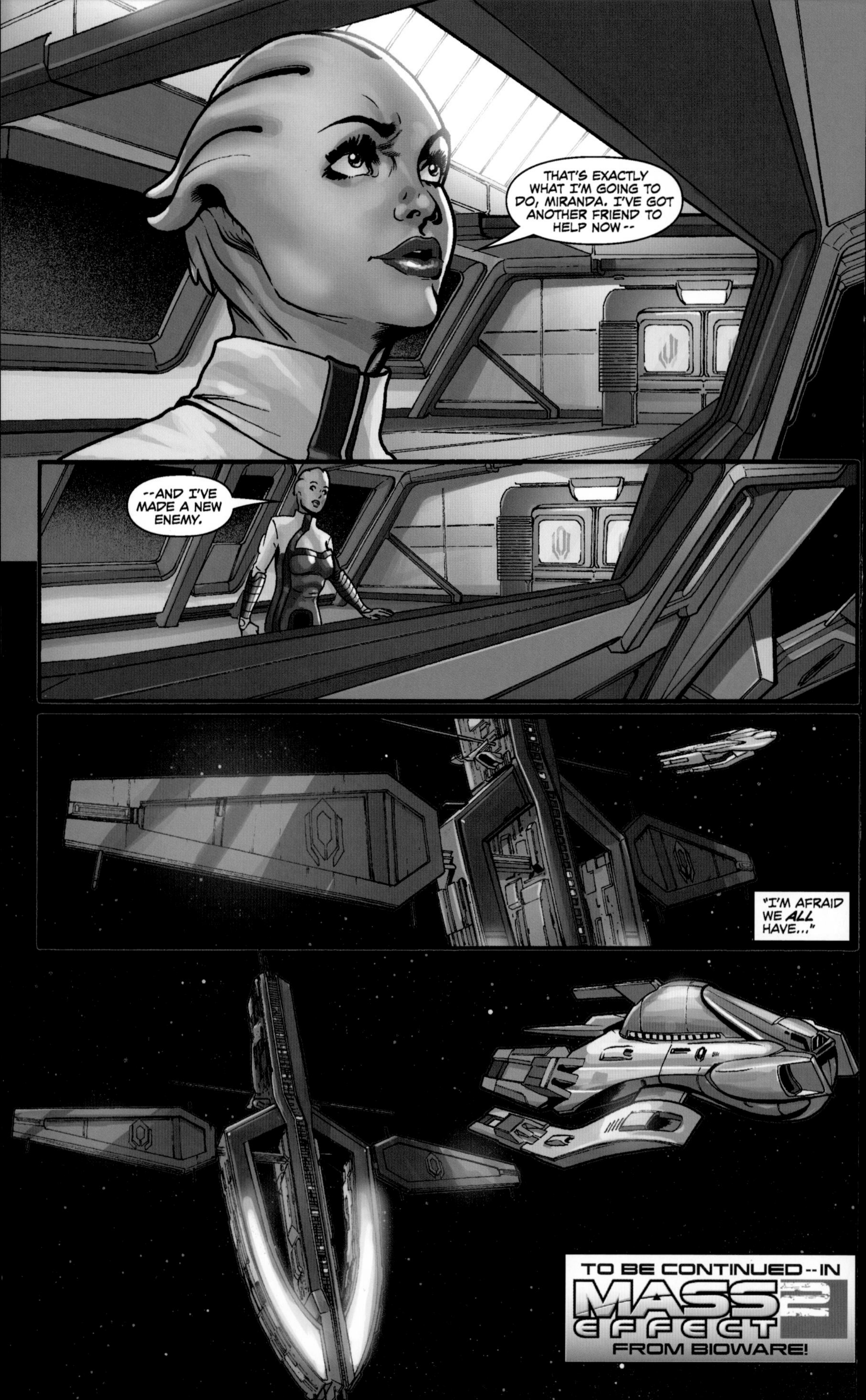
THAT'S EXACTLY WHAT I'M GOING TO DO, MIRANDA. I'VE GOT ANOTHER FRIEND TO HELP NOW--
--AND I'VE MADE A NEW ENEMY.
"I'M AFRAID WE ALL HAVE..."
TO BE CONTINUED--IN MASS EFFECT 2 FROM BIOWARE!

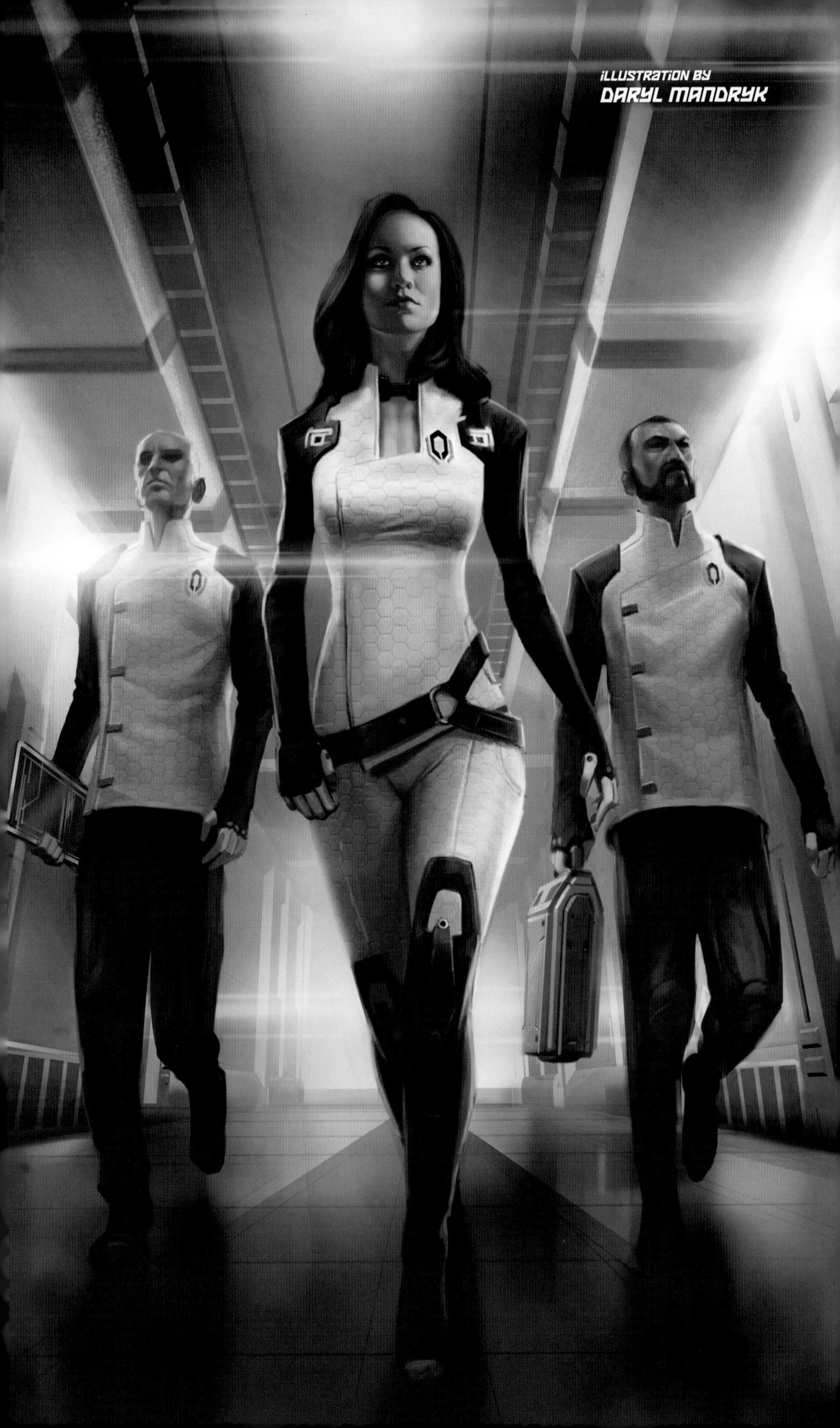

ILLUSTRATION BY
DARYL MANDRYK

BY OMAR FRANCIA

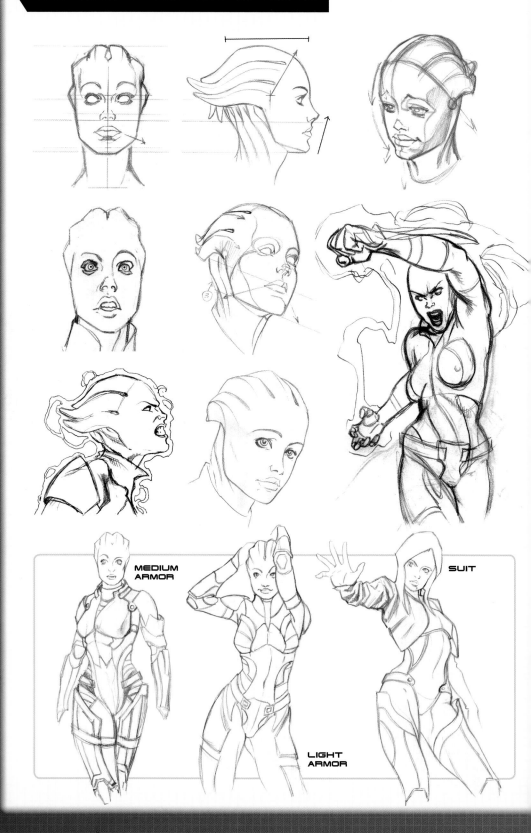

MEDIUM
ARMOR

SUIT

LIGHT
ARMOR

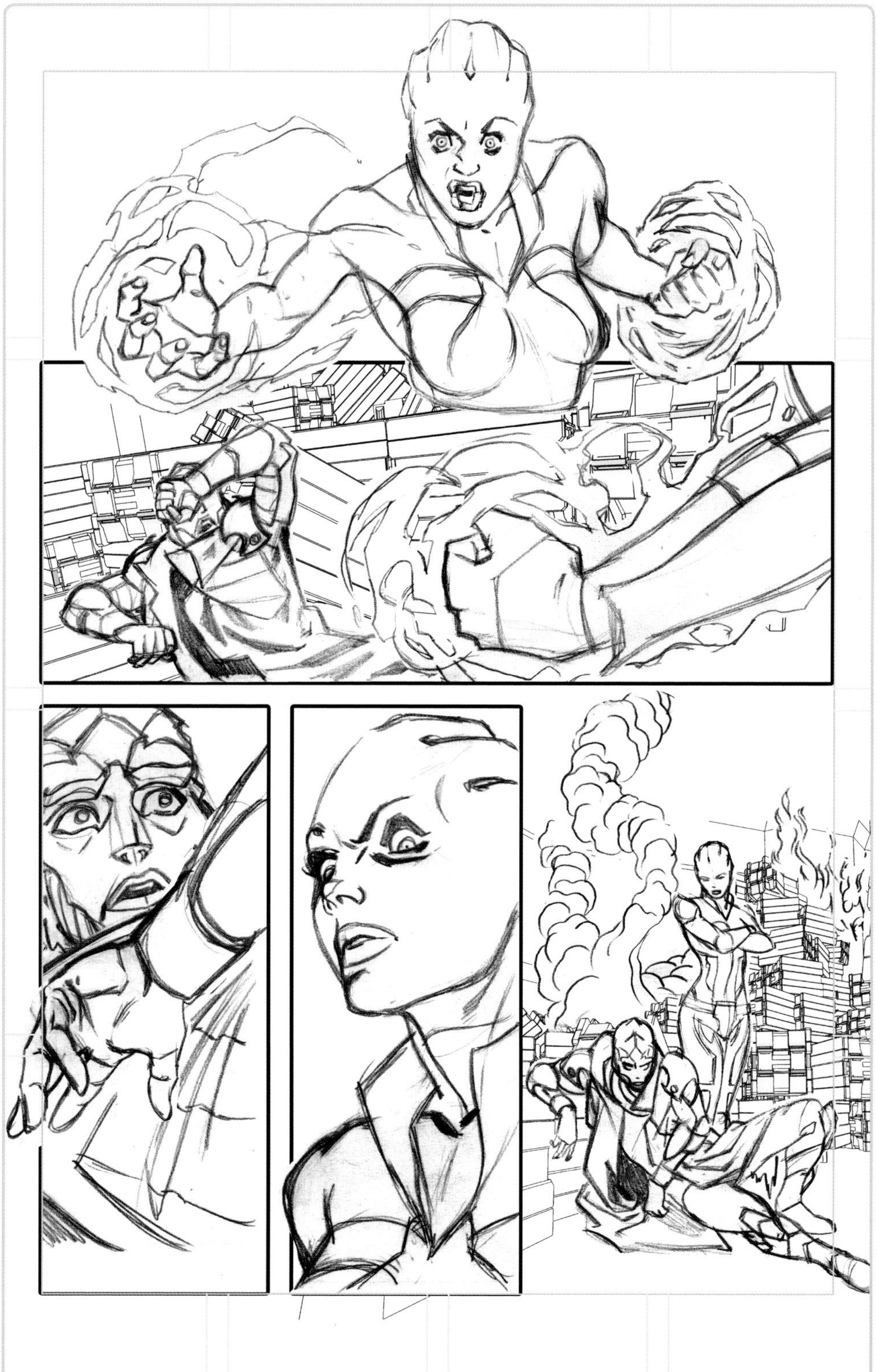

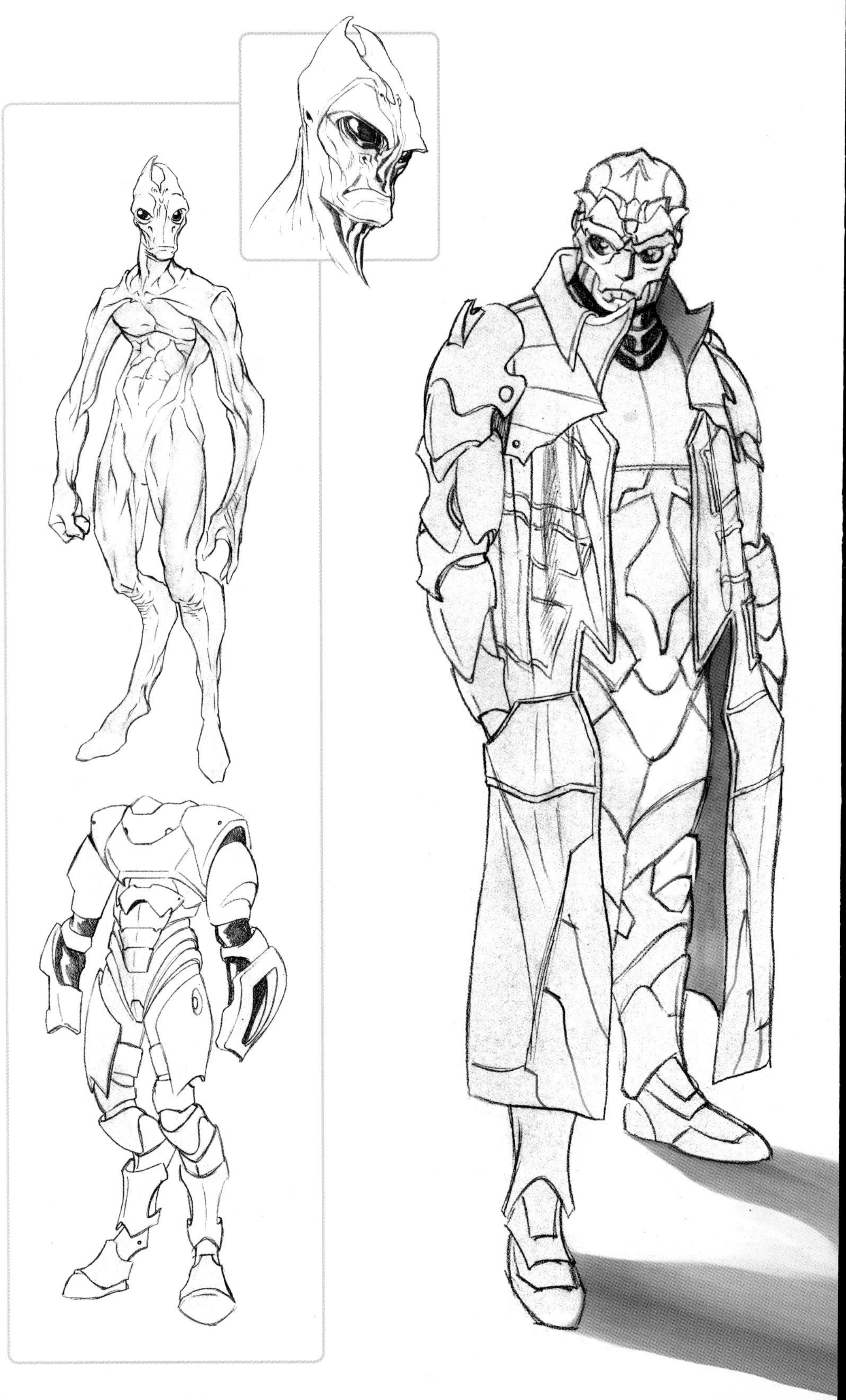

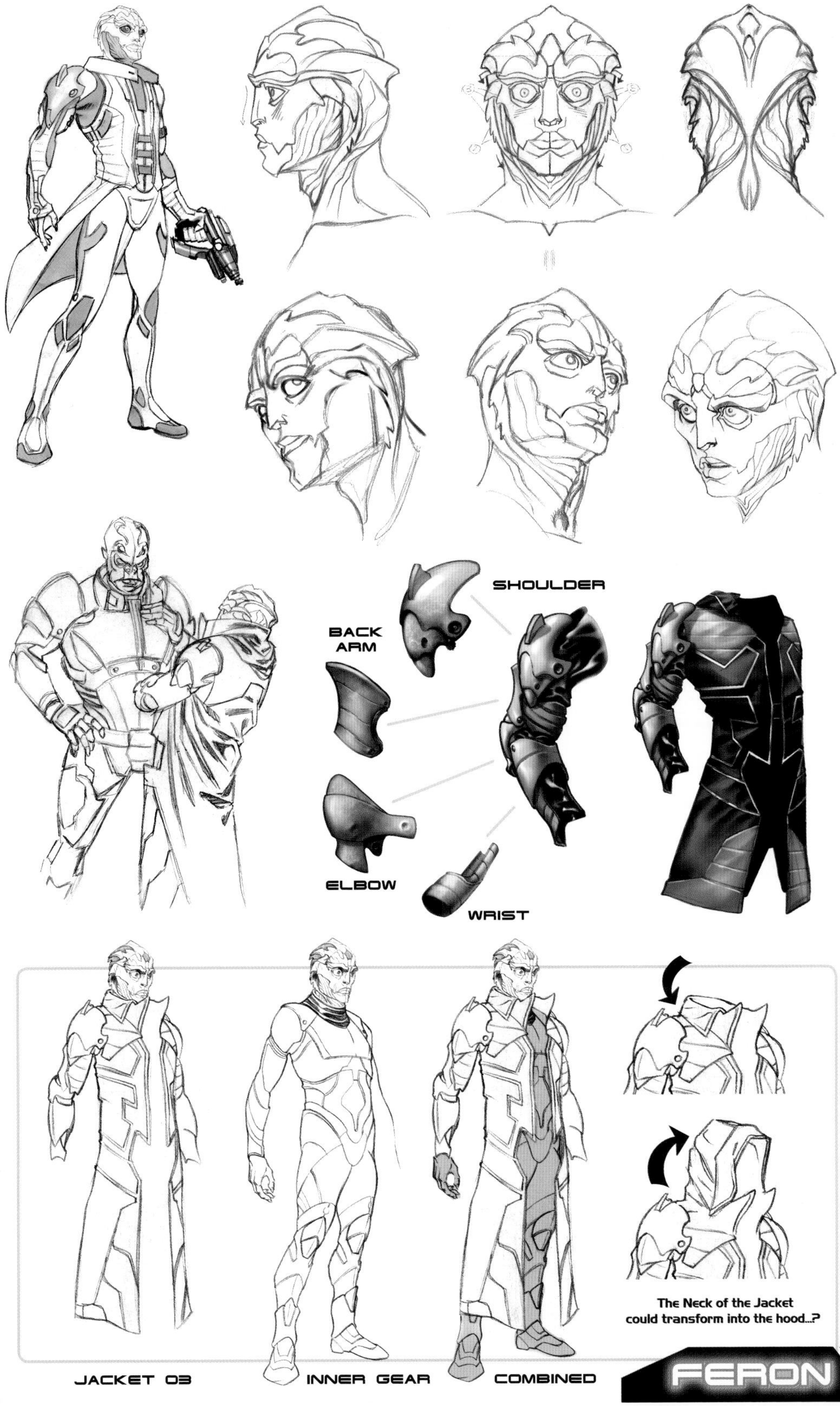
SHOULDER
BACK ARM
ELBOW
WRIST
The Neck of the Jacket could transform into the hood...?
JACKET 03
INNER GEAR
COMBINED

FERON

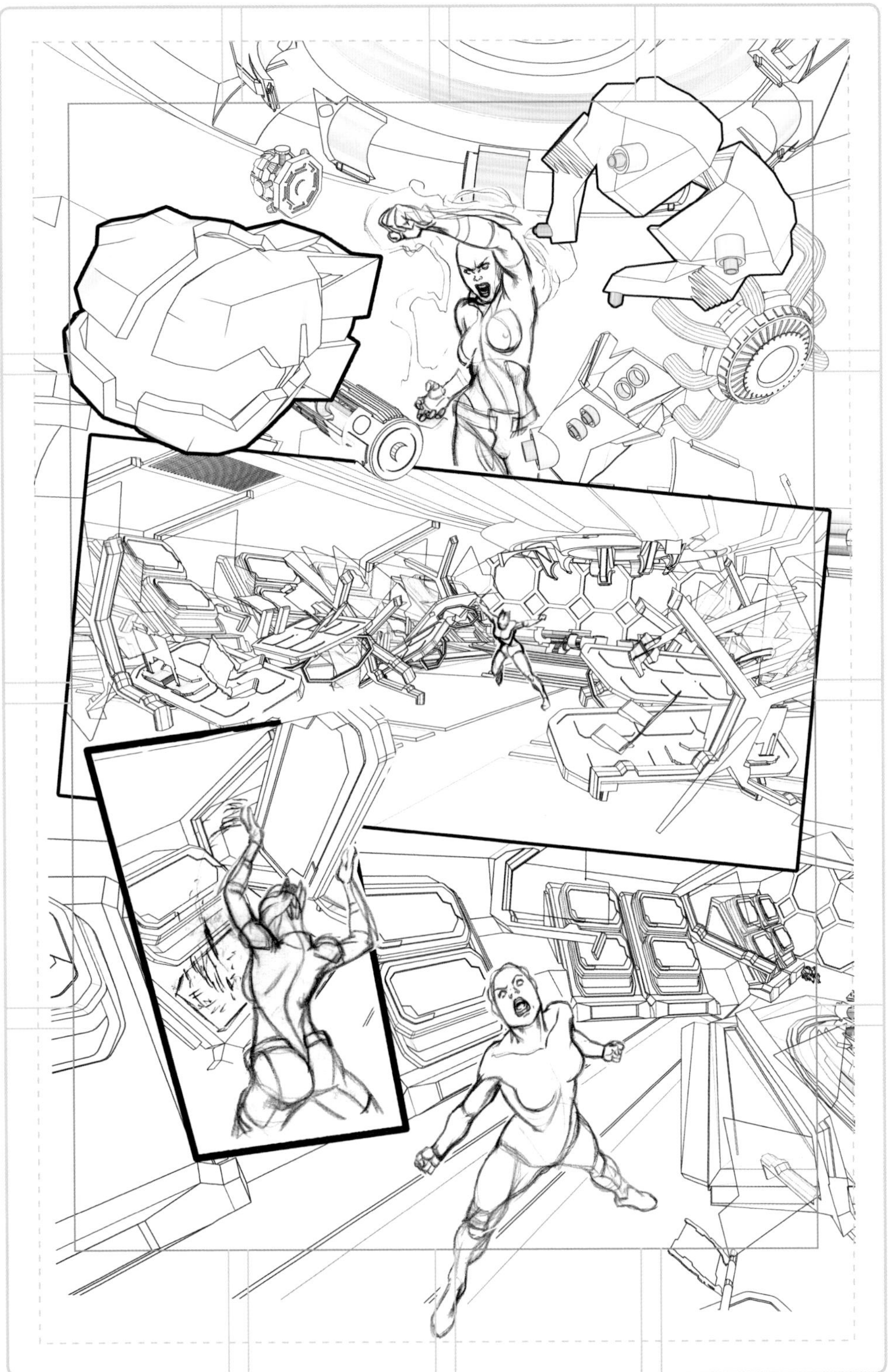

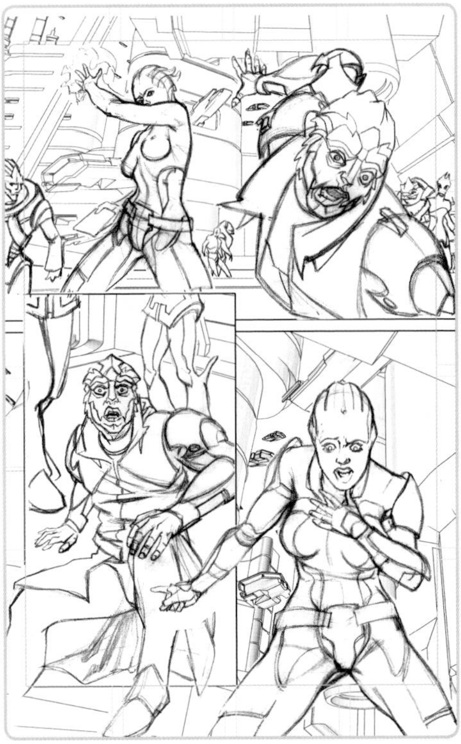
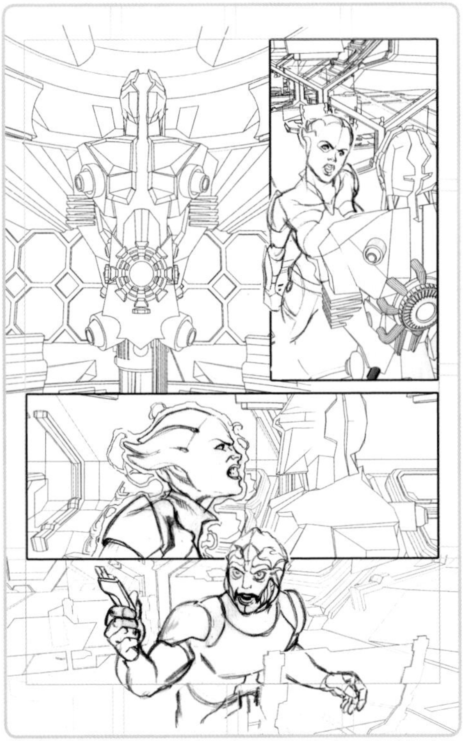
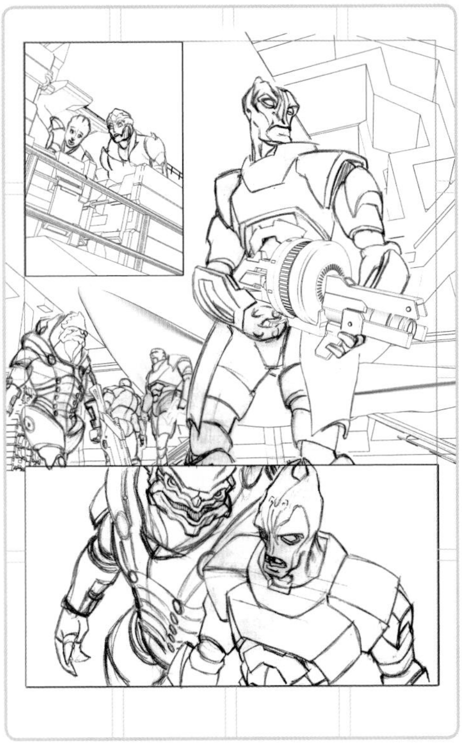
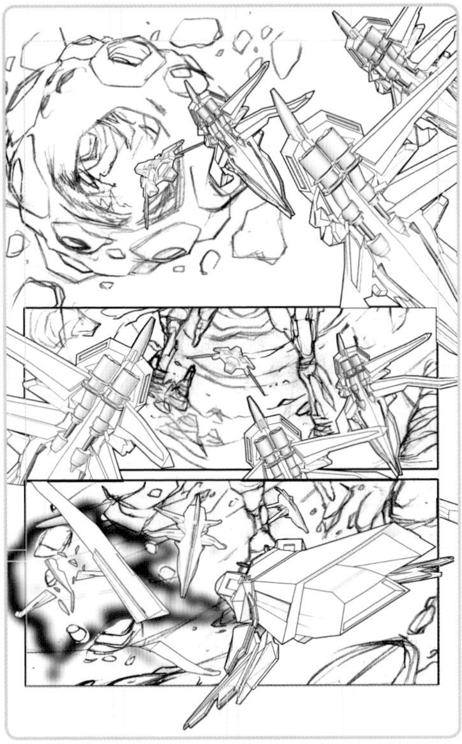

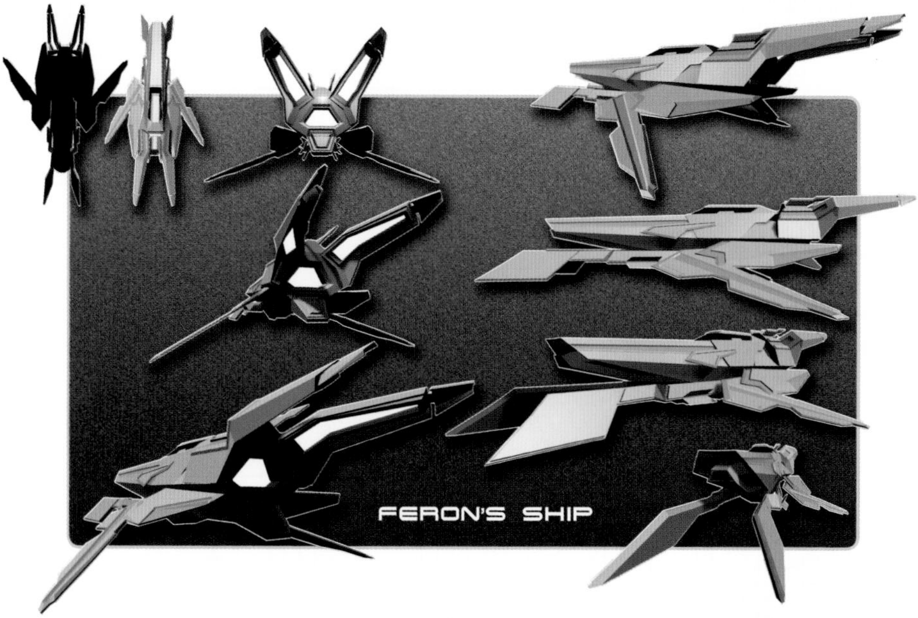
FERON'S SHIP

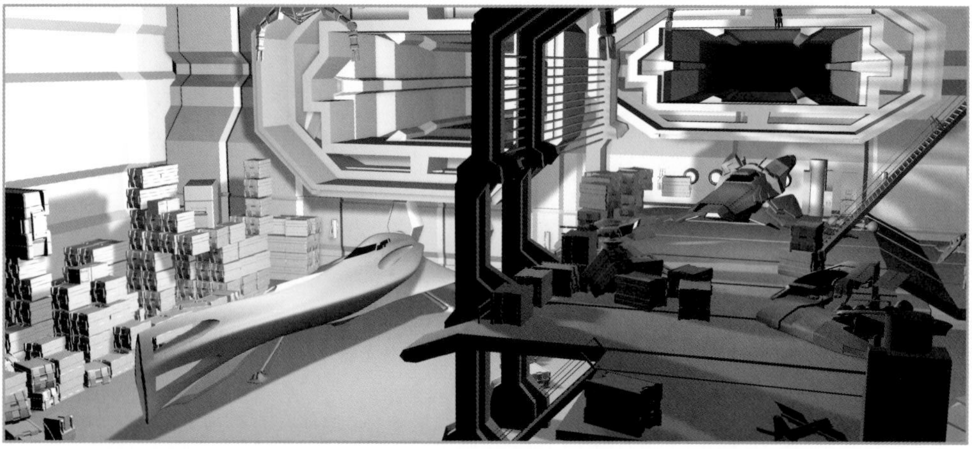

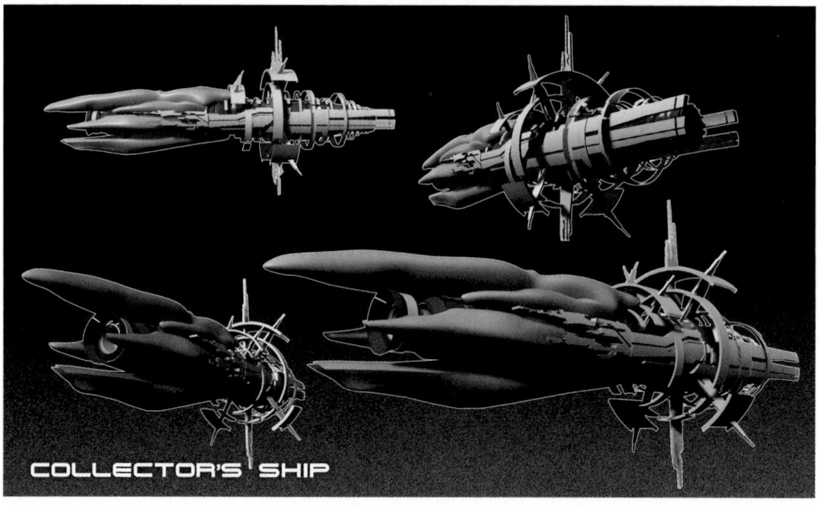
COLLECTOR'S SHIP

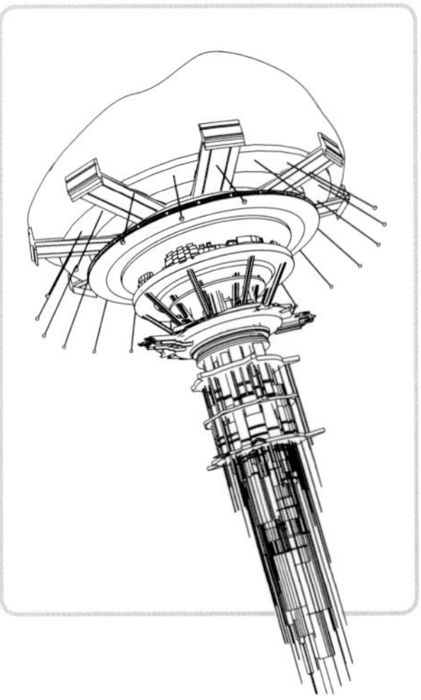

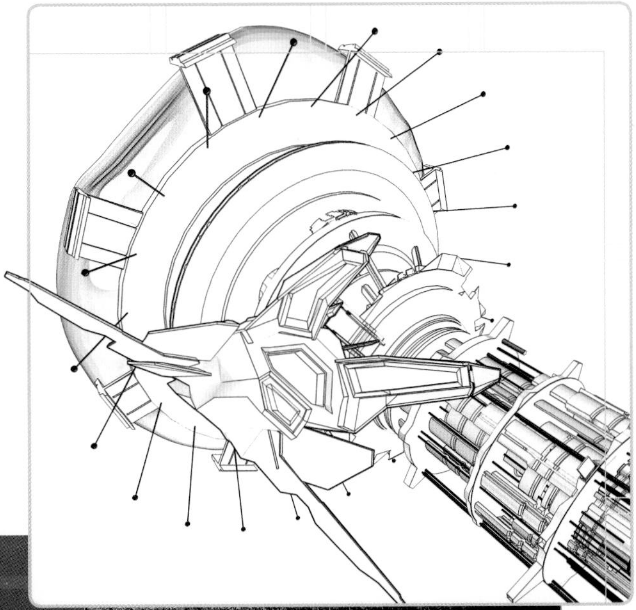

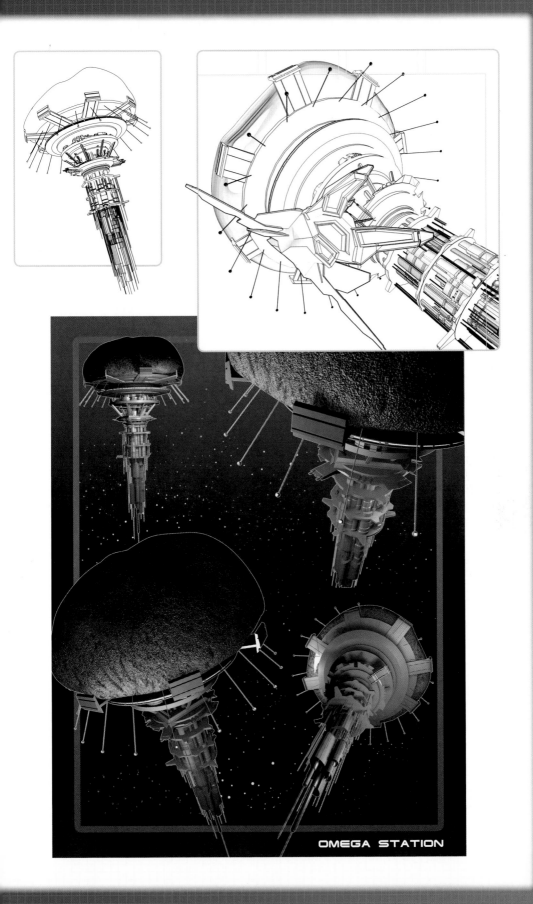

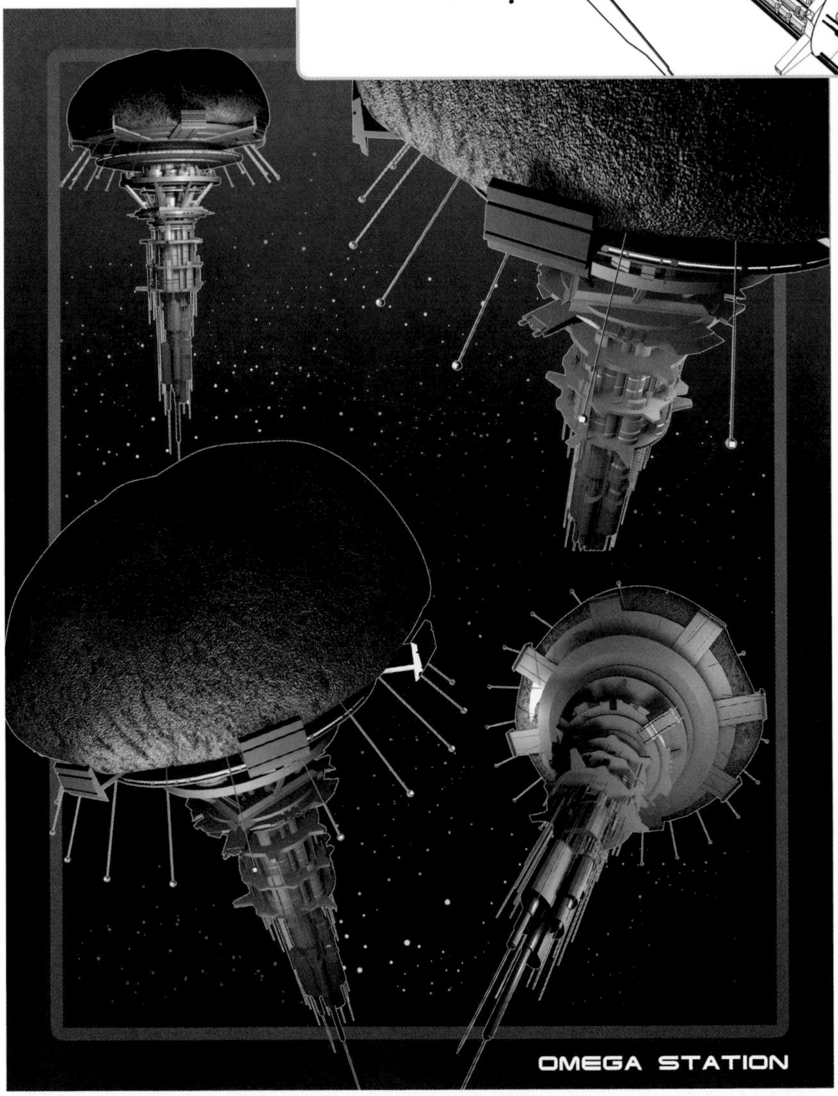
OMEGA STATION

STAR WARS®
KNIGHTS OF THE OLD REPUBLIC

Volume 1: Commencement
ISBN 978-1-59307-640-5 | $18.99

Volume 2: Flashpoint
ISBN 978-1-59307-761-7 | $18.99

**Volume 3: Days of Fear,
Nights of Anger**
ISBN 978-1-59307-867-6 | $18.99

**Volume 4: Daze of Hate,
Knights of Suffering**
ISBN 978-1-59582-208-6 | $18.99

Volume 5: Vector
ISBN 978-1-59582-227-7 | $17.99

Volume 6: Vindication
ISBN 978-1-59582-274-1 | $19.99

Volume 7: Dueling Ambitions
ISBN 978-1-59582-348-9 | $18.99

Volume 8: Destroyer
ISBN 978-1-59582-419-6 | $17.99

Volume 9: Demon
ISBN 978-1-59582-476-9 | $16.99

TO FIND A COMICS SHOP IN YOUR AREA, CALL 1-888-266-4226.

For more information or to order direct: *On the web: darkhorse.com *E-mail: mailorder@darkhorse.com
*Phone: 1-800-862-0052 Mon.-Fri. 9 A.M. to 5 P.M. Pacific Time.

*prices and availability subject to change without notice. STAR WARS © 2010 Lucasfilm Ltd. & TM (BL 8023)